Creative Teaching

Creative Teaching

A Practical Approach

Alfred DeVito
Purdue University

Gerald H. Krockover
Purdue University

Kathleen J. Steele
Crawfordsville Community Schools

HarperCollins*College*Publishers

Acquisitions Editor: Chris Jennison
Project Editor: Melonie Parnes
Design Supervisor and Cover Design: Wendy Ann Fredericks
Cover Illustration: Tom Fluharty
Production Administrator: Valerie A. Sawyer
Compositor: Black Dot Graphics/Typo•Graphics
Printer and Binder: R. R. Donnelley & Sons Company
Cover Printer: The Lehigh Press, Inc.

Creative Teaching: A Practical Approach

Library of Congress Cataloging-in-Publication Data

DeVito, Alfred.
    Creative teaching: a practical approach / Alfred DeVito, Gerald
H. Krockover, Kathleen J. Steele.
      p. cm.
    Includes index.
    ISBN 0-06-500320-9
    1. Teaching—Aids and devices. 2. Classroom management.
I. Krockover, Gerald H. II. Steele, Kathleen J. III. Title.
LB1044.88.D48   1993
370.3'078—dc20   92-31797
                                            CIP

92 93 94 95 9 8 7 6 5 4 3 2 1

Contents

2
Creative Teaching—If It Is Too Much Trouble, It's Probably Worth It!   32

3
What They Neglected to Tell Me About . . . Does It Matter?   66

4
Alternative Skills and Techniques— Teaching Children to Teach Themselves   118

5
Creative Evaluations— Evaluations and Trust 220

Appendixes

Preface

This is a book about teaching children. More specifically, it is a book about *Creative Teaching* for children. Increased societal complexities necessitate the preparation of teachers who are creative, innovative, independent thinkers who can develop these traits in children under their charge. This book is intended to help you develop the knowledge, skills, and teaching strategies needed to become a creative teacher who can prepare and present lessons in an exciting way to a variety of children in a variety of situations.

Creative Teaching is designed to provide preservice and in-service elementary teachers with guides for creative instruction. It may be used as the basic text for an introductory elementary methods course, or as a resource for classroom use.

Chapter 1 explores the creative aspects of teaching. It examines the changes affecting current educational trends and sets the stage for active learning.

Chapter 2 presents personal, creative teaching approaches that help teachers promote academic progress with children. Attitudes and practices, questioning techniques, individualized instruction, technology, and creative teaching aids are examined.

Chapter 3, "What They Neglected to Tell Me," features practical approaches to initiate and to maintain instruction. It offers age-level profiles of children; information on maintaining order in the classroom; working with gifted, exceptional, and multicultural children; and developing a positive teaching approach.

Chapter 4 presents methods and techniques for teaching children to teach themselves. It includes theme interest centers, task cards, puzzler activities, audiotutorial tapes, invitations to investigate, file-folder games, jigsaw teaching activities, book kits, modules, and ways to present controversial issues.

Chapter 5, "Creative Evaluation—Evaluation and Trust," examines evaluation in all three domains of learning—cognitive, affective, and psychomotor. A number of evaluation ideas and techniques are included for self-evaluation and portfolio assessment. Additional sections are devoted to evaluating yourself as a teacher, including interviewing, obtaining, and maintaining a teaching position.

Useful information can be found in Appendixes I through V, which list education journals and museum resources, state teacher-certification offices, personal computer communication resources, and sources for ordering creative teaching materials.

The authors would like to thank the following reviewers, whose comments and suggestions were very helpful: Morris Anderson, Wayne State College; Nancy Bacharach, St. Cloud State University; Joseph Baust, Murray State University; Patricia Hanley, University of South Florida; Judith Reiff, University of Georgia; and Evelyn Swartz, University of Kansas.

Alfred DeVito
Gerald H. Krockover
Kathleen J. Steele

Chapter
1

Setting the Stage

You Can Make the Difference

It is a fact nothing short of a miracle that the modern methods of instruction have not yet entirely strangled the holy curiosity of inquiry: for this delicate little plant, aside from stimulation, stands mainly in need of freedom: without this it goes to wrack and ruin without fail.

Albert Einstein

This is a book about teaching in elementary and middle schools. It is a book about skills, techniques, and the general mechanics of teaching. More than that, it is a book written to communicate the joy, the excitement, the pleasure, and the honor of being a creative teacher. Knowledge of content, knowledge of the methods of teaching, and an acquisition of what it takes to experience the joy of creative teaching are all necessary for effective teaching. Teachers who weave these attributes together make a difference in the lives of their students. Your touch can make a difference.

WHAT IS IT LIKE TO BE A CREATIVE TEACHER?

Teaching is not just a job. It is a vocation filled with the excitement of helping children discover themselves and the full range of their capabilities. In this undertaking, teachers also discover themselves and amplify their own full range of capabilities. Teaching is a people-oriented vocation. Children are unique

1

people. Teaching is like being a parent over and over. Children are on loan to teachers. It is like inheriting a family for a year, a process that repeats itself year after year. Teachers inherit children at their best. We get to love and enjoy them without having to worry about scratches, bruises, toothaches, or any of the other trials and tribulations associated with their growing up. We inherit them reasonably healthy, clean, and eager to please us. The teaching challenge begins with, "May I please have your attention . . . ?" A thank-you note to parents might be in order.

Teaching is a vocation where one constantly strives to bring out the best in oneself for those under one's charge. Teaching requires a degree of gentle mental toughness. It seems the better one teaches and the more skillful one is in accomplishing one's goals in the learning process, the more the learners think they did it all by themselves. They wonder why they ever needed you. Creative teachers interpret this as a compliment and bravely continue on. Teaching is a gregarious vocation and, at the same time, a lonely one. Any rewards, pats on the back, and possible "hail good teacher" comments must all be inferred, for they rarely are forthcoming even when justified. Teachers make the difference, but the salutations are few. In many instances you stand alone. Nonetheless, creative teachers smile and carry on undaunted. Teachers occasionally are thanked for past efforts well done. Any acknowledgment, recognition, or applause, if it happens, is often far removed by time and distance from the teacher's ears. Creative teachers accept this and dig deeper. Teachers plant seeds that then grow. But teachers rarely see the harvest. Some say teaching is a thankless vocation. Creative teachers say it is a thankful vocation with gains that far exceed the losses.

What is a creative teacher's day like? Each day is a new experience. It is a day full of challenges for the students and from the students. It is a day of surprises for you and for them. It is a day of gladness. Every day is a brand new day and a fresh start for everyone. It is a day of your being resilient, flexible, creative, and reacting to the numerous nuances, both verbal and nonverbal, emanating from children. It is a day of acting cheery when you are dreary and being energetic and enthusiastic even when you feel you might be "losing" it. It is a day in which you grow in maturity as you learn to weather the cheers, tears, and jeers of the day-to-day engagements with children and their foibles. It is a day filled with the multitude of engagements that place you in the role of audio-visual repair person, occasional plumber, human vacuum cleaner, counselor, social and medical adviser, referee, judge, oracle, and master ad-libber. It is a day on the firing line, but every day you become more capable and resourceful.

Being a creative teacher is being onstage, in charge, responsible, a clerical wizard, an actor, a weaver of sorts, and an imperfect perfectionist of human interactions and understanding guiding children to mastery of themselves. Sometimes the roadmap for this excursion is illegible, but creative teachers get the job done with style and grace.

Being a creative teacher is receiving a stream of warm vibes from loving, caring children. Being a captive audience, children are extremely loyal to their teacher. They know they belong to you for a period of time. They like you. If perchance a drought of vibes occurs, creative teachers know it does not matter, for a few warm vibes will suffice.

Creative teachers know that each child is a unique, one of a kind, hand-crafted individual, and that the responsibilities associated with teaching unique children require a personal, deft touch to achieve maximum results. Creative teachers know that to flourish, children's potentials must be nurtured in a free environment. Creative teachers know that diverse alternatives must be designed and made available for consumption to allow for maximum individual growth enhancing the acquisition of a strong self-concept. Creative teachers should be trained, gentle, caring, responsible individuals who know and understand children, know where they are going with them, how to get them there, and when they have arrived at the chosen destination. Creative teachers also know the parameters of society and the system within which they operate, and they strive to reach full fruition while maintaining harmony within existing constraints. At times this seems like an impossible undertaking. Yet, the challenge breathes fire into one's being as one subsumes oneself to the exhilarating engagement with children and learning.

THE TEACHER IS CHANGING

Change is constant. If you are doing something in the same manner you did it ten years ago, with all the advances in technology and research, there probably exists a new or improved method of performing this task. This is true for the task of teaching. Accepting change as constant, inevitable, and eternal does not mean that teachers should pursue change for its own sake. All changes are not necessarily good or appropriate. The notion of "If it ain't broke, don't fix it" could, in some instances, be a viable consideration. Change does not have to occur, but it does. And creative teachers entertain constructive changes if and when they are needed. It has often been stated that things must change so they can remain the same. If things did not change, things would not be like they are. Change is everywhere, and creative teachers adjust to it, occasionally initiate it, and expect change to be part of their lives and of their teaching careers.

Miss Leederkranz's day ran the gamut from providing instruction to a host of managerial and custodial chores such as feeding the furnace. Ms. DeFaugraw's day is also taken up with providing instruction. Although her day is devoid of feeding, stoking, and cleaning the furnace, Ms. DeFaugraw performs a host of ancillary instructional tasks. Things in teaching have changed; however, many similarities still exist. Present-day teachers do many of the same tasks that occupied teachers in the past, and basic concerns still exist. The children come to learn. The teachers prepare to teach. A proper learning setting that complements the children's social, physical, and mental requirements is provided. Within such a disciplined environment, learning is sustained.

Figure 1.1 How are they alike? How are they different?

Miss Alveeta Leederkranz
Then

Ms. Patty DeFaugraw
Now

WHAT HAS CHANGED FOR TEACHERS?

Some changes are:

- Teacher preparation for certification
- A requirement for continuous learning throughout one's teaching career
- Expectations, objectives, and goals of the children, parents, community, and administration
- The child and the family
- Class size, length of the day, and school year
- Composition of class population; for example, differences in cultures, languages, and abilities, such as the average, the gifted, the slow, the physically handicapped, and the special children

- More active involvement in educational negotiations affecting teaching and learning
- Time constraints, plus year-round teaching considerations
- The curriculum
- The mobility of the society
- Status of the teacher
- Increased litigation
- Sex and drug education
- Values clarification
- New technologies for instructional improvement
- The world

Read "Welcome to Pedagogical Paradise." Then decide what changes you would add to the list above.

Welcome to Pedagogical Paradise

Join the club. As a teacher of children, you will become one of the chosen few. Your job will be simple! Anyone with real talents can do it. You may often be called upon to perform miracles. You will teach nonreaders to read. You will teach readers to comprehend. And you will teach comprehenders to persevere in the constant pursuit of knowledge and to love the engagement. Concomitantly, you will have the responsibility for mastery of a few other "Rs." You will chart numerous pathways for individual successes and interest in (w)riting, (a)rithmetic, and responsibility. You will plan something for special-needs children, average children, and a little something different for gifted and talented children. Your outstanding performances and contributions will occur with such frequency that you will smile and accept these accomplishments as "just part of the job."

You will love teaching. You will particularly love the first year of teaching. Preparation, inspiration, and perspiration all will be at their peak. You will revel in your successes and on occasion think, "It did not happen today. I just could not get it together. I think I am losing it. Why did I switch from electrical engineering?" Several deep breaths, a tightening of the intellectual mechanism, plus a sigh or two, and you will be off and running with your usual success patterns. You will love the children. They, in turn, will love you. They are yours for a year. You will be responsible for their progress, their continued thirst for learning, their social growth, some of their health concerns, and their level of satisfaction within the group and with you. You are the "keeper and stroker" who develops and sustains individual, positive self-concept growth in children. For a given critical period, you are the greatest influence in children's lives.

You will be parent, friend, and confidant to those in your charge. You will dream of goals to be fulfilled by all; yet, you must accept that not all dreams are fulfilled. You plan. You act. You replan. You rebound. You will be forever enthusiastic and vigorous despite those swollen legs and feet that signal Friday has arrived. Monday brings renewed vigor. You will be recognized as the clever teacher who discovered elastic stockings and those adorable space shoes only to be exposed as a purveyor of what all veteran teachers have already found out. Teaching can be a leathery profession, and requires cunning and skill to survive. You will learn this with time. You must stay healthy. A sick shepherd cannot lead the flock well.

(continued)

You will vacillate in your role as teacher. Shifting from lofty thespian moments of grandeur staged in front of the class, you may find yourself at times keeper of dental retainers or contact lenses; coach; counselor of children with problems; pacifier of differences in children of varying religions, colors, and social and ethnic backgrounds; accepter of the world as it is and planner of how it might be. You will become ambidextrous with paper towels and rubber gloves, swiping through art accidents and children's bodily inconsistencies with equal ease. Head lice will be your forte. You may even become known as the fastest toweler in the entire school district. Occasionally sabbaticals are awarded for mastery of such skills. You may also become the economic wizard you have always dreamed of being. You will transact milk monies, picture monies, field trip monies, book club monies, "gift for the janitor" monies, and become keeper of the computer coupons. You will quickly fill those lonely evenings becoming an expert in rolling coins for acceptance at the local bank.

You will never be alone. True, you occupy the trenches. You are where it's at. But you have a fantastic support system behind you. Parents stand behind you as your first line of defense. Win them over, and you will never have to know the meaning of "burn out." Start with Back to School Night by wowing them with your winsome teaching demeanor, organization, astuteness, and general knowledge of "their" child. They will love you, if you let them. The school is also behind you; it needs successful teachers. Work hard. Plan your work and work your plan. Do all the *right* things. Volunteer to coach the volleyball team even though you have two left feet. Be creative, but not too creative. Stay off the salary committee until you achieve tenure or a continuing contract. Ask questions, but don't ask too many questions—again, until you have a continuing contract. Remember when the door of your classroom is closed, you are on your own. Like a rare mountain flower you will blossom into an outstanding teacher. Grow as you go. Always be aware of the subtleties that impinge on learning. Be aware of the impact you can and do make on children. You will revel in your part in the process and product. Surely you will be a teacher extraordinaire in the paradise you create.

Sincerely,

Emma Ritis

Teaching is changing. Creative teachers expect change. They anticipate and accept change knowing that it is a natural phenomenon. They do, however, analyze and critique all changes to ensure they result in positive outcomes. Reinhold Niebuhr's literary contribution is worthy of examination as one confronts contemplated changes.

Prayer for Serenity

O God
Give us serenity to accept
   what cannot be changed.
Courage to change what
   should be changed

and wisdom to distinguish
  the one from the other.

Reinhold Niebuhr (1892–1971)

THE STUDENT IS CHANGING

The demographics of our nation are changing and, as a result, the students who are enrolled in our schools are also changing. National demographics indicate that as we enter the twenty-first century there will be the following changes:

1. Seventeen percent fewer school-age children.
2. One out of every five 18-year-olds will be functionally illiterate. (This is the highest percentage of any industrialized nation in the world.)
3. Only 15 percent of net additions to the work force will be white males. Three out of five additions will be women and 25 percent will be minorities.
4. By the year 2020, two-thirds of American workers will be female and minorities.

Presently, one in four children under age 18 lives in a single-parent family compared with one in ten in 1960. Fifty-one percent of those children also live in poverty.

POINTS TO PONDER

What inferences can you make about these changes and the students entering your classroom?

Additional studies provide new insights into how students are changing. For example, a major study of 3000 students in grades 4 through 10 (Rothman, 1991) found that schools are a major contributor to the dramatic drop in self-esteem and aspirations that girls experience during adolescence. This study also found that teachers often inadvertently foster girls' lack of confidence in their academic abilities by sending subtle cues that boys are more able than girls.

Another study found that racial and ethnic prejudices are still prevalent. This study found that while support for racial equality has grown, "negative images of members of other racial and ethnic groups are widespread among whites." It also found that "most groups have at least some prejudice against all other groups." Education was found to help change such attitudes and to be one of the "strongest influences toward a person having positive or at least neutral attitudes toward others." Moreover, if tolerance and the history and contributions of diverse cultures are emphasized, stereotyping declines (Armstrong 1991).

As a result, what we say and do can have a lasting effect upon children. Whether we wish to admit it or not, we convey our likes and dislikes, our strengths and weaknesses, our values and opinions, and our prejudices to our students.

Two students who are now in college have these comments to make about teaching. Could either of them be our former students?

BETTY: When I think of past approaches to teaching, I can only be reminded of the horrible experience I had when I was in elementary school. We had a science lesson once a week. It usually was on a Friday afternoon. For half an hour we would take turns reading from a science book. We would never do any of the experiments we read about. Then, at the end of each section, several questions would arise concerning the material covered. If the class was confused or did not understand a point, the teacher would never discuss the problem. Instead, that question was assigned as homework due the next day. The teacher would hand back our papers with next to no discussion on the issue. All through elementary school I had the feeling that my teachers' favorite subject was anything but science. In one of my classes we had a choice of either art or science. Needless to say, art would always win.

SANDY: I feel that today's children are basically no different from me as I was 12 years ago. I was always bored with social studies class, thinking there was nothing worse than memorizing facts about something I could not even visualize. I actually thought that was all there was to social studies because, from the time I entered first grade until high school, I was only acquainted with memorizing facts and maybe seeing one or two videos per year. The other students and I were not presented with any alternatives; therefore, we knew of nothing better and swallowed what the teachers offered.

Read Edsel Memorial High School and think back to your own education from elementary through high school.

THE CURRICULUM IS CHANGING

"If it is February 9th, I should be on page 178, especially if I plan to cover the book by the end of the year." This is definitely a thought from the past, when the basic content did not change from year to year and the textbook was the primary source of information.

We are living in an age of instant information. The curriculum must change to meet the needs of a society that has current information at its fingertips and expects its members to access and utilize that information. The use of on-line data bases and CD-ROM should be infused into the curriculum activities so students will have access to current data bases of encyclopedias, newspapers, and periodicals. They must be able to search for and retrieve articles within

Edsel Memorial High School
Anywhere, U.S.A.

Dear Parents of Our Graduates:

As you are aware, one of your offspring was graduated from our high school this June. Since that time it has been brought to our attention that certain insufficiencies are present in our graduates, so we are recalling all students for further education.

We have learned that in the process of the instruction we provided we forgot to install one or more of the following:

—at least one salable skill;

—a comprehensive and utilitarian set of values;

—a readiness for and understanding of the responsibilities of citizenship.

A recent consumer study consisting of follow-up of our graduates has revealed that many of them have been released with defective parts. Racism and materialism are serious flaws and we have discovered they are a part of the makeup of almost all our products. These defects have been determined to be of such magnitude that the model produced in June is considered highly dangerous and should be removed from circulation as a hazard to the nation.

Some of the equipment which was in the past classified as optional has been reclassified as standard and should be a part of every product of our school. Therefore we plan to equip each graduate with:

—a desire to continue to learn;

—a dedication to solving problems of local, national, and international concern;

—several productive ways to use leisure time;

—a commitment to the democratic way of life;

—extensive contact with the world outside the school;

—experience in making decisions.

In addition, we found we had inadvertently removed from your child his interest, enthusiasm, motivation, trust, and joy. We are sorry to report that these items have been mislaid and have not been turned in at the school Lost and Found Department. If you will inform us as to the value you place on these qualities, we will reimburse you promptly by check or cash.

As you can see, it is to your interest, and vitally necessary for your safety and the welfare of all, that graduates be returned so that these errors and oversights can be corrected. We admit that it would have been more effective and less costly in the first place, but we hope you will forgive our error and continue to respect and support your public schools.

Sincerely,

P. Dantic

P. Dantic, Principal

Source: William C. Miller, "Recalled for Revision," *Phi Delta Kappan*. vol. 53 (December 1971), back cover. Copyright 1971. Phi Delta Kappa, Inc. By permission.

minutes. Interactive videodisks can inform, tutor, and enhance oral presentations. Through electronic bulletin boards, students can receive up-to-date weather and satellite data for science, prices and stock market reports for mathematics and economics, and current news for social studies.

Curriculum should extend beyond the classroom. Community resource persons and mentorships are valuable in personalizing education. Field trips provide firsthand experiences, and a view of the real world of business and industry. Electronic bulletin boards offer students the opportunity to ask questions of business executives, college professors, scientists, and researchers in various fields. Interactive computer programs such as National Geographic KidsNetwork allow students to research topics such as acid rain or weather and compare their results through the use of modems, which connect computers through the use of phone lines with student research teams in different schools across the United States and Canada.

Curriculum must be designed to be activity oriented so students can be engaged in the learning process. Retention is greater than 90 percent if students see the material, hear the material, perform a task related to the material with coaching, and teach the material to someone else. In order to meet the needs of all students, they should have the opportunity to work individually and in cooperative groups. Controversial topics such as pesticides, drug testing, and nuclear waste need to be included in the changing curriculum to permit students to think about the moral and ethical issues facing our society today and in the future. Important topics such as AIDS, drug abuse, alcoholism, suicide, and sex education must also be addressed.

But what about the basics? How will you know what to teach in every subject for every grade and ability level? There may be state guidelines, school district curriculum documents, and textbook scope and sequence charts to assist you in determining the basic curriculum. Be inquisitive. Ask. Discover what documents are available. Use them if they are current: check the publication dates. Are the resources available? Where? Do the resources include computer software and other innovative materials? Remember that curriculum materials continue to change. If the paper is brittle and a little yellow, the best curriculum guide may be the teacher next door.

Creative Lesson Planning: Content, Process, Product

What are you going to teach? What level of knowledge or skill do you want to target? What do you want students to verbalize, draw, write, or perform? If you can answer these three questions, you have already mastered the essence of creative lesson planning. Creative teachers ask themselves these questions informally as they plan, brainstorm, and organize innovative learning activities for students.

Content is what you want students to learn. The key element of a fable; the political, economic, and social aspects of the Civil War; how to use the various problem-solving strategies; the constantly changing geology of the earth; or the effects of smoking on the human body are all content materials that students can learn.

Process is the thinking skill or affective skill that you want the student to implement. Do you want students to memorize fables, list the elements of a fable, analyze the moral of a fable, compare two fables, or create and write an original fable? (Bloom 1956; see also Krathwohl, Bloom, and Masia 1964).

Developing product lists in the categories of verbal-spoken, verbal-written, media-performing, and media-visual can expand your vision and help you think of a greater variety of products (Sato, 1988). Verbal-spoken includes products such as oral presentations, panel discussions, and debates. Essays, journal entries, stories, lab reports, and newspaper articles are considered verbal-written. Media-performing ideas are puppet plays, dances, songs, dramatic presentations, and newscasts. Dioramas, charts, graphs, posters, time lines, and computer printouts are included in the media-visual area. A diverse list will spark new and creative ideas. It can also make the same content seem fresh after you have taught third grade for the fifth time.

Teachers can select one product, such as creating a poster to inform others about the effects of smoking on the human body. At other times it is important to allow students to choose from several projects. For example, a student could write a report, give an oral presentation, create an informative pamphlet, tape interviews with a smoker and a nonsmoker, or write a song about the effects of smoking. Students with different learning styles like to develop different kinds of products. Students also take responsibility for their actions when they have a choice in the decision.

When writing creative lesson plans, remember to add content, process, and product to your objectives and activities. It will give you, your principal, and the curriculum director a clear idea of what you are teaching. Be generous with your creative ideas. Write at least 15 dynamic activities for each unit. Generating a pool of ideas from which to choose will stretch your imagination and force you to be more creative and innovative. Some of your best ideas will materialize after you have written the first five or six activities.

Notice that listing the page numbers to be covered per week was not mentioned. Creative lesson planning takes a competent teacher who understands the content that needs to be addressed. He or she can turn routine activities such as reading, doing the questions at the end of the chapter, and taking the test into high-level activities where students research, analyze, brainstorm, evaluate, and create original products such as pedigree charts, posters, graphs, essays, slide shows, computer programs, games, and books.

Now you are ready to write a creative lesson plan. Give it a try. Remember to include a variety of cognitive and affective activities.

Broad-based Themes for an Integrated Approach

Broad-based themes such as freedom, change, and diversity provide continuity and flexibility for interdisciplinary units. Select a theme that provides a focus for all curricular areas. An individual teacher in a self-contained classroom or a team of teachers working together can plan activities that relate different subject areas to a central theme.

For example, if frontiers is selected as a theme, students could study the historical aspects of the American westward movement. In language arts, students could read *Little House on the Prairie* or *The Bears of Blue River* and compare the authors' visualizations of this period. Personal frontier journals could be started by each student to record his/her individual history. In mathematics, students could participate in a simulation where they would estimate the amount of various supplies needed to travel the Oregon Trail and calculate the cost of supplies. Geology and geography of the United States could be studied as students plot their way across the Appalachian Mountains in search of the new frontier. Mileage could be recorded and graphed during the frontier simulation. Simple machines of the frontier period could be investigated and modeled in science. Students could make a time line to show the relationship of this period of history to the development of machines. Music, dance, and art of the American frontier could be emphasized by the music, physical education, and art teachers.

Saturation? Maybe, but interdisciplinary units using broad-based themes give students the opportunity to learn about a topic in depth instead of having numerous brief encounters with a topic in isolation.

A good source for broad-based themes is Adler's (1952) *The Great Ideas: A Syntopicon of Great Books of the Western World.* The Syntopicon contains a set of 102 concepts that can be used as a springboard when planning curriculum and writing interdisciplinary units.

THE SCHOOL IS CHANGING

Carpeting softens the footsteps and warms the appearance of many new and remodeled schools. Near the office an electronic sign flashes daily announcements and birthdays. A letter press is available in the teachers' lounge next to the copy machine. Computer-generated notices and banners adorn the walls. Recycling bins are located at the ends of hallways. Computers are visible throughout the building, and a walking track encircles the school yard. These are some of the physical changes you will see as you enter a school today, but this is only one aspect.

School management and accountability are also changing. At Laura Hose Elementary School in Crawfordsville, Indiana, the school's mission statement is posted in the main hallway for all to see.

The mission of Hose Elementary School is to promote:

the growth of the whole child (academically, intellectually, emotionally, socially, and physically);

the development of responsibility; and

the desire to learn so that each child may make progress toward achieving his/her potential.

This statement, prompted by performance-based accreditation through the Indiana Department of Education, was written by a committee of teachers, staff members, parents, and the school principal. The goal of shared decision making is to empower administrators, faculty members, and parents to make decisions that will improve their local schools. Schools are becoming more accountable for the academic progress of their students. State-mandated testing programs give schools a clearer picture of their strengths and weaknesses. Funding associated with improved test scores and attendance records has encouraged schools to be more accountable.

The school day is being lengthened and school services are being increased to meet the needs of a changing society. Students are arriving earlier and staying later due to the schedules of working parents. In many schools, breakfast is part of the daily routine in conjunction with special after-school programs to assist latchkey children. Bilingual programs are being established in many communities to meet the needs of diverse populations. Preschool programs are being offered by many schools to provide educational opportunities for at-risk students. More elementary school counselors, psychologists, and substance-abuse counselors are being hired to meet the affective needs of students. Seeing a growing need for parental support, many schools have instituted parenting classes.

THE BIG THREE AND THE TERRIBLE THREE

The basic purpose of education is to assist students in developing the ability to think. Numerous studies support this notion. Benjamin S. Bloom (1976) points out that it is possible for 95 percent (yes, 95 percent) of our students to learn all the school has to teach, all at near the same mastery level. However, rather than meeting this goal, instruction in school tends to widen the gap between high- and low-achieving students. Unsuccessful students become more unsuccessful, and successful students become more successful as they advance through each grade level.

Instilling in children the basic values of learning should be the goal of every school program, and we need to decide what learning categories are basic to education. Which of these categories do you think students would retain after one year? Rank the six categories listed from 1 (retained the longest) to 6 (the shortest).

My Ranking	*Learning Category*
_____	**Factual Material**

Examples: Elements are made up of only one kind of atom. The speed of light is 300,000 kilometers per second.

| _____ | **Attitudes About Self in Relation to Subjects, Studies, and Others** |

Examples: I like math. I enjoy doing reading activities. My teacher is a big bore.

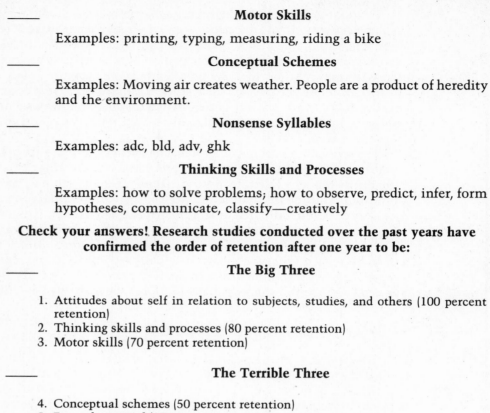

_____ **Motor Skills**

Examples: printing, typing, measuring, riding a bike

_____ **Conceptual Schemes**

Examples: Moving air creates weather. People are a product of heredity and the environment.

_____ **Nonsense Syllables**

Examples: adc, bld, adv, ghk

_____ **Thinking Skills and Processes**

Examples: how to solve problems; how to observe, predict, infer, form hypotheses, communicate, classify—creatively

Check your answers! Research studies conducted over the past years have confirmed the order of retention after one year to be:

_____ **The Big Three**

1. Attitudes about self in relation to subjects, studies, and others (100 percent retention)
2. Thinking skills and processes (80 percent retention)
3. Motor skills (70 percent retention)

_____ **The Terrible Three**

4. Conceptual schemes (50 percent retention)
5. Factual material (35 percent retention)
6. Nonsense syllables (10 percent retention) (Cronbach 1963).

Does the order surprise you? While the results of research indicate that instruction should concentrate on the categories in the Big Three, concepts and facts should not be eliminated from the teaching repertoire. Facts and concepts in isolation are of little value; they need to be used to develop the three higher learning categories.

POINTS TO PONDER

- In what categories does most instruction in our schools take place: the Big Three or the Terrible Three? Why?
- In which categories should most instruction in our schools take place? Why doesn't it?
- What are the implications of these results for the way we plan learning experiences? Should experiences be planned for the Big Three or the Terrible Three? Cite reasons for your answers.
- If you teach for the Big Three, should you neglect the Terrible Three? Explain your answer.

The following example illustrates how the Big Three can be implemented using a science-technology-society approach to learning. Identify the Big Three elements shown in the example.

One Example of Emphasizing the Big Three Using a Science/Technology/Society (STS) Approach

TRADITIONAL	STS
Connections and Applications	
Students see no value and/or use for their studies.	Students can relate their studies to their daily lives.
Students see no value in their studies for resolving current societal problems.	Students become involved in resolving social issues and see science as a way of fulfilling their responsibilities as citizens.
Students can recite information/concepts studied.	Students seek out information and use it.
Students cannot relate the science they study to any current technology.	Students are engrossed in current technological developments and, through them, see the importance and relevance of scientific concepts.
Creativity	
Students decline in their ability to question; the questions they do raise are often ignored because they do not conform to the course outline.	Students ask more questions, and these questions are used to develop STS activities and materials.
Students rarely ask unique questions.	Students frequently ask unique questions that excite their own interest, that of other students, and of the teacher.
Students are ineffective in identifying possible causes and effects in specific situations.	Students are skilled in identifying possible causes and effects of certain observations and actions.
Attitude	
Students have few original ideas.	Students continually offer ideas.
Student interest in science declines at all grade levels.	Student interest increases from grade level to grade level and in specific courses.
Science seems to decrease curiosity.	Students become more curious about the material world.

(continued)

Students see their teacher as a purveyor of information.	Students see their teacher as a facilitator/guide.
Students see science as information to learn.	Students see science as a way of dealing with problems.

Process

Students see science processes as skills scientists possess.	Students see science processes as skills they can use.
Students see processes as something to practice as a course requirement.	Students see processes as skills they need to refine and develop more fully for themselves.
Teacher concerns for process are not understood by students, especially since they rarely affect the course grade.	Students readily see the relationship of science processes to their own actions.
Students see science processes as abstract, glorified, unattainable skills that are unapproachable.	Students see process as a vital part of what they do in science class.

Knowledge

Knowledge is information mastered for a teacher test.	Students see science knowledge as personally useful.
Knowledge is seen as an outcome in itself.	Knowledge is seen as a needed commodity for dealing with problems.
"Learning" is principally for testing.	Learning occurs because of activity; it is an important happening, but not a focus in and of itself.
Retention is very short lived.	Students who learn by experience retain information and can often relate it to new situations.

Source: From: Yager, R. E. (1990). "Instructional Outcomes Change With STS." *Iowa Science Teachers Journal,* Spring, 2–21.

BE CREATIVE!

Creativity, although deemed a valuable trait, is probably our least developed talent. It is a thinking process, the power to recombine things that already exist into something new. Creativity can also be described as a succession of acts, each dependent on the one before and suggesting the one after. Creative recombinations can produce a new object, a new technique for performing a familiar task, or a new solution to a problem. Creativity provides you with options.

Attributes of Creative Teachers

Creative teachers tolerate uncertainty. They have an innate ability to be comfortable with strange and doubtful situations. They have an incessant desire to create order out of chaos. And they have the courage to persist to create that order to suit their own terms. Creative teachers are more concerned with satisfying themselves and their students' needs than with pleasing others. Creative teachers usually:

- enjoy variety in all engagements.
- respect supervision. While they may have their own ideas, they do listen and then carefully consider all facets of directives before acting or reacting.
- analyze conditions and seek alternative solutions. They have strong self-concepts.
- immerse themselves in more than one undertaking at a time.
- possess an abundance of energy and apply it in a disciplined manner.
- are willing to take chances, to go that extra mile to accomplish their goals.
- possess an insatiable curiosity. They risk security to explore new and uncharted areas.
- enjoy accepting challenges and "running" with the ball. They are persistent in their search for solutions to problems and questions.
- enjoy manipulating objects and ideas to see how they might work in a different situation.
- are intuitive, curious, and not overly concerned with inconsistencies. They do not get bogged down in minutia. They fight it.
- are less concerned with such labels as nonconformist. They distinguish blind conformity from deliberate or purposeful conformity.
- are well disciplined and persist with the demands of the task at hand.
- are hard workers. They can muster their energies, and recognize that success comes from sustained work accompanied by extensive training and perseverance.

Creativity can be developed by applying oneself. See every act as a challenge. Is there a better way to do this? Why are we doing it this way? How can I change it? Is the proposed change going to result in an improvement? Brainstorm into tomorrow; don't sit on yesterday.

Creativity is not fragile, but creative vitality is. Vitality, enthusiasm, and positive thinking lubricate the creative process. Stimulate both the analytical and the intuitive hemispheres of the mind, capitalizing on the advantages of both. Believe in your creative potential. Pass it on to others.

WHY TEACH SKILLS?

The school curriculum is claimed by some people to be a "many splendor'd thing." It is often described as fascinating, challenging, beautiful, interesting, and intellectually satisfying. But not everyone agrees; for many people, unfortunately, the curriculum is an unpleasant sortie into a vast sea of facts, formulas, concepts, vocabularies, laws, theories, and generalizations coupled with unfamiliar intellectual applications. So it is not unusual for students and, occasionally, teachers to ask the question, "Who needs the curriculum (and why)?"

The need to know subject matter content does not answer the question or satisfy these questioners. If subject matter is to gain stature in the eyes of those discontented with the school curriculum, it must be promoted not on the basis of the value of content acquisition but, rather, on the basis of what subject matter can do for the individual's ability to think. There is no substitute for knowledge, the content of the curriculum. However, isolated facts, while vital and necessary components of subject matter, are only part of the learning process.

What Is Unique to Using a Thinking Skills Approach?

Why should skills be given equal time with the subject matter of the curriculum? While each discipline has its own particular approach, tools, and methods for discovering and ordering information, all learning has in common the processes of exploration and experimentation. They are unique to a skills approach. Exploration and experimentation are the processes of establishing the existence of something or finding the solution to a problem. Concomitant with the acquisition of the skill of experimentation, elementary and middle-school children should acquire from a skills approach to learning:

> the habit of questioning all things;
>
> the ability to evaluate premises, impinging variables, and the consequence of anticipated action;
>
> the spirit of demonstrative replication and verification;
>
> a desire to search for data and their meanings;
>
> a respect for logic in the development of a strategy for inquiry.

If there is a joy to learning, it is in the awareness and development of skills acquisition as a primary outcome of learning. The learner will see the facts, concepts, formulas, vocabularies, laws, theories, and generalizations of the subject matter as justifiable and even desirable.

What Should Determine the School Curriculum?

Determination of the curriculum content is contingent on several factors—the goals of society, the structure of the discipline, and the goals of the learner. The goals of society are usually broad and pervade the entire curriculum, K–12. The discipline, while seemingly well delineated, is often confounded by the nature and geographic mobility of the learners. The goals of the learner should be of primary importance. A more detailed discussion of these factors follows.

The Goals of Society   The structure of a democratic society demands that its citizens be responsible, competent, and ethical. The curriculum can assist children to understand the dependence of society upon educational achievement and to accept the fact that education is basic to living. Children should be led to understand the relationship of technological innovations and human affairs to society.

The Structure of the Discipline   Desirable outcomes of the curriculum should include:

- the acquisition of knowledge;
- the communication of knowledge;
- the use of knowledge by children in the solution of problems;
- the means for survival;
- the personal fulfillment reached from applying the newly acquired knowledge as a consumer and, perhaps, as a vocation.

Education should be structured to help individuals acquire skills and knowledge and to nurture their emotional adjustment to relate successfully to themselves and to the world around them. Children should be afforded a maximum education so that they can best manage their personal and collective lives to survive in the face of change.

The Goals of the Learner   Education is the human enterprise of striving to explain natural phenomena. It should extend children's ability to learn, choose, communicate, question, and respond to challenges. Such abilities will enable them, as individuals, to live with purpose in the world of today and tomorrow, achieving pleasure and satisfaction in the process.

The school curriculum should present appropriate content. Further, the curriculum should help students learn processes that will make them capable of observing with discrimination, of classifying observations of data, of quantifying their observations and communicating through the use of graphs, of synthesizing and modifying explanations, and of making and testing predictions against theory.

Content Selection in the School Curriculum

Over the past 20 years much that has happened in public school instruction has been good. Numerous federally funded projects at the elementary and secondary school levels have pointed the way for what might be generally accepted as appropriate content instruction for public-school students. Fallout from these projects has carried their spirit and intent into commercially prepared textbooks, visual aids, and a wide assortment of hands-on equipment and manipulatives. A variety of good materials is available for instruction tied to all disciplines.

Generally speaking, the curriculum should be exploratory. The nature of the learner rather than the structure of the content should dictate the curriculum. The curriculum in the primary grades should concentrate on the development of the basic process skills such as observing, classifying, measuring, communicating, inferring, predicting, and recognizing space/time relationships.

These skills should be developed around hands-on curricular activities that:

- stimulate curiosity and enthusiasm;
- capitalize on the creative nature of young children;
- foster continuous creativity;
- nurture the habits of systematic observations;
- initiate and sustain qualitative and quantitative thinking and representations;
- promote the development of problem solving.

A discipline vocabulary, while important, should not be acquired at the expense of the acquisition of ideas. Ideas should precede the vocabulary of the discipline.

The curriculum content of both intermediate and middle schools should focus on the enlargement and continuity of these skills. In these grades the curriculum should concentrate on content acquisition as a vehicle for the development of such integrated process skills as experimenting, controlling for variables, collecting and interpreting data, and models.

The vitality of the discipline should be promoted by constantly presenting it as a challenge. Inquiry, the spirit of searching for answers, should not be sacrificed to the tedium of the subject. This is not to deny that the tedium exists, but it is tolerated best when the discipline's vitality is fully appreciated by the learner.

Curricula, like everything else, must change, but that change must be carefully monitored. Priorities must be delineated. Given an exponentially increasing body of knowledge, the school's curriculum content must be organized to assign appropriate material to different grade levels and student groups. Historians, history educators, and teachers, for example, need to agree on appropriate topics in history for students at the elementary and middle-school levels.

The capstone to any curricular instruction should be the capacity of an individual to relate sensitively, to think divergently, and to perform imaginatively in confrontations with people and ideas. For every complex problem there is usually a short, simple answer. Unfortunately, it is usually the wrong answer. The right answer is the one we want badly enough to work hard enough to obtain.

WHAT IS YOUR STYLE? (LEARNING STYLES/TEACHING STYLES)

The 4MAT System (McCarthy 1980) compared the findings of well-known learning styles researchers such as David Kolb, Carl Jung, and Anthony Gregorc, and identified four similar strands about how people perceive and process information. McCarthy combined the research findings into four distinct learning styles.

Style One learners or "Innovative Learners" like to work in groups, discuss ideas, listen to the point of view of others, and share experiences. They are sensitive individuals and do not like conflict or impersonal teachers.

Style Two learners or "Analytic Learners" are interested in facts and ideas. They like traditional classrooms where there is one right answer, peace and quiet, rows of desks, and structured assignments. They enjoy a well-organized lecture and learn by reading and thinking through ideas. They do not like group work and group grades.

Style Three or "Common Sense Learners" want to know how things work and need hands-on experiences. Information should be useful and practical. These learners like to go on field trips and to get actively involved. They do not like sitting in one place and listening to lectures.

Style Four or "Dynamic Learners" seek hidden possibilities. They learn by trial and error and self-discovery. Freedom to discover and create is important for these risk takers. They do not like rigid schedules or routine work.

As a learner, you will prefer one of these styles. As a teacher, you usually teach and design activities that correspond to your learning style. If this is the case, you are teaching to about 25 percent of the students in your class. Bernice McCarthy suggests that it is important to rotate your teaching style so the other 75 percent of the students in your class have a chance to participate in activities that are meaningful and enjoyable to them.

As you walk down the hall of any school and peer into classrooms, you see differences in teaching styles. Some rooms are meticulous: orderly printing on the chalkboard, desks neatly arranged in rows, a place for everything and everything in its place, a quiet tone of orderly children, and a well-organized teacher's desk. Across the hall is an active classroom: individualized learning centers positioned on available tables, students on the move, desks pushed into groups, sounds of computer activities and busy chatter, the chalkboard covered with magnetic clips holding student art work, and the teacher's desk partially hidden behind a screen to conceal the pile of papers and clutter accrued during the day.

Both classrooms are excellent environments where children can enjoy learning as long as the teachers are competent, enthusiastic, and caring. Is one classroom better than the other? No. The way a teacher structures classroom environment, interacts with students and parents, plans activities, attends to paperwork, and assigns grades is related to personal temperament (Keirsey and Bates 1984). You probably will not be able to alter your teaching style or the style of the teacher across the hall, but by learning more about your personality type and temperament you can identify your strengths and weaknesses and work conscientiously to appreciate the positive aspects found in yourself and in the other teachers in your building.

Just think: Within one faculty you have the opportunity to interact with teachers who are open-minded, knowledgeable about important facts and details, like to organize and complete projects, and think of new and hidden possibilities. Together you can be a dynamic team, a powerful change agent that can encourage, inform, coach, challenge, and accommodate every young mind that enters your school.

POINTS TO PONDER

What is your teaching style? What assessments can you take to find out?

DO YOU HAVE A PREFERENCE? (RIGHT, LEFT, OR WHOLE BRAIN)

Sperry (1973) discovered that the functions of the two hemispheres of the brain were different. Bogen (1975) concluded in his research that the two hemispheres of the brain process information differently. The left hemisphere processes information in a linear or sequential pattern where the right hemisphere uses a global process. Since students process information differently, teachers need to be aware of how they present information.

Some students process information in a linear manner using the left hemisphere. They need factual material, presented in a sequential and organized manner. They like carefully planned, structured assignments. They can follow verbal instructions. Even though they like to talk and can write effectively, they prefer multiple choice tests because there is only one right answer.

Other students process information globally using the right hemisphere. They learn best by seeing and doing. They like demonstrations and illustrations. They like to draw and use manipulatives. When doing a report, they will research everything, but have difficulty narrowing down the topic. They probably will write the paper first, then write the outline. They like working with others; it helps their ideas flow. They are spontaneous and use their intuition to solve problems. They like open-ended assignments so they can be creative and use different resources and various forms of media.

Other students process information using both hemispheres of the brain. They feel comfortable learning in a variety of ways.

As a teacher it is important to be aware of your brain preference, because you will have a tendency to teach and assign projects that reflect that preference.

RIGHT-BRAINED/LEFT-BRAINED SURVEY

Choose the description that is most like you by placing a check by the letter.

_____ **A.** Prefers verbal directions, uses names of streets when giving directions.

_____ **B.** Prefers visual directions, uses maps and names of landmarks when giving directions.

_____ **C.** Uses both verbal and visual directions.

_____ **A.** Likes a clean, organized desk.

_____ **B.** Likes to have a variety of materials handy. May have a few piles of papers or books on desk.

_____ **C.** Has a semiorganized desk with a few essential materials available.

_____ **A.** Likes to finish one task before starting on another project.
_____ **B.** Works on several tasks simultaneously.
_____ **C.** Can work on one task at a time or several projects simultaneously.

_____ **A.** Proceeds at a task in a logical and sequential order.
_____ **B.** Works at a task in a random order.
_____ **C.** Proceeds at some tasks in logical, sequential order, but handles other tasks in random order.

_____ **A.** Likes to plan and structure the day.
_____ **B.** Likes variety in the day, is very spontaneous.
_____ **C.** Likes both structure and spontaneity in a day.

_____ **A.** Uses a "To Do" list.
_____ **B.** On occasion makes a "To Do" list, but loses it.
_____ **C.** Uses a "To Do" list when necessary.

_____ **A.** Solves problems in a logical manner.
_____ **B.** Uses hunches and past experience to solve problems.
_____ **C.** Solves some problems logically and others intuitively.

_____ **A.** Learns best by listening.
_____ **B.** Learns best by seeing visuals, pictures, and diagrams.
_____ **C.** Learns best by both listening and seeing visuals.

_____ **A.** Likes details and facts.
_____ **B.** Understands the main ideas.
_____ **C.** Understands the main ideas and retains selected facts and details.

_____ **A.** Prefers multiple-choice tests.
_____ **B.** Prefers essay tests.
_____ **C.** Likes both multiple-choice and essay tests.

_____ **A.** Analyzes information, likes to outline and classify.
_____ **B.** Synthesizes information, likes to summarize.
_____ **C.** Can outline and summarize information equally.

_____ **A.** Works well with an authority figure.
_____ **B.** Enjoys working in a collegial or team effort.
_____ **C.** Enjoys working with an authority figure as well as working in leadership roles with a team of colleagues.

_____ **A.** Prefers to work in a quiet atmosphere without interruptions.
_____ **B.** Prefers to work in an active environment with a degree of noise.
_____ **C.** Can work in both quiet and active settings.

_____ **A.** Controls emotions, internalizes feelings.
_____ **B.** Displays emotions, shares feelings.
_____ **C.** Internalizes as well as shares feelings and emotions.

_____ **A.** Likes to improve or fix something.
_____ **B.** Likes to invent or create something.
_____ **C.** Likes to fix as well as create items.

_____ **A.** Remembers what people say.
_____ **B.** Remembers what people do.
_____ **C.** Remembers what people say and do equally.

_____ **A.** Feels it is important to be on time.
_____ **B.** Loses track of time, is often late.
_____ **C.** No preference relating to time.

_____ **A.** Gains energy by being organized.
_____ **B.** Gains energy by being creative and flexible.
_____ **C.** Gains energy by being both organized and flexible.

_____ **A.** Likes being right.
_____ **B.** Likes being insightful.
_____ **C.** Has no preference.

_____ **A.** Squeezes toothpaste tube from the bottom, rolls tube.
_____ **B.** Squeezes toothpaste tube in the middle, only rolls tube when necessary.
_____ **C.** No preference, probably uses pump.

Count the number of As, Bs, and Cs. A high number (13 or above) of only As, Bs, or Cs indicates that:

If it is As, the left side of the brain is more active in processing information.

If it is Bs, the right side of the brain is more active in processing information.

If it is Cs, both sides of the brain are processing information.

If the scores are equally divided or you have a blend of Cs and As or Bs, you are using the whole brain, but may be favoring one side.

If you have a right-brain preference, you will give open-ended assignments. Left-brained students may become frustrated. They will not begin the assignment until they have the specific details, due dates, and requirements. On the other hand, if you have a left-brain preference, you may give so many directions that the right-brained students may feel suffocated. The key is balance. Remember to consider your preference and your students' preferences when introducing new topics, planning group work, and assigning projects.

IMAGINE THAT! (GUIDED IMAGERY FOR CREATIVE THOUGHT)

There is just not enough time. With textbooks in every subject, plus workbooks, black-line masters, enrichment pages, skill sheets, and tests, students do not have time to use their imaginations.

All week students record the one correct answer on hundreds of black lines, then during the last 20 minutes on Friday afternoon teachers ask them to write a creative story. Does it surprise you that students groan and fall short at their attempts? Besides, teachers have to grade all of those assignments, so they lack the time and energy to plan for guided imagery.

Creative ideas flow when you are relaxed. Many times the solution to a problem is evident as you wake from sleep. New ideas pop into your head as you drive to work, exercise, doodle, or take a bath. Students also need time to relax, reflect, and imagine.

Guided imagery is simple to do, it can be done in short blocks of time, and is easy to plan if you have a couple of visualization or imagery books handy. Start by having the students sit quietly and close their eyes. Have them focus on their breathing and relax their bodies. After the students are relaxed and centered, begin a guided imagery exercise that will allow them to focus on their senses.

Imagine what it would feel like to be sitting in a boat in the middle of a lake on a warm day. Feel the warmth of the sun and the coolness of the breezes. What sounds do you hear? What do you see in the water around you? What do you visualize in the distance? Be aware of the smells that surround you.

After the guided imagery exercise, encourage students to draw, write, tape, or make a concept map of visualizations. When students have recorded their own creative thoughts, allow time for them to share. Students will be very responsive and willing to discuss. All visualizations are correct and, therefore, help to build self-esteem. Lines of communication are opened. Guided imagery can be used to stimulate creative writing and artistic production. It can also be used to help students relax before a test, increase concentration, and improve memory skills (Murdock 1987).

If your goal is to meet the cognitive, creative, and affective needs of students, you will find time to schedule guided imagery.

CONCEPT MAPPING

Have you ever started to write a story, unit plan, research paper, speech, or journal article, and the blank sheet of paper overwhelmed you? Concept mapping is a way to brainstorm ideas, tie unrelated thoughts together, and start the creative juices flowing.

Begin with a nucleus word or phrase, then write clusters of words or phrases that relate to the main idea (Rico 1983). As you write each word, circle it and then draw an arrow to connect your thoughts. It is important to let your ideas flow. In the final writing phase, you may not use all of the words you generated, but any word may spark a better idea. The concept map will give you a visual presentation of your ideas as shown in Figure 1.2, and the poem will illustrate the final writing phase.

Figure 1.2 Concept map

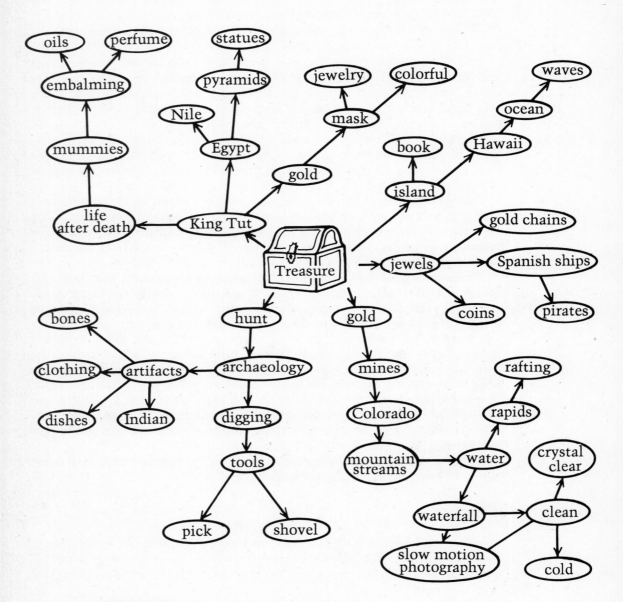

Treasures

A treasure may glisten in the pages of a book,
as the reader internalizes the adventure within.
Or it may be in the depths of a fearsome sea,
ready to be claimed by the seeker of Spanish ships and golden coins.

A treasure may be a fragment of a bone or a shard of pottery;
unearthed by the toil and determination of a patient
archaeologist.
Or it may be the solitude of a Polynesian island;
where the waves tickle the shy, peaceful sand.

A treasure may reveal the story of powerful kings;
who were preserved in cloth and oils to wait for a life beyond.
Or it may be a crystal clear waterfall, tucked high in the mountains;
ready for a photographer to capture each sparkling crystal.

Kathleen J. Steele

Individuals with a left-brain preference organize ideas in a sequential, out-line format. Concept mapping may help them to generate more original and cre-ative ideas. Concept mapping for an individual with a right-brain preference quickly presents a holistic picture providing a visual framework from which to start.

Concept mapping can be very useful when creating interdisciplinary units. Concepts such as power, conflict, future, energy, or change can be used as spring-boards to generate activities that relate to several subject areas, allowing stu-dents to see how art, music, history, science, mathematics, and/or literature are connected.

WHY BOTHER?

All is not right with the world, and much of the blame for this is placed on educa-tion—or lack of education. It has been predicted that by the year 2000, high-school seniors will be exposed to more information in one year than their grandparents may have encountered in their entire lives. These same students will have had to assimilate more information, innovations, and inventions than have appeared on the scene in the past 150 years. And, yet, many high-school students still struggle with reading. Nearly one million high-school students drop out of school each year and another 750,000 receive diplomas, even though they barely can read. Reading seems out of date. Even though students may mas-ter the basic academics, many find school a joyless experience, devoid of the excitement of learning. If they don't drop out, they may simply stay on and be classified as "students at risk."

Despite numerous advances in our society, the same subjects are taught now as they were taught 50 years ago. A piece of chalk is still the dominant tool used to promote learning. The teacher is still the dominant figure. And the teacher is least trained in what is prime to learning—questioning, inquiry, and problem solving, all well seasoned with tender loving care, gentleness, patience, and humility. Students are asked to do too much thinking without acting, then are criticized for acting without thinking. The academic world is unlike reality.

Students exit schools feeling they don't count for much; that feelings don't count; that nothing much matters; that they never have any good ideas; and that one can get by, by sliding by. This is not acceptable. Unskilled, semiliterate individuals cannot compete. They produce inferior, noncompetitive products. Competition is not an evil act. Competing is an experience that engages one's knowledge, pride, tenacity, discipline, creativity, stamina, and personality to the maximum. Students need to work smarter, compete smarter, live smarter, rather than merely working harder. Lower literacy is a competitive disadvantage.

Why do creative teachers bother? We bother because we care. We bother because we do not wish to tolerate inconsistencies in quality. We bother because we wish to correct or change inequalities and improve things for all. We care because we recognize the value of human resources: A generation is a terrible thing to waste. Creative teachers are concerned with inflexible learning organizations that are authoritarian and highly resistant to change, children who "doom" themselves even before engaging life, programs that do not test students' mettle. We are concerned about a class of illiterate individuals disenfranchised from a class with access to education, information, and advanced technology. We concern ourselves with the question, "Will the bottom portion pull the top down faster than the top portion can pull the bottom up?" We bother because we care and wish to be involved in the improvement of education.

RESEARCH SAYS . . .

PAST AND FUTURE OF THE NATION'S REPORT CARD

GROWTH OF SINGLE-PARENT FAMILIES

SCHOOLS PARTLY RESPONSIBLE FOR DROP IN SELF-ESTEEM AMONG GIRLS

RACIAL, ETHNIC PREJUDICE STILL PREVALENT

MANY STUDENTS SPEND SCHOOL DAY AS PASSIVE "SPONGES"

Each week we are bombarded with headlines regarding the status of education in our schools with respect to its most important product: our students. We are constantly provided with facts and figures about the students enrolled in school today. For more than 20 years, the National Assessment of Educational Progress (NAEP) periodically has been testing American students to see how much they know about mathematics, reading, writing, science, U.S. history, civics, and geography. A number of conclusions can be drawn about student performance from those results:

1. More students are gaining basic skills, but fewer are demonstrating higher level applications of those skills.
2. Minority students, particularly African Americans, have made substantial progress in narrowing the gaps between them and their white counterparts, especially in reading. Nonetheless, the differences in performance remain unacceptably large—by age 17, the equivalent of two grades in reading and four grades in science.
3. Reading, writing, and mathematics performance has changed little over the past 20 years. Science has shown minor achievement gains.
4. Little progress has been made in reducing the gender gaps that favor males in mathematics and science and females in writing.

NAEP looked at what is being done to improve student achievement. They concluded that over the past 20 years little seems to have changed in how students are taught. For example:

1. Despite much research suggesting better alternatives, classrooms still are dominated by textbooks, teachers' lectures, and short-answer activity sheets.
2. Students still spend little time reading at school or at home.
3. Students spend little time discussing or writing about what they read.
4. Students receive little writing instruction and rarely work on independent activities and group projects.

By providing measurements of American educational achievement, NAEP will be critically important in assessing the success of our National Education Goals over the next ten years. NAEP information will assist both researchers and practitioners in setting the stage for learning and in helping to make a difference in how children learn.

PAUSE FOR A SUMMARY

- What we say and do as teachers can have a lasting effect upon children.
- Creative teaching advocates the integration of all areas of the curriculum with the attitudes, ideals, and spirit of each discipline.
- Creative teaching develops observational skills in making distinctions, in critical thinking, and in experimenting.
- The basic purpose of education is to help students learn to think.
- The approach to teaching should vary to accommodate all learners.
- The curriculum is a natural for developing attitudes, thinking skills, and motor skills.
- Determination of the content in the school curriculum depends on several factors, including societal goals, the structure of the discipline, and learner goals.

- The elementary and middle-school curriculum should be exploratory in nature with the learner, rather than the structure of the disciplines dictating the curriculum.
- The elementary and middle school curriculum should center on broad-based themes to encourage interdisciplinary study and continuity.
- There is no shortage of outstanding materials or teaching strategies for meaningful curricular instruction at the elementary and middle-school levels.
- Education must continue to change to meet the needs of a diverse and evolving society.

REFERENCES

Adler, M. (1952). "The Great Ideas: A Syntopicon of Great Books of the Western World." In J. VanTassel-Baska, (1988). *Comprehensive Curriculum for Gifted Learners*. Needham Heights, MA: Allyn and Bacon.

Armstrong, L. S. (1991). "Racial, Ethnic Prejudice Still Prevalent, Survey Finds." *Education Week*, vol. 10, no. 17, p. 6.

Bagley, M., and Hess, K. (1987). *200 Ways of Using Imagery In the Classroom*. Monroe, NY: Trillium Press.

Bagley, M., and Lavin, C. (1988). *Reading Through Imagery: K to 5*. Monroe, NY: Trillium Press.

Bloom, B. S. (1956). *Taxonomy of Educational Objectives: Handbook I: Cognitive Domain*. New York: David McKay.

Bloom, B. S. (1976). *Human Characteristics and School Learning*. New York: McGraw-Hill.

Bogen, J. E. (1975). "Some Educational Aspects of Hemisphere Specialization." *UCLA Education*, vol. 17, pp. 24–32.

Cronbach, L. J. (1963). *Educational Psychology*. New York: Harcourt Brace Jovanovich, p. 10.

De Mille, R. (1976). *Put Your Mother on the Ceiling*. New York: Penguin Books.

Hess, K. (1987). *Enhancing Writing Through Imagery*. Monroe, NY: Trillium Press.

Keirsey, O., and Bates, M. (1984). *Please Understand Me: Character and Temperament Types*. Del Mar, CA: Prometheus Nemesis Book Company.

Krathwohl, D. R.; Bloom, B. S.; and Masia, B. B. (1964). *Taxonomy of Educational Objectives, Handbook II: Affective Domain*. New York: David McKay.

McCarthy, B. (1980). *The 4MAT System: Teaching to Learning Styles with Right/Left Mode Techniques*. Oak Brook: Excel, Inc.

McGuigan, F. J., and Schoonover, R. A., eds. (1973). *The Psychophysiology of Thinking*. New York: Academic Press.

Murdock, M. (1987). *Spinning Inward*. Boston: Shambhala.

"Past and Future of the Nation's Report Card." (1990) *Office of Educational Research and Improvement Bulletin*. Washington: U.S. Department of Education.

Rico, G. (1983). *Writing the Natural Way*. Los Angeles: J. P. Tarcher, Inc.

Rothman, R. (1991). "Schools Are Called Partly Responsible For Drop in Self-Esteem Among Girls." *Education Week*, vol. 10, no. 17, p. 6.

Sato, I. S. (1988). "The C-3 Model: Resolving Critical Curricular Issues Through Comprehensive Curriculum Coordination." *Journal for the Education of the Gifted*, vol. 11, pp. 92–115.

Sperry, R. (1973). "Lateral Specialization of Cerebral Function in the Surgically Separated Hemispheres." In F. J. McGuigan and R. A. Schoonover, eds. *The Psychophysiology of Thinking*. New York: Academic Press.

VanTassel-Baska, J. (1988). *Comprehensive Curriculum for Gifted Learners*. Needham Heights, MA: Allyn and Bacon.

Chapter
2

Creative Teaching
If It Is Too Much Trouble, It's Probably Worth It!

Where children are encouraged to make many choices, they increase in confidence and self-awareness. . . . If children have many choices to make, the teacher is able to observe each child in a wide variety of situations. The broader [the] observation, the better [the teacher] is able to plan for a child's further learning.

Laura D. Dittmann

A TRUE FAIRY TALE

Once upon a time, a long time ago (it really only happened a minute ago) a new, open-concept, continuous-progress, individualized, self-pacing school opened. It was a beautiful sight. The interior was shiny and sparkling (you could dine on the polished tile floor). There were intermittent walls, few doors, no room designations, and nothing was out of bounds. As the week preceding the start of school began, the teachers arrived at the building and readied themselves for the new year. They met their principal (he had a one-hour break from his role as tour guide), heard his inspiring speech, and went on their way. It was a busy week. They had to set up the bulletin boards to welcome the children to school, arrange the desks in neat rows, divide the coat racks and storage cabinets, and arrange them to encircle each area. The teachers of each grade level had to predetermine the division of the children into groups (the blues, greens, golds, and purples), order the movies, prepare the lesson plans, and post the rules of conduct in the school.

Happy children with smiling faces entered the school the following Monday morning. They were pretested for grouping in reading, mathematics, science, and social studies (the major subjects).

Oh, yes, we almost forgot to tell you that this school used the integrated-day approach, except:

Art had to be from 9 to 9:50 on Mondays and Wednesdays.

Music had to be from 1 to 2:15 on Thursdays.

Physical education had to be from 2 to 2:30 on Fridays, and so on.

At the end of the first week, the principal and his administrative staff (the secretary, the coach, and the janitor) decided that homerooms should be instituted, based upon grade level.

At the end of the second week, the teachers requested that the children remain with them all morning for skill work in a self-contained setting.

At the end of the third week, the skill work was continued all day.

By the second semester, dividers had been installed throughout the school along with room doors. The children stayed with their one teacher all day, except for "specials."

And they all lived happily ever after—all except the children.

Educational jargon is overwhelming. Some of the jargon words are used in our true fairy tale. Unfortunately, in education, more often than not the vocabulary changes but the instruction doesn't. Before we present you with skills and techniques that are useful as alternatives to the traditional instruction, let us examine alternative approaches to traditional educational problems and the use of creative teaching aids.

CHANGING YOUR SCHOOL

Grandmother, daughter, and granddaughter were all reminiscing about their school days. Each, in turn, described a typical classroom of her era. At the finish they looked at each other in amazement. Each had described the same room. Well, not really, but nearly so. So few changes in the classrooms had taken place in the 65-year gap between grandmother's and granddaughter's time that, for all practical purposes, they seemed to be talking about the same room. Is your classroom much the same as the classrooms in your childhood? Most assuredly paint colors and furniture have changed, but it is surprising that classrooms now are more like than unlike classrooms of the past. When changing the school, what better place to start than with your classroom and yourself?

CHANGING YOUR PHILOSOPHY

Every teacher has a philosophy underlying classroom teaching, whether it is written or unwritten, spoken or unspoken. Our actions reveal our philosophy. We can hardly conceal our views of education. Our every action bespeaks our beliefs. Some of us are steadfast in our philosophies; others are meandering, searching for a philosophy. In either event, review these thoughts: Some may cause you to alter your philosophy.

As you teach children the many wondrous things of life, remember you are growing, changing, maturing, learning, loving, just like your students. You and they are eternal learners.

Education is not just preparation for life; it is a portion of life. Education is a highly personal, fragile thing. It is nurtured internally, digested slowly, and is powerful enough to move the universe. It is a glorious thing you do, encouraging learning in others. Yours is an awesome task.

Take some risk. A turtle can only progress when its neck is stuck out. Push a little for what you believe. Keep pushing. Perseverance counts.

Start each day thinking—to children with love.

Raise your sights. Aim high. Even if you miss the highest target, you may strike a target of value a little lower down. If you aim low and miss, you will strike the dust. Children should leave your class one step closer to being creative, innovative, independent thinkers. Aim high.

Being a good teacher is like being a good parent—at times, extremely difficult. At times you will not know if what you are doing is right or wrong until it is too late to change it. Nevertheless, you must make decisions.

You don't have to know everything, but it helps. Improve your posture. Be yourself. Relax, and let the good teaching roll out. Think positively. You are okay. The children are great. The sun rises every day even though some days are cloudy. Remember that you may not be the best teacher in the world, but you'll do until he or she comes along.

Slow down. Most teachers have a tendency to rush learning. A teacher cannot teach faster than the students can learn. Allow children time to reflect on and respond to your teaching and their learning.

CHANGING YOUR ATTITUDE

Children are amazing. They are basically patient with, tolerant of, and sympathetic to the inconsistencies of education. Some even love us. The loyalty that children exhibit toward the system reflects their acceptance, or perhaps resignation, during 180 days a year for at least 9 years. In any event they deserve a round of applause—tempered with the awareness that not everyone you teach will have the same excitement for learning that you have. Different appetites require different menus. Avoid the negatives in teaching. Don't, can't, won't, haven't, and similar words should be supplanted, where possible, by positive statements. Confidence is a good teacher trait—and a good child trait.

Love children. Become an affection giver. If you can't love them, at least like them. Not all children are easy to like; nevertheless, they welcome and need affection.

Smile. Don't wait until Thanksgiving Day to launch your personality.

Laugh. It is amazing how few students can describe their teacher's laughter. It happens too rarely. Laugh with the children, not at them.

Rarely do teachers fail because they are not intelligent enough to teach. Most fail because they lack personality to communicate and relate to children and adults. No one owes you anything. You owe yourself something. Smile. Enjoy the job. Teaching is fun. Children are great. Give a little—then a lot.

gold and silver have their price—

learning is priceless

CHANGE FOR ALL CHILDREN

Things must change so they can remain the same. Change is universal. Change is life. You are not the same as you were when you started to read this paragraph. Education must change. The change should not be for its own sake, but it should be in response to educational needs as they arise.

Creative teachers are not afraid to change. The words, "I tried that, but it didn't work, so I'm trying another plan of attack today," are often used. The creative teacher's motto is, "Change for all children." No idea, method, or activity that has potential for helping children to learn and to succeed is eliminated before it has been tested and evaluated in the classroom.

Creative teachers place children first. The children are their overriding concern, more important than the school, the superintendent, the school board, other teachers, other jobs, or anything else.

Think of how you would change to meet the following situations:

- if children came to school only when they wanted to;
- if you could teach what you wanted to, when you wanted to, as long as you wanted to;
- if you had no supervisors;
- if you got paid by the number of students you attracted to your class;
- if you could regulate the curriculum;
- if you did not have to worry about the calendar;
- if you got paid in direct proportion to the scholastic achievements of your students;
- if teachers were not granted tenure;
- if you taught 11 months of the year;
- if children chose their teachers and changed teachers as they saw fit;
- if you had a parent helper in your class;
- if you were asked to televise your lessons to children being taught at home several days a week instead of attending school five days a week;
- if children graded teachers.

Problems outnumber solutions. It is easy to raise questions, and even easier to give advice. Were it not so easy, not everyone would be so eager to donate something to this pastime. Solutions to problems are bandied about by professionals who expound and then resolve the problem by using the eternal, "We ought to. . ." When the din fades and you reflect on the "we," you will quickly find that we is you. Authorities can identify problems, society can demand satisfactory solutions, but final solutions rest in the hands of the classroom teachers. The individual teacher is the vital catalyst in the process of education. The we must be you or woe is us. You are the axle about which education turns.

CHANGING YOUR OBJECTIVES

In preparing to teach a specific lesson, a teacher might legitimately ask two questions. First, what do I want the students to learn? A response to this question necessitates a rationale for the instruction and performance objectives (or what the students will be doing to acquire the learning). Second, do the students already know this? A response to this question may be found through preassessment measures.

A major complaint about performance objectives is that teachers tend to prepare the majority of them along the path of least resistance. This path follows the cognitive, or knowledge, domain. Performance objectives that merit consideration but receive less attention are those concerned with the development of attitudes, values, interests, and appreciation—all part of the affective domain. The objectives of the psychomotor domain are also slighted in favor of objectives in the cognitive domain. Teachers are rightly faulted for restricting performance objectives in the cognitive domain to simple recall rather than spreading them throughout the hierarchy of thinking skills. Little attention is directed to higher orders of thinking such as analysis and synthesis.

Change your objectives by including a variety of levels within each domain, be it cognitive, affective, or psychomotor.

When preparing performance objectives, consider the fact that we don't demand accuracy in art or creative writing, but we have permitted ourselves to require accuracy in content areas supporting past accomplishments. As a result, we may be paying a high price in lost interest, enthusiasm, vitality, and creativity in school. For example, teaching is not always exact. It is a creative engagement with ideas to solve problems. Many proposed ideas, at first, are seemingly harebrained, but they may well give rise to a brilliant solution.

EFFECTIVE TEACHING: DEVELOPING LIFELONG LEARNERS

Education does not end the instant you have a mortarboard on your head and a diploma in your hand. Education is the self-directed pursuit of knowledge. Teachers need to be able to train students to become lifelong learners.

Traditional Student	*Lifelong Learner*
Memorizes information	Knows where to find and how to use information
Fills in the blanks	Writes reports, letters, memos, and research documents
Answers questions	Asks questions
Solves problems that have one correct answer	Solves problems that have multiple answers
Works alone	Works with associates and teams of students
Listens to the teacher	Communicates with others, gives presentations, leads group discussions
Uses textbook as a primary information source	Gets information from multiple sources
Uses computer for drill and practice	Uses computer for word processing, data storage and retrieval, and communication
Uses teacher as a resource	Uses resource professionals outside the school and community
Has English as the major language	Speaks at least one foreign language
Wastes time	Manages time efficiently
Is bored	Meets new challenges with a positive attitude
Is teacher directed	Is self-directed

POINTS TO PONDER

Compare the differences between the traditional learner and the lifelong learner. What learning opportunities do you plan to provide for your students? Where will you place your emphasis? What would you add to the list?

Emphasis must be placed on how to find and use information instead of remembering isolated facts for a test. Students must be actively involved in solving real-world problems cooperatively and presenting their solutions orally or through written reports and articles. Students need to take an active role in making decisions about the way they learn and how they will demonstrate their knowledge. Students need to be trained to use all forms of technology such as slide projectors, overhead projectors, copy machines, interactive videodisks, teleconferencing equipment, video cameras, computers, CD-ROM, scanners, and laser printers. Word processing and on-line retrieval systems must be available for students of the twenty-first century. Schools must prepare students to become lifelong learners so they will continue to learn, to value education, and to be productive citizens.

REMOVING THE EDUCATIONAL STRANGLEHOLD

A favorite story in education circles tells of a time in the late 1960s when a European educator visiting the United States chose to investigate a so-called modern school. On visiting a fair-sized community and meeting a fair-sized superintendent, he inquired, "What is a modern school?" The superintendent hesitated momentarily and then said: "I don't understand it myself. I know only two people who understand it. One is a second grade elementary teacher on the east side of town and the other is one of the custodians in this building. Unfortunately, these two don't agree."

Things are not that bad, but sometimes they approach that level of confusion. We talk of traditional schools, modern schools, cooperative learning, and so on, ad infinitum. To refer to any one type as unique is, of course, unwarranted and incorrect. Each has a bit of the other. Regardless of title, each has a bit of a stranglehold on children. The title may be different, but the noose is the same.

Nooses are formed by dedicated teachers who have spent some 16 or 17 years preparing to teach. They intend to teach, and teach they do. Being intelligent, red-blooded, strongly motivated, well-organized, hardy, and determined to succeed, they plunge forward attacking the besieged learners with a barrage of facts, concepts, generalizations, and ditto sheets, all of which are supposed to result in significant learning for students. The result may be summed up thus: "Never have so many waited so long for so little." This commitment to exposition has existed long enough for researchers to have evolved what is termed the rule of two-thirds. It says that, on the average, in elementary and secondary schools, almost irrespective of subject areas, two-thirds of the class time is spent talking—two-thirds of that time the teacher is talking, and two-thirds of the teacher's talk is telling or demonstrating rather than interacting with students.

Many teachers seem compelled to see that every detail they feel responsible to transmit is transmitted. It must be crammed into the hapless, and often numb, children. But children are nice—they still love us. At least they tolerate us, despite our attempt to strangle them with knowledge.

It doesn't matter in what setting you operate or what title you assign to your teaching strategy. It does matter that you create a learning environment that will recognize and respond to individual needs and differences.

This commitment carries with it a prime consideration to change from a pedantic dispenser of knowledge to a facilitator of learning and a responder to children's behavior. Such a change results in inquiry learning. The important location is no longer in front of your audience; it is among your audience. No longer do teachers perform in front of children; they set the stage and then move out of the way so that children can learn.

The age-old question of who learns most in the classroom need not always be answered, "The teacher, naturally!" This may seem a valid response inasmuch as some teachers do most of the work and the thinking, all of the talking and questioning and, in many cases, most of the answering. We know this approach impedes individual progress. It shortchanges the learner by making him or her a spectator rather than a participator in learning.

Only when children make real choices in identifying their goals, planning strategies for learning, and evaluating their progress by questioning themselves and others can real learning take place.

We may never know exactly how we learn or how any other individual learns. Students learn by themselves as well as with their peers and teachers. It is said that no man is an island, but in some ways he is. Learning is personal, internal, and unique. Each child learns for himself or herself. We have done a poor job of convincing children that learning is for them. Most children go to school to please parents, teachers, and truant officers.

There is a joy and an intellectual power to learning. If there are elements of belief and trust in a learning environment, if the value of each child is respected, and if each child is free from total dependence on a particular individual or particular approach to learning, perhaps this joy and power can be realized.

CHANGING YOUR QUESTIONING TECHNIQUE

Teachers talk. They talk a lot. Often they talk too much. Teachers ask questions. They ask a lot of questions. Often they ask too many questions.

Recent tallies of teacher-pupil interaction revealed that 60 to 70 percent of the words spoken in a classroom were spoken by the teacher. The remaining 30 to 40 percent of the spoken words divided by the class population reduced down to a small number of spoken words per student per day. On the average, for every question asked by a pupil, a teacher asked 27 questions. The teacher's questioning rate averaged three and one-half questions a minute. Unfortunately, this domination does not develop an aggressive attitude toward thinking in students. Most questions teachers ask are trivial. Few stimulate students to think, and few draw well-thought-out responses from students. Most teacher's questions call for answers falling into the categories of memory, information giving, criticism, and comparison, with the heavy emphasis on memory and information giving. Rarely are questions directed to a problem-solving situation.

It is clear that in the teaching-learning situation, the teacher is the dominant figure. Teachers are prone to try to do student's thinking instead of motivating the students to think for themselves. Teachers who dominate the learning scene do little to stimulate inquiry or creativity. In fact, they discourage it. Inasmuch as so many of the questions teachers direct at students require only the use of memory to answer them, students tend to think the main purpose of education is memorization. Teachers concerned with training students who engage in the pursuit of learning for the purpose of understanding trade the quantity of questions for the quality of questions.

Questioning is akin to good investigating. A scientist formulating a well-thought-out hypothesis is questioning. If one asks good questions, one usually gets good answers. Teachers who practice poor questioning techniques promote student guessing and slovenly habits of thinking. Students as well as teachers should be aware of good questioning techniques. The teacher needs to provide the model.

Most successful teachers are good questioners. They ask open-ended questions that promote discussion rather than closed questions that call for single-word answers.

Open-ended Questions	*Closed Questions*
What do you observe?	What color is it?
Can you suggest a way to classify these?	Can you classify this by color?
What inferences can you make?	Is the cloth wet?

Often closed questions are strictly of the yes-no type, and they evoke little discussion or student involvement. Open-ended questions promote discussion and often require the student to use decision-making skills.

The Think-Pair-Share method (Lymon 1988) encourages teachers to ask open-ended questions and then to allow ten seconds of thinking time. After this period of time, the students discuss their ideas in pairs and then share them with the entire class. Changing the format of your instruction from lecture to seminar groups also promotes student and teacher dialogue. It encourages students to think, to visualize, to question, and to respond. A cueing bookmark (Figure 2.1), which includes question starters and discussion strategies, is helpful for the teacher and students to develop more thought-provoking questions. The teacher who asks critical and open-ended questions provides a model for students. Students' questions usually reveal little interest or serious thought. When teachers ask, "Are there any questions?" the response is meek and weak. The rule for questioning should be, "Don't tell what you can ask. Don't ask what the students should be asking." Challenge your students to be creative questioners.

Remember: Creative teachers promote discussion by asking the question first, then calling a student by name to answer it. They may ask another student to comment, and another, then another, rather than simply responding to one student's answer.

Creative teachers encourage rather than discourage student-to-student interaction.

Creative teachers allow sufficient time for student responses to questions. They practice waiting from 5 to 15 seconds for each student response rather than using the machine-gun approach—a question every two or three seconds. Open-ended questions cannot be answered in one or two seconds. Children need time to respond to questions and they need to have their answers accepted, temporarily at least (Johnson 1990).

How many times will a student try to respond to a question if continually told that his or her answers are wrong? Wrong answers should be reserved for quiz shows on television. Children should be encouraged to respond to questions, and their answers should be accepted until a "better" answer is discovered either through discussion, experimentation, or in reference materials.

Creative teachers are not afraid to say, "I'm not sure," "I don't know," "Maybe you're right and I'm wrong," "That's a great idea." They think positively and encourage lots of happy faces rather than sad ones.

Front	Back
QUESTIONING FOR QUALITY THINKING	**STRATEGIES TO EXTEND STUDENT THINKING**

Front

QUESTIONING FOR QUALITY THINKING

Knowledge—Identification and recall of information
  Who, what, when, where, how _____ ?
  Describe _____ .

Comprehension—Organization and selection of facts and ideas
  Retell _____ in your own words.
  What is the main idea of _____ ?

Application—Use of facts, rules, principles
  How is an example of _____ ?
  How is related to _____ ?
  Why is Significant _____ ?

Analysis—Separation of a whole into component parts
  What are the parts or features of _____ ?
  Classify according to _____ .
  Outline/diagram/web _____ .
  How does ____ Compare/contrast with ___ ?

Synthesis—Combination of ideas to form a new whole
  What would you predict/infer from _____ ?
  What ideas can you add to _____?
  How would you create/design a new _____ ?
  What might happen if you combined _____
    with _____ ?
  What solutions would you suggest for ____ ?

Evaluation—Development of opinons, judgments, or decisions
  Do you agree _____ ?
  What do you think about _____ ?
  What is the most important_____ ?
  Prioritize_____ .
  How would you decide about _____ ?
  What criteria would you use to assess ____ ?

Back

STRATEGIES TO EXTEND STUDENT THINKING

- **Remember "wait time I and II"**
  Provide at least three seconds of thinking time after a question and after a response
- **Utilize "think-pair-share"**
  Allow individual thinking time, discussion with a partner, and then open up the class discussion
- **Ask "follow-ups"**
  Why? Do you agree? Can you elaborate? Tell me more. Can you give an example?
- **Withhold judgment**
  Respond to student answers in a non-evaluative fashion
- **Ask for summary (to promote active listening)**
  "Could you please summarize John's point?"
- **Survey the class**
  "How many people agree with the author's point of view?' ("thumbs up, thumbs down")
- **Allow for student calling**
  "Richard, will you please call on someone else to respond?"
- **Play devil's advocate**
  Require students to defend their reasoning against different points of view
- **Ask student to "unpack their thinking"**
  "Describe how you arrived at your answer." (think aloud")
- **Call on students randomly**
  Not just those with raised hands
- **Student questioning**
  Let the student develop their own questions
- **Cue student responses**
  "There is not a single correct answer for this question. I want you to consider alternatives."

Source: Language and Learning Improvement Branch, Division of Instruction, Maryland State Department of Education.

Creative teachers have developed many positive responses to student answers rather than just okay, yeah, right, or wrong. They include:

Good job!

Well done!

Good for you!

Wow!

I like that!

You're doing a great job!

Outstanding!

Very nice!

Superior!

I'm impressed!

Interesting.

Excellent!

Terrific!

Super!

Creative teachers are concerned about their students' feelings and often ask them to evaluate what has been occurring in their class.

What are their favorite subjects? Why?

Are they doing things they don't like? How could these situations be changed?

What do they like or prefer?

What would they like to change? And for what reasons?

Evaluation is a continual process, not a once-a-semester or once-a-year thing. Try improving your questioning technique by:

- limiting yourself to one question in a 15-minute period;
- never answering your own questions;
- eliminating questions that call for yes-or-no responses;
- not asking questions that invite aimless or guessing responses;
- making sure that each child in your class is asked at least one meaningful question a day;
- asking both narrow- and broad-response questions;
- limiting memory questions to one an hour;
- letting the students ask the questions;

- mixing up your questions (thought-provoking questions, what-if questions, evaluation questions, and a variety of other types);
- asking a question and then listening. (Teachers are not always good listeners, particularly with children.)

CHANGING YOUR DISCUSSIONS

Talk to students. Don't always talk teaching-learning talk. Children need the faith and courage that come from your consideration of them as individuals who can make contributions. They need this more than they need to know the associative and distributive law or how to spell the word artichoke. Talk to them about many things, as you would talk to invited guests in your home. If necessary, change your conversational style. Communicate with individual children, not classes of children. Make every child feel you are talking directly to and for him or her.

Listen to students. Consider all students' responses. They say many things that have implications for improving your teaching. Learning that significantly influences behavior is self-discovered, self-appropriated learning. Instead of directing, ordering, meting out assignments, monitoring a practical rest-room schedule, or disciplining, step off the merry-go-round and strike out in new directions.

You say you can't. Remember the old adages such as "Where there's a will there's a way," "If you want to do something badly enough, you'll do it," "If there is something you want to do badly enough, you'll find the time." By and large these statements are true. We are not advocating a complete remodeling of your teaching style, but we are advocating your consideration of the changing role of a teacher. Your discussions should reflect this changing role. You are not a dispenser of knowledge, but rather one who elicits and clarifies learning. You are the one who convinces children that they have worth and that you have faith in them. You are the mood or climate setter. You are an organizer and facilitator of learning. And you recognize that you have limitations.

CHANGING HARD ROOMS TO SOFT ROOMS

Most children look forward to their first year of school with indescribable anticipation. They love their teachers. A book bag and a pencil box are exciting parts of the grown-up process of getting educated. This enthusiasm slowly dims until it bottoms out in what is called the fourth-grade slump. The excitement has worn off. September school attendance is only highlighted as a replacement for a long summer vacation. After the first few days when old friends have been revisited and new teachers scrutinized, rationalized, and categorized, the resignation sets in. It never ceases to be a wonder that so many students can tolerate so much, so long, with such reasonable—under the circumstances—politeness.

The decline of interest in school can be attributed largely to the artificial environment that exists in schools. It is unnatural for students to become a captive audience corralled in a room or several rooms and subjected to teachers who have decided in advance who shall learn what, when, to what extent, and in what period of time.

The classroom should be an extension of the home. Granted, children in your class may come from a variety of homes—some far better than any classroom, some as good, and some grossly inferior to any classroom. In terms of what the learner needs, any school, the best school, is inferior because the school exists for adults, not children. Although principals invite them to do so, children rarely think of the school as their home. Yet, many children spend more waking hours in school than in any other single place.

What does a school lack, or have, that causes students to reject it as their home? The biggest single factor is that there is no place to hide. This factor affects teachers as well as students. There is no place for privacy or private thoughts.

Not only is privacy lacking, but everything needs a sanction. At home you don't need permission to invade the refrigerator, retreat to the basement, use the bathroom, or step outdoors. In school you can't talk, move, shout hallelujah, or whistle. You sit or move in a prescribed manner. You play games. You have to please one adult continuously.

The parameters for running a school rule out its ever becoming the equivalent of a home. It need not be. Children, teachers, and principals all know this. Schools have other things to offer that a home never could. Schools have, for example, 30 or more constant companions, a team, a spirit, a publication, and so on. We all know what is desirable, but many of us are reluctant to teach as well as we know how. We teach as we have been taught. We honor our past heritage even though we know better. Somehow we feel this is the way we are expected to act.

Listen to the Sounds a Child Makes

Patricia R. Burgette

Listen to the sounds a child makes,
The spoken pleas, the silent message.
It is the child we teach,
Not the content, the morals, the skills.

Listen for the child who needs to be seen.
He needs to be known as unique,
Not just another one of the group.
The message may come
As a flurry of temper,
A shouted word,

A carefully spoken question,
Or a soft intent look.

Listen to our own needs,
The problems of the teacher,
The principal, the counselor.
How are these needs met?
Whose desires determine the course of the day?
All are there and should be heard,
Never forgotten or put aside.
We are all there and all must be a part.

Listen to the world outside,
Beyond the walls of the room.
Move as a part of life;
Share the warmth and reality of today.

Traditional, safe teaching is hastily saluted, and the merit raises go on. Teaching and reaching out are a bit more frightening. The ground is not as solid as in a subject area. Statements like, "If I let the children do as they please, it will be chaos; they'll never learn; they won't be ready," show a few of the fears of teachers making a transition to an alternative approach in the classroom. What does one do to soften a classroom? Here are a few suggestions:

- Periodically rearrange the room. Let the students assist you in deciding what to place where.
- Arrange the room so students can have private areas.
- Bring in a rocking chair. A recliner would do nicely. Why not? Some people study best in a prone position, others in a rocker.
- Have a few radios available. Periodic news and weather forecasts are part of the curriculum of the world around us.
- Have a junk box or "creativity bin" available.
- Include a box of modeling clay and a set of blocks.
- Provide greater storage space for children. The only private areas most children have are their desks. And those aren't very private.
- Allow children to get involved in decorating the room.
- Allow their ideas to come through. Remember that it's their room, too.
- Eliminate requests for permissions. Have the class provide the ground rules.
- Let each child get involved in a project of his or her choosing.
- Bring in a refrigerator. Let the class rule on what the behavior will be.
- Look at every conceivable space and surface area in light of a new purpose. What can you do with a ceiling? Is a floor just a floor? Are you really short of bulletin board space?
- How many musical instruments do you have readily available in the room?

- Have one or more computers available.
- Create a student message center.
- Build a reading loft to highlight your class library.
- If your room doesn't already have a rug, get a rug. Even a small one will do.
- Ask individuals to describe the conditions under which they work best. Try to duplicate some of the conditions that suit the largest number of students.

Some critics would howl long and hard at these changes. Some teachers might renege on accepting any or all of these changes. Some principals would be upset if the school looked too "lived in," if the children looked as though they were loafing instead of learning, or if the noise were beyond their personal expectations. They would be right to criticize. Anything can be carried to extremes. Anything that resembles a free-swinging circus with no learning going on can be an educational disaster. The rub is: How does one know when real learning is going on? There is no assurance that any more, or any less, learning is taking place in a "traditional" as opposed to a "creative" classroom. The only consolation a teacher has is in the acceptance of the notion that learning occurs best when individuals have a greater degree of freedom to explore, manipulate, and experiment within an environment. Associated with this latitude must be the provision of conditions that foster an attitude of "search" for learning. This attitude must be cultivated in an atmosphere of acceptance and approval, but at times it must forbid specific acts by individuals.

The learning process is to teach students to exercise individual control—control of themselves. If rigid controls are forever clamped on students, when do they mature?

A teacher doesn't need to be an educational interior decorator to make a sterile room come alive. If you think of yourself as a merchandiser, revitalizing a classroom can be a pleasant challenge. You are in business—the business of education. You are selling a product. To make your room livable, with learning space that entices learning, try adapting some standard business practices:

- Change the display counter. (Alter the decor, bulletin boards, interest centers, and anything else to improve the teaching environment.)
- Issue credit. (Give everyone an A at the start of the semester.)
- Welcome the customer. (Greet the students as they arrive each day.)
- Let the customers test-drive the product. (Provide some of the benefits that supposedly accrue from education.)
- Rent property. (Allow students to rent desks in the locations of their choice.)
- Give refunds. (Anyone unhappy with his/her education can come back for a refund.)
- Exchange the product when the customer is dissatisfied. (Remember that there should be no unhappy customers.)
- Offer discounts, bonuses, stamps, and other incentives.

- Have a clearance sale. (Raffle off incompletes, Ds, and Fs.)
- Establish a preferred mailing list to alert interested students to unique learning events.

Some children's suggestions have evolved into highly satisfactory rehabilitations of so-called traditional classrooms. Plans for two such rehabilitations follow:

Room 1 The components and their uses are:

  a. storage of large objects such as maps, large posters, and so on
  b. individual cubbyholes for each student, for the purpose of storing projects
  c. storage of equipment needed in an action-involvement classroom such as microscopes, balances, cameras, calculators, flashlights, and globes
  d. a magazine rack for periodicals and books
  e. students' desks and tables
  f. a raised, off-the-floor, center-of-the-classroom sandbox for action demonstrations and activities
  g. collection and specimen cabinets
  h. blackboard and movie screen
  i. teacher's desk

Figure 2.2

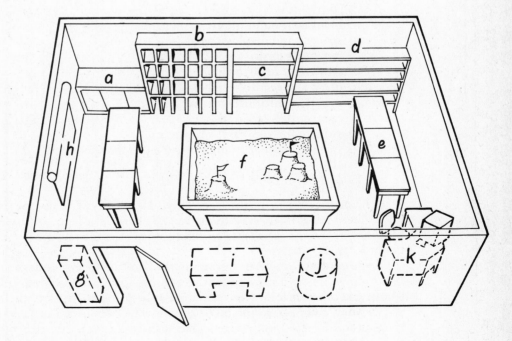

> **j.** creativity bin for odds and ends
> **k.** technology area, including a computer

The most unusual feature of this room is the center-of-the-room, raised sandbox, with the height suitable for the grade level for which it is being used. This sandbox does what the blackboard cannot do—it gives you the third dimension. Using a blackboard conveys the impression that we live in a two-dimensional world. How much easier it would be to reconstruct the Battle of Gettysburg by quickly scooping out areas, building up others, inserting a road, adding a farmhouse, establishing a railroad, and developing other details, than to read about it. The battle can be reviewed as you develop and change the conditions within the sandbox. What better way to teach history and geography?

Also what better way to teach the volume of a cone and a cylinder? Using a cone and a cylinder of similar heights, the volume of a sand-filled cone when poured into the cylinder fills the cylinder one-third full. Seeing, feeling, and listening make learning more lasting.

Mapping exercises, geology units, social studies units, reenacting reading stories—your imagination is the only limit—all done in relation to the sandbox concept can enhance learning. What else could you add or change in this room to improve instruction?

Room 2   Here we have another classroom designed by children. The components are:

> **a.** blackboard and movie screen
> **b.** storage and display space
> **c.** teacher's desk
> **d.** students' desks or tables
> **e.** book and reading shelves
> **f.** mobile multipurpose cart
> **g.** creativity bin
> **h.** storage for sporting equipment
> **i.** storage space for radio, video equipment, records
> **j.** sink
> **k.** computer table

The primary asset of this room is its flexibility. The teacher is in the audience. The students are free to move and work in a place of their choice. The mobility of the furniture and equipment permits arrangements to meet a variety of learning situations.

In designing a creative classroom, think of the spaces you may not currently use such as the window space, the ceiling, the wall space outside your classroom, and other spaces. Here are some suggestions: Think of the ceiling as the sky. Several constellations can be shown. The path of the sun and the phases of the moon can be plotted. Somewhere in the room note true north and magnetic north. Other compass directions can also be recorded around the room.

Figure 2.3

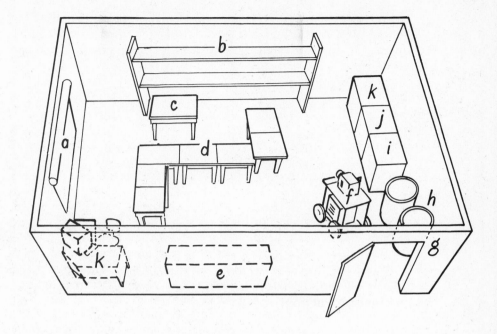

Windows have many uses. They can be used for decorative purposes or for experiments with light and temperature changes. Beekeeping is a fascinating window observation exercise. Your window, as the inside wall of the hive, can make everything easily visible. One teacher built birdhouses and feeders so that things could be viewed from inside the room. Herb gardens are also great window activities.

Hallways are great for displays and time lines. If you need to string a wire across the room to support draperies, fishnet artistry, or hanging gardens, do it! Just take the necessary safety precautions to insure that what goes up will stay up until you want it to come down.

Many valuable and highly usable room items such as display cases, advertisements, or card-display racks are yours just for the asking. When you spot something in a market or shopping center that looks usable, ask: "What happens to that when you (the grocer, the druggist, the lumberyard man) want to get rid of it? Really! Please save it for me. Call me collect! The number is . . . ." Better yet, give them your business card; you are a professional.

A local collecting station for recycling newspaper, aluminum articles, and glass furnished one entire school with trays and glassware for science and art. The children used the objects, then recycled them back whence they came. This is ecology in action. You and your students can practice what you preach.

The key to instituting a creative classroom is thinking about what better uses can be made of particular objects or places in order to bring about an improved learning environment. This is not constant change for change's sake, but it is the application of thought to the solution of problems as they arise. This thinking involves the consideration of all components of the room, school, and school yard. Try taking your class outdoors for science or to the gym for a mathematics lesson. Redesign your classroom using your own ideas and those of your students.

SELF-CHECKING FOR SUCCESS

Smiley faces abound. Stickers brighten the corners of ditto sheets that filter into the homes of eager-faced children who want proudly to show off their As and Bs. But what happens to the papers plagued with the indelible red letters of C, D, and F? This mass of refuse is flung into wastepaper baskets, folded into tight paper wads, and hidden in the dark recesses of desks and lockers or stuck into secret compartments of last winter's coats, old book bags, or even underwear, where nobody, not even the student, can view the fatal marks.

Teachers constantly tell children that practice makes perfect and then they promptly take each practice sheet, check it, score it, and give the student a grade. Practice should be just that—a time to try, to experiment, to get some answers right, and to make some mistakes. The most important part of learning is finding out what you do and do not know. Students need to be graded on the knowledge they have mastered, not the trial runs. When you work with a computer program and make a mistake, you are politely reminded to try again or to correct your error. The red letter F does not flash on the screen to attack your self-esteem or to squelch your motivation. Teachers need to celebrate correct answers and encourage students to learn from their mistakes.

Allowing students to check their own drill work permits students to evaluate their own progress in a nonthreatening manner. Immediate feedback is received, and students have the opportunity to learn necessary skills. The teacher can concentrate on developing pre- and posttests to monitor the progress of each student and assist students individually in mastering the concepts. Learning centers and educational games can also provide opportunities for students to practice skills without fear of failure. Self-checking games encourage students to work together, to teach each other, and to enjoy learning. The benefits for teachers are that learning becomes a positive experience in their classrooms, and teachers have fewer stacks of papers to grade. Students learn that they can be trusted and are responsible for their own learning. Isn't this the real goal of education?

THE INNOVATIVE, INTEGRATED CLASSROOM

The Way Things Were

The next time you are passing through a new town and happen to be driving by a public school building, stop and observe it. Does it look much like your school? Assume that the school is not in session and that no students are about. Without referring to the name of the school, could you, from the observed outward signs, state what grade levels are taught in this school? Is it an elementary school, an elementary/middle school, a junior high school, or a senior high school? What observations would allow you to state the grade levels that occupy this school when it is in session? What visible signs would help you with your decision? Would it be the nature of the artwork posted on the interior of the windows? Would it be the type and variety of playground equipment? Would it be the size and dominance of the gymnasium? Or would it be the size of the smokestack?

Would gaining access to the interior of this building have facilitated your decision? What internal clues would aid you in your decision? Physical objects such as extremely small chairs and desks, if they existed, would communicate something. What other clues might exist? Would the dimensions of the various classrooms be a clue? Would the presence of sophisticated equipment such as microscopes, chemical vents for exiting dangerous fumes from laboratory benches, computers, or trophy-filled cases be important clues?

As you wander through the building, could you select a room that is similar to yours? Or are the classrooms so diverse that you could not possibly find a room just like yours? Oddly enough, most schools look more alike than unalike, and this is generally true for classrooms within schools. Elementary classrooms across the country look very much alike, whether they are located in Begonia, Indiana or Bubblestart, California. There are many legitimate reasons for this, including policy, habit, economics, and preference. Nonetheless, there is an amazing similarity among public school learning settings. Commonalities extend to the horizontal alphabet line prominently placed over the blackboard in the front of the room. Bulletin boards are highly visible, and they are gaily festooned with children's art and other curriculum achievements. Rugs may cover portions of the floor. Well-worn paths are easily identified leading to and from the classroom drinking facilities, the pencil sharpener, and the wash-rooms. One almost always knows when one is in an elementary classroom, and that is the way it should be. Some elementary classrooms have been beautifully described as "living" circuses or "learning" communes. It seems like many things are going on at the same time, each in harmony with each other. These classrooms are integrated around children and the curriculum.

A classroom should have a personality. A classroom should mirror the teacher's personality and interests as well as the academic subjects being taught. The gestalt of any room should broadcast what transpires there. Upper grade level classrooms almost defy identification as to who teaches what to whom. Few clues exist within some rooms to communicate such information. More often than not, one can rarely ascertain what the instructor is like or likes. Some classrooms are devoid of any input from the instructor's personality. A classroom should reflect the personality of the school, the students, and the teacher. The message should be, "Hey, this is our room, your room, my room! We live here and we learn here." The classroom should be more than a room in a building.

The classroom is one of many learning arenas for children and teachers. Children learn all day in all ways from all people and all things. The classroom, however, is a unique setting for interactive group learning. As closely as possible it should complement and reinforce the total learning process as it exists in life. The classroom setting, by the very nature of its assemblage, offers unique situations for advancing learning, and in the process it should mimic the natural path of learning. This is best done through a creative, innovative approach to an integrated curriculum classroom.

The Way Things Might Be

An integrated classroom is anchored in the belief that nothing exists in isolation, that learning is connected in one way or another to all of life's processes, and that broad-based knowledge is preferred to narrow or limited-based knowledge. Integrating the classroom involves a meshing of the curriculum areas both with the physical attributes of the classroom and with the personalities of the teacher and the students. No prescriptive, step-by-step, integrated classroom process can be dictated inasmuch as curriculums, classroom physical attributes, and human personalities vary. Nonetheless, some broad, across-the-board commonalities prevail.

Curriculum Concerns

If a hierarchy of subject areas were to be assigned, traditionally reading and language arts would occupy the top position. The old adage, "You learn to read so that you can read to learn," is not totally unfounded. So these two areas must infiltrate all instruction. Every continued opportunity to promote better reading and language arts skills should be made. Attributes are accrued as they impinge on science, mathematics, and social studies. One does not read without reading about something. And that something supports other areas of the curriculum. Readers who comprehend are thinkers who question. Those who question, search, and those who search, read. Reading is at the hub of learning. Reading books, at every level, should be available, embellishing all areas of the curriculum. The teaching of art, mathematics, science, and social studies involves knowledge of the history of each. One can create history, but more often than not one reads about history.

As reading and language arts are bonded together, so are mathematics, science, and social studies. These three areas of the curriculum enjoy a special relationship. Mathematics complements science, and vice versa. One is incomplete without the other. A circle in mathematics can be a cycle in science. Scientists solve problems using mathematics. Mathematicians and scientists communicate through their writings, incorporating much prior research gained by reading. Proficiency in all of these areas can aid in the successful search for solutions to problems.

Social studies can be considered an extension of mathematics and science and the application of these skills to human-related problems. The interconnectedness of learning is strengthened by the continued articulation of this linkage.

Art is an expression of life. It embodies balance, proportions, rhythm, spatial relationships, color, composition, emphasis, perception, and so on. Art is mathematics, science, and an expression of human relations and reactions to the environment. Every piece of art embodies a story the artist intends to communicate to others. Art is about people, and people are about learning. Art is another strand in the web of learning. Art is creative. And so are mathematics, science, and writing as they offer or suggest unique solutions to social problems.

Physical education is a vital part of the integrated classroom. Physical education involves the physics of the human body, the mathematics of proportions, the chemistry of energy systems within the body, the biology of living, and more as they all interact in the process of living and surviving. Physical education should extend beyond deep breathing, push-ups, and kickball.

Classrooms are integrated into the learning schema when attention is given to those ancillary embellishments that augment the instructional lesson. The physical components of the classroom can be rearranged; for example, the furniture can be moved to mimic a setting for a story, an arrangement of a mathematical lattice, or a spatial maze for a science lesson. Mathematical assignments can be made for each chair and desk to connote paired sets, a correspondent, or an arrangement by some assigned ranking to communicate ordering. Classroom bulletin boards should reflect and complement these actions.

The classroom is a three-dimensional space. The floor tiles form a grid. The classroom has an orientation within the school and on the earth. What are these compass orientations? In cubic meters, what is the volume of the room? What is the history of the architectural design of the schools? It goes on and on. An integrated classroom cannot be mapped out in advance; it evolves out of the integration of the curriculum. It happens as you let it happen. It is an unstructured evolution that, when nurtured, blossoms into a unified learning experience unfettered by strained objectives, time constraints, and a set number of pages to be covered.

A classroom is a reflection of the teacher within. The ambiance of the classroom usually matches that individual's personality. The personal books that line the teacher's shelves speak of interests, likes, loves. The items that adorn the walls, shelves, desk, window sills, and the items that are displayed on the bulletin boards and the frequency of change of these items tell an observer much about the instructional leader and the climate for learning.

An integrated classroom is best served by a relaxed teacher who takes calculated risks and enjoys seeing the totality of the learning process unfold; by a teacher who constantly is alert to learning situations and what can be gained by their inclusion in part or in whole; by a teacher who has tolerance for what occasionally seems like chaos but with patience unfolds in a sensible, natural order; by a teacher who has a strong self-concept and imparts the acquisition of this to his or her students.

MOTIVATING CHILDREN

School attendance for children is a mandate. Children attend school with varying expectations of the outcome, which change over time. Among these expectations are the fulfillment of wishes to succeed for themselves, their parents, and/or their peers. Generally, they all want to achieve. Success is a highly desirable commodity. Few of us envy failure. Children seek to derive pleasure from working, applying themselves, being disciplined to the task of learning, and reaping the rewards of their efforts. They wish to find some level of performance that affords them the pleasure of engaging the learning process and emerging from it with some sense of accomplishment. They desire recognition in one form or another. They require love, or at least some measure of affection or recognition that attests to their worth as an individual. They need acceptance tempered with respect. They desire to be tested in terms of their abilities to achieve and to revel in the feeling that comes from doing things well on their own. They wish to grow and mature into capable, thinking individuals. Fulfillment of these desires is not solely the teacher's responsibility. The teacher provides the thrust for promoting a "lust" for learning.

Motivating children is a cyclic endeavor. Children come to school eager, sometimes frightened, but nonetheless eager to learn. Eagerness is readily tempered by the regimented routine of the day-to-day instructional procedures and the general mechanics of being part of the academic community. Children's interests wax and wane, and they persist. Motivating children can best be achieved by promoting those processes that promote the continued improvement of critical thinking as a personal acquisition.

Motivation is achieved most readily when the learner knows that learning is personal and a do-it-yourself activity. The responsibility for learning belongs first to the child; it is nurtured by the teacher and parents. The primary goal of personal improvements through self-growth via learning makes it easier for the learner to handle the joys and the frustrations of acquiring an education. Teachers become advocates of self-concept improvement when they see children become aware of the value of disciplining themselves for success in school and in life. Children are motivated when they see personal growth, when they recognize the effort necessary for success in academia, and when they develop a strong self-concept rooted in performance and content knowledge sufficient for them to carry on independently in the search for solutions to their problems.

MOTIVATING CHILDREN THROUGH INDIVIDUALIZED INSTRUCTION

Everyone is for it, few know what it connotes, and fewer know how to do it.

Individualized instruction is centered around the student—not the teacher, the school, the program, a computer, or a tape recorder. Individualized instruction should be for every student enrolled in your course, whether at the elementary school or college level. Individualized instruction is a specific program of instruction for each student, based on his/her previous experiences, interests, and abilities.

In individualized instruction, all students do not proceed through the same materials at their own rates as they do with self-paced instruction. All students do not proceed through the same taped sequence of materials as they do in audio-tutorial instruction. Furthermore, all students do not proceed through a sequence of frames with immediate answer confirmation as they do in pro-grammed instruction or computer-assisted instruction.

Individualized instruction involves student-teacher planning (the order is important) of materials based upon the entering behaviors of each student. Individualized instruction involves teachers' preparing individualized materials for individual students.

An excellent way to begin individualizing your creative teaching is to write down what you plan to offer your students as a program of instruction. Use action verbs that emphasize skills such as observing, clarifying, predicting, measuring, and so on. Make sure you don't limit your list to the areas of knowledge and recall. Your goals or objectives should also include those drawn from the affective and psychomotor domains.

With your set of goals and objectives, you must ask yourself if all your students will need to proceed to all of the goals and objectives you have delineated for your creative teaching endeavor. Do some of your students already have many of these capabilities? If, for example, one of your objectives is to be able to measure the density of an object to the nearest tenth of a gram per milliliter and four students already can do this, should they have to do it along with the rest of the class? Could their time be better spent working on some of the other objectives? This prior assessment will enable you to identify, before instruction begins, those students who can adequately perform specific portions of your creative teaching program.

Whether or not you realize it, through the process of constructing goals, objectives, and preassessment evaluations, you are already beginning to individualize your instruction. The next step is to meet with your students (they should have a part in deciding what they need to do and how they must proceed in order to acquire creative teaching skills). Together you should prepare an instructional outline or sequence of activities or procedures that they will need to follow in order to master the material presented. But that's still not individualized instruction. If you think it is, reread the definition. Does this alter your decision? The interests and abilities of each student still need to be taken into account. From the preassessment measure, you have an idea of an individual's background experiences in science. Meeting with each student for a general discussion as well as examining the student's past record in other classes and at other grade levels will provide additional information. An attitude inventory as well as past performance on standardized tests (whether the Sequential Tests of Educational Progress at the elementary level, Iowa Tests of Basic Skills at the junior high level, or the statewide assessment) provide you with a good cross section of the student's background experience, interests, and abilities. As a result, you and the student should be able to begin to make some decisions about performance in your creative teaching classroom. The student may have already met some of your goals and objectives, and others may not be applicable. The list you make now is this individual's, and probably no other student in the class will have the same list. Now you're on the road to individualizing instruction. Are you getting uneasy? Will this take too much time?

Remember: Nothing is as hard as just getting started! Keep reading!

Many of your students may be experiencing their first contact with an individually prepared creative teaching program. Consequently, at first they may be confused. Be patient. They will miss meeting every day as a group with a teacher who tells them what to do each step of the way in a lockstep learning environment. They may feel uncomfortable in having individual programs of study. The weight of the transferred responsibility can cause difficulties. An individualized course at a higher grade level can cause confusion and frustration. To assist students in the changeover to individualized instruction, many teachers have used student contracts like the one on page 57 (Figure 2.4). They are truly contracts, signed by the student and the teacher and dated. These contracts specify when certain parts of the individualized program will be completed and turned in for either teacher evaluation or self-evaluation or both. Students say these contracts help them keep track of their direction and serve as a valuable substitute for daily teacher assignments. Most students who have progressed through one individualized course probably will not need contracts in future individualized courses of instruction.

It will be helpful if you ask students who have completed your individualized creative teaching program to return and assist you as student guides. Classroom assistants can serve the same purpose as student guides. They can assist with the teaching (often doing an excellent job) as well as setting up materials and equipment. Furthermore, student guides serving as part of the learning team can provide an effective learning environment.

If you're still with us, but not yet convinced about all this—don't despair! For individualized instruction to be successful in creative teaching, the roles of the teacher and the student in our classrooms must be modified. Teachers no longer are the content experts or lecturers; instead, they are guides. They guide individuals. They are the stage setters for learning. Teachers who teach an individualized class often remark that they know these students better than they have ever known students before. They know their background experiences, interests, abilities, moods, whims, and life goals. They also find that the students have a greater interest in school—it's no longer boring and remote from their daily lives. However, teachers who teach individualized classes need time—time to meet with students individually, time to prepare materials (many different types), time to evaluate their students' progress, time to work with student guides, and time to think and be creative.

Good teachers of individualized learning are more important than facilities. Most existing facilities are adaptable to individualized procedures. A variety of areas in the room are needed as well as a good instructional-materials center in the school where students can work independently.

Figure 2.4

STUDENT LEARNING
CONTRACT

I _____ , agree to successfully
(STUDENT'S NAME)
complete the following activities and objectives on or before _____ .
(DATE)

Objective or activity

1.

2.

3.

4.

5.

Signed_____
(STUDENT)

Approved_____
(TEACHER)

Today's Date_____

What about the student's role in an individualized class? The student is no longer a passive learner who sits back in class and, for one reason or another, daydreams. The student who daydreams may either know the material already or can't understand the material because it is not being presented at his or her level. Students in an individualized class are using materials designed for them, that they helped to design. They become active learners. They are using materials they can cope with. Superior students in the class can go as far and as broad as they wish. Less able students can work on those areas of learning in which they most need assistance as well as pursue their own interests. With the trend toward mainstreaming, special-education children can easily participate in the creative teaching class. Gifted students can soar with this approach, too. It takes time.

A majority of students will not cover as much material as you may have covered in the past. These students however, will have a greater knowledge and understanding of the material they do cover than they would have had if taught by traditional methods. If one of your goals is to cover lots of material, individualized instruction may not meet that goal. Students have a greater responsibility for learning in an individualized program than in the traditional program; that is, the main responsibility for learning is now placed upon the student's shoulders, not the teacher's.

Critics of individualized instruction say many students waste classroom time—according to these observers, "They don't do anything!" There are two reasons for this impression. First, students new to an individualized program often do not know how to handle this new freedom for learning and, as a result, they need assistance (student contracts help to get them started). Second, students probably aren't wasting any more time than in any other class, but it seems more obvious to an observer of an individualized class.

An efficient way to assist teachers and students in adapting to their new roles is through the development of modules, interest centers, or packages of materials developed by teachers. Students can use these as part of their learning program (as discussed in Chapter 4). Many materials on the market can be adapted for use in modules and interest centers. Many existing materials have components that can be used for interest centers and module development. Don't worry if you can't think of a module or interest center on your own—initially most people have difficulty preparing these. You need to collect many representative materials that are available in topics for your grade level or subject area. From these you can select those materials that may best fit your needs and then adapt them. Most of your students will be able to assist you with the development. They might suggest areas they wish to include in the course of study or areas where individual packages may assist them.

Teachers who attempt alternative creative teaching approaches often have the problem of keeping track of the progress of each child and the materials with which each is involved. Computer software programs are one way. However, those who do not have access to this software may wish to use the Keysort Kid Cards approach.

KEYSORT KID CARDS

The Keysort Kid Card method will enable you to keep track of each child—to know immediately who needs additional help, who has successfully completed an activity or who hasn't. Keysort Kid Cards take up little space and little teacher time.

To use Keysort Kid Cards, you will need to prepare a set of cards. One is shown in Figure 2.5. Copy or duplicate the card, and tape or glue it to a piece of cardboard or manila folder the same size. You will need at least one copy for each student in your class, so be sure to make lots of duplicates.

Forty punch-holes on this card will allow you to use up to 40 topics or evaluation ideas for each child (if you use two cards you will have 80). Write the name of each child in your class on a separate card (30 children, 30 cards). When a child completes an activity, the hole for the corresponding activity number on the

Figure 2.5 Keysort Kid Card

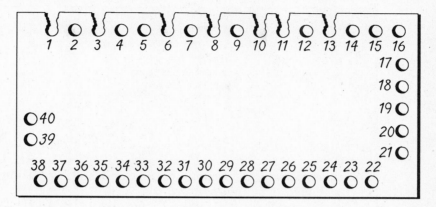

card will be punched out. Be careful not to punch through the edge of the card (or through the numbers).

Let's consider a typical third-grade class of 28 children. Keep in mind that virtually any subject or topic can be used. You are limited only by your creativity.

Suppose you have a list of 25 reading activities and you want each child to successfully complete at least ten of them. These 25 activities can be represented by the first 25 numbers on the card. When Jerry, for example, successfully completes his first activity, punch out the hole through the margin of his card for number 1 as shown in the illustration.

A knitting needle or any similar object that will fit through all the holes of any stack of cards will assist you in determining who has completed what activity and how many activities have been completed by each child. The cards of the students who have not completed a particular activity will stay in the stack. Another excellent feature is that if a small-group discussion relating to activity 4 is desired, you can pass the knitting needle through the fourth hole of all the class cards. Those cards that drop out have successfully completed the fourth activity and are ready for the discussion.

You can also use this method for keeping track of children with reference to other skills such as mathematics, group work, and for evaluation purposes.

USING PERSONAL COMPUTERS CREATIVELY

Each day schools in America add a new topic to their teaching repertoire—the personal computer. Usually the computer has one or two disk drives and/or a hard drive, plus a printer (dot matrix, letter quality, or laser) and monitor (amber, green, or color). The computer may also include a graphics card.

As this computer "package" is appearing in the classrooms, teachers are facing a dilemma: What do you do with one, two, five, or ten personal computers in the creative teaching classroom? Most classrooms use a personal computer as

Figure 2.6 Levels of Computer Usage

HIGH	6	Electronic Communication
	5	Data Base (Information Retrieval)
	4	Experimenting, Collecting and Analyzing Data
	3	Word Processing
	2	Simulations and Games
LOW	1	Drill and Practice

an electronic workbook. That is, they use software of a drill and practice nature. This is the most fundamental level, or level 1 of computer usage (see Figure 2.6). Other classrooms use the computer for games and simulations. This is the next level, or level 2 of computer usage.

Creative teachers work at level 3 and above. They utilize the computer as a word processing tool (level 3) enabling students to prepare papers and reports. As teachers, they use the computer to keep track of student progress. They utilize the computer for laboratory experiments (level 4), attaching sensors to the computer that allow the students to collect and analyze information.

Software is readily available for level 5 activities, which involve the use of data bases. Data bases provide students with a resource base of information that can be accessed utilizing key words such as author, title, subject, or general topic. Data bases can be very useful when preparing a paper, doing an activity, or exploring a research topic. It can be utilized in the literature search.

The highest level (level 6) of computer usage is as an electronic communication system. The following additional items are needed: a modem (1200 or 2400 baud are most often used), communication software, and a telephone line.

Electronic communication can open up the world to you and your students. One aspect of electronic communication is electronic mail or e-mail. With e-mail, messages can be sent around the world to other students and teachers. This allows for instant, worldwide communication. With e-mail, pen pals take on a new meaning.

Special-interest clubs or forums called bulletin boards are available through the use of electronic communication. There are hundreds of choices available, with topics ranging from weather to environment to literature to languages.

Commercial bulletin boards also offer a wide variety of information services from special references to e-mail to on-line shopping to airline reservations. Specialized bibliographic retrieval services also offer access to vast amounts of reference materials.

With the addition of a facsimile (FAX) board to your computer, graphic images can also be sent around the world. This allows student diagrams and art work to be shared easily on a worldwide basis.

When personal computers are used at level 3 and above, the world is made available to you and your students. Next let's look at other creative teaching aids that can be used to enhance instruction.

CREATIVE TEACHING AIDS

The volume of aids available for creative teaching alternatives is overwhelming. The mere use of an aid—for example, a cassette tape recorder—does not constitute an alternative program, however. This section will give you a representative list of common aids that can assist you and your students in your creative teaching endeavors. Many of these aids can serve as substitutes for the real thing when it is impossible or impractical to bring the real thing into your classroom. Animals such as the white whale, elephant, seal, octopus, squid, or lion are fascinating subjects for children. Most principals would cringe, however, should you requisition hay to feed your class pet, the elephant!

Excellent media aids are available that will do the job. Videotapes are outstanding for individual or small-group use. Tapes that duplicate experiments that would be difficult for you to duplicate and tapes that feature microscopic animals, like brine shrimp, are recommended. If you can easily duplicate what the videotape does, then, of course, you needn't buy or rent that video.

Many teachers and students enjoy preparing their own videotapes. This technique provides the student with direct experience in photographic preparation and use of videotapes. They are less expensive than commercial videotapes, and student-prepared videotapes may be more closely related to the materials being used in your classroom. Most photographic stores would be happy to advise you and your children on how to prepare a videotape.

Computer-assisted instruction (CAI) is making rapid inroads in our school programs. Many schools are purchasing personal computers in order to provide CAI experiences for their students. CAI can be utilized with each individual student and can serve as a teacher's aid by taking care of many bookkeeping duties such as attendance, individual progress, and evaluation measures.

Schools are also purchasing calculators to replace the long, tedious workbooks for mathematics. We have not begun to comprehend the potential in this area. Calculators can assist students in solving many problems in science and mathematics that often take long hours of tedious, mechanical manipulation if done by hand. Students should receive instruction of a hands-on nature in using calculators. Remember that their world is not our world, and they will be living in a world vastly different from today's.

Audiocassette tapes, of course, have been used successfully in assisting students in all curricular areas. Students of almost any age can successfully use a tape recorder after a short introductory session. Audiotapes can be useful in assisting children with reading problems. The narrative is recorded, and children can read along with it. Each child can have a personal story (it's the number one topic that children of all ages prefer) presented on his or her own reading level. The child need not be penalized for not understanding the story because of its original difficult reading level. On the other hand, students at a higher reading level can be presented with stories in their original form. After a few years, you will have developed an excellent library of stories at a variety of reading levels for use with your students. By the way, children enjoy preparing story tapes for other children—it also helps them improve their reading, writing, and speech skills.

Sound films (16mm) are also excellent media aids. However, they probably are the most abused aids in use today. Unfortunately, most of the films are encyclopedic presentations stating either all of the parts of the grasshopper in 15 minutes or showing unimaginative, complex experiments.

Select only those films or videotapes that add to your teaching endeavors. They should include one or more of the following features:

- They should present the children with a problem to be solved.
- They should, when appropriate, have children in the film or videotape.
- They should, when possible, use simple, everyday, homemade equipment.
- They should cause you to think by asking questions, some of which are not necessarily fully answerable.
- They should provoke children to want to discuss the film at its conclusion.
- Finally, the films or videotapes should present the content subject as it really is: for example, the scientist as a real person, not always as the man in the long, white coat.

Let's not forget the aid that every teacher uses (and abuses)—the bulletin board. Many school bulletin boards are merely that—boards for bulletins, made by teachers mainly to please other adults. We prefer bulletin boards designed for children as "action" bulletin boards, with the following characteristics:

- They often present the children with a problem in the form of a question.
- They involve the children by using task cards or by having the children contribute to the bulletin board.
- They are continually changed as children perceive that they need changing.
- They are often tied to an interest center.

Are your bulletin boards action bulletin boards? We've provided an example of a real action bulletin board in Figure 2.7. Compare it to your own!

Schools are also adding CD-ROM and videodisk capability to the learning environment. CD-ROM and videodisks allow students to access data bases and interact with text and graphics including photographs. They allow for rapid retrieval of information that is useful as students pursue individual projects.

RESEARCH SAYS . . .

According to a 1990 study by the Hudson Institute based in Indianapolis, the central problem facing education in America today is a lack of investment in modern technology. The report states that the U.S. educational system

Figure 2.7 Action bulletin boards

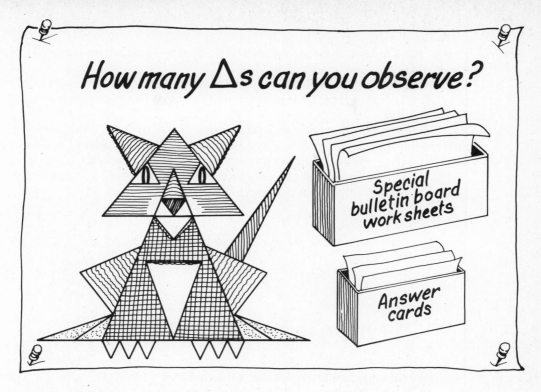

How many △s can you observe?

Special bulletin board work sheets

Answer cards

Find the numbers...

1. in the rectangle, but not in the circle, square, or triangle.

2. in the square, but not in the circle or triangle.

3. in the circle, but not in the triangle or rectangle.

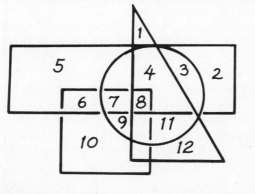

Answer cards

undervalues innovation and wastes $100 billion per year with a bloated bureau-cracy and outmoded teaching methods.

Education has the lowest level of capital investment of any major industry, providing $1,000 in capital for each student compared with a national average of $50,000 per job.

The report recommends new teaching methods to make better use of computers and improved communications. It also says that students and teachers should be given choices in what public schools they may attend or teach at.

Student testing should put greater stress on job knowledge and skills and less on academic achievement (Perelman 1990).

POINTS TO PONDER

What does this research tell you about what you should be doing in your classroom?

How does this research report relate to the title of Chapter 2?

How does this study indicate the need for change in American education? Defend or refute your position. (Come on, take a stand: You can do it.)

PAUSE FOR A SUMMARY

- Creative teachers are always open to change, particularly when the change may improve learning for children.
- Creative teachers need to expand their role as educational agents for change and continued improvement of their school, philosophy, attitude, objectives, and curriculum.
- Successful teachers are good questioners. They promote open-ended questions rather than closed questions with single-word answers.
- Creative teachers encourage student-to-student interaction and allow sufficient time for student responses to questions.
- The key to a creative classroom is thinking about what better use can be made of particular objects or places in order to improve the learning environment.
- Direct experiences are the vehicles whereby students apply concepts and theories to reality.
- A creative teaching environment allows for maximum student involvement and minimum teacher direction.
- Individualized instruction is a specific program of instruction for each student, based on his/her previous experiences, interests, and abilities.
- The Keysort Kid Card method enables you to quickly assess each child and to know his/her orientation in discrete areas of the curriculum.
- Creative teaching aids include: computer-assisted instruction, computers, calculators, audiocassette tapes, video tapes, 16mm films, bulletin boards, CD-ROM, and videodisks.

REFERENCES

Bloom, B. S., ed. (1956). *Taxonomy of Educational Objectives: Handbook I: Cognitive Domain.* New York: McKay.

Harrow, A. J. (1972). *A Taxonomy of the Psychomotor Domain: A Guide for Developing Behavioral Objectives.* New York: McKay.

Johnson, N. L. (1990). *Questioning Makes the Difference.* Dayton, OH: Creative Learning Consultants.

Krathwohl, D. R. (1964). *Taxonomy of Educational Objectives: Handbook II: Affective Domain.* New York: McKay.

Lymon, F. T. (1988). "Cueing Thinking in the Classroom: The Promise of Theory-Embedded Tools." *Educational Leadership*, vol. 45, no. 7, pp. 18–24.

Perelman, L. J. (1990). *Central Problem Facing Education Today.* Indianapolis: Hudson Institute.

Chapter
3

What They Neglected To Tell Me About . . .

Does It Matter?

What you don't know will hurt you.

DeKro

Are educational cliches such as, "Start tough, you can always ease up later," "Plan your work and work your plan," "Teach them to read so they can read to learn," "Never lay a hand on a child in love or in hate," valid? Useful? A smug educational stance might well be, "It depends." And well it does. No prescription or teaching formula exists. Each teacher finds his or her own way, which can change from class to class. No one can tell you how to act or react under all circumstances. When it becomes your turn, you will draw on all that has been previously made available to you and, using your innate talents and abilities, you will do the best you are capable of doing. You do not always know if you have done the right thing or the wrong thing until after you have done it. Another appropriate cliche is applicable here: "Hindsight is always twenty/twenty vision." Retrospective, constructive evaluation always enhances progress.

If done properly, teaching is one of the most difficult, challenging, and demanding professions in the world. It is the passion to teach that swells the ranks and propels the profession forward. To be well prepared, trained, drilled, and forewarned makes the complex task of teaching more palatable. Knowledge, preparation, desire, enthusiasm, vitality, and energy are the wellsprings of exciting, creative teaching.

Things matter if one cares. Teachers are educational evangelists, and they have a need to play out this social role. They espouse education. Recognizing its value, they will broadcast it from any stage. It matters to them that people are informed about and are challenged by education. It matters that they give of themselves and express themselves with people in a manner that few people are privileged to do. They get close to humanity. They touch souls. It matters to them that they make a positive difference in the lives of those around them. It matters to them that they be part of the continuing parade of learners.

OBTAINING A TEACHING POSITION

Some individuals view a teaching license as a passport to the world. It can be. Children are enrolled in schools all over the world. You could teach in any number of schools, provided you meet the requirements and conditions. They are in your backyard, down the street, across town, or in the next town. You will make your selection based on your own discrete reasons. The choice is yours. In Appendix III, we have included a list of state certification offices that may be contacted.

Once you have selected the geographical area in which you wish to teach, select a town where you would like to live. Using a map of the region and a compass, swing an arc the radius of which is equal to no more than a one-hour drive (preferably less) from your selected city. This city should be located at the center of your circle. You have now circumscribed an area that would be the maximum daily one-way drive for you. How many towns are of the size you desire to teach in? Is there a university or college located within this area? This would be advantageous, for teachers need to continue their schooling either to maintain their position or to move up the pay scale. Close proximity to a university is a decided plus.

Your next action is to select schools where you would like to submit letters of application for employment. Random selection of schools is not the best course of action; resource books are available listing schools in your state, their addresses, the names of the school's administrators, and other pertinent data. These resources are usually available in university or college education libraries and placement offices, and your state department of education office, usually located in the state capital. Using this reference and any other leads, compile a list of schools that appear to interest you. Rank these from best to least for you. Formulate a letter expressing your desire to work for that particular school system, inquiring about possible openings in your area of expertise, and requesting an application form and an interview (even if there is not a position open). Mail your letters to schools of your choice in accordance with your previously established priority list. Express the reason for your interest in this unique school system and, if necessary, offer them a few days of free substitute teaching. This is a bold offer and, while it may not be accepted, it and you will be remembered. If you are invited to substitute for one of the school's teachers, this opportunity will be invaluable. It will provide you with a feel for the school system and assist you in deciding if you would want to teach within this system. Conversely, it gives the school system an opportunity to view you in action. Your letter should be at least one page and not more than two pages. The optimum length is about one page and a half. If it is too short, the reader may infer that your capabilities are limited. If it is too long, he or she may lose interest. Be brief! Stress the salient points of your abilities. Let the reader know who you are, what you are seeking, and in a gentle manner communicate why a school system might be pleased to call you one of their own.

Include your vita. Make sure it contains everything of importance and nothing that is unimportant. Don't write one résumé to fit all occasions. Keep key information on the computer and personalize it for each school district. Distinct schools and situations call for hand-tailored revisions to highlight how you meet their particular needs. Be sure that the vita is neat and tidy, that all rules of grammar are observed, and double-check to be sure that all spellings are **correkt.** Nothing stands out so vividly as misspelled words.

AN INTERVIEW—PART OF THE PROCESS AND PART OF THE REWARD

An interview is usually offered in response to an interest stemming from a review of your letter of inquiry and the accompanying résumé. This is an opportunity for the prospective employer to view the candidate for the position in person. They have read about you and now they wish to see what you look like, how you act, and how you conduct yourself, what kinds of questions are of concern to you, and in general to make an assessment as to how well you fill their requirements and fit into the system. The first impression can be lasting. Some recommendations are:

—Dress in a simple, professional manner. Avoid high fashion clothes. Avoid overly bright or loud colors. Wear clothes that project a firm, calm, mature, in-charge image.

—Good posture is a plus. Don't slouch until you reach your car after the interview. Remember that nuances add up. Don't revert to a small mannerism that might be deemed annoying.

—Watch your language. As a prospective employee, you will be expected to speak well. Avoid "yeah," "yep," "nope," and other nonacceptable colloquialisms. Avoid run-on conversations. Be direct. Be pleasant. Listen carefully. An occasional "yes, sir" or "no, sir" response perks up the ears of the interviewer. Even if you don't regularly use these terms, they could be dusted off, used, and buried later. Remember that you are selling yourself. While you would not want to falsify your image, these responses plus others such as "thank you" and "please" are expected to be taught to the children in your future classes.

—Come prepared to ask several good questions; for example, "What reading program do you use?" "Are your expectations being met by this program?" "Do students have access to technology such as computers in the classroom, in a laboratory, or both?" Avoid global questions that may extend into lengthy and ethereal responses by the interviewer. It is not unusual for interviews to end on a "do you have any questions?" note. Be prepared with one or two questions of substance. Avoid questions such as "What might my salary be?" or "How many paid convention trips away from school will I be reimbursed for?" If you are interested in salaries, and most of us are, simply request a copy of the current salary guide. This will tell you everything you wish to know. You can study it later on your own.

—It may also be helpful to bring to the interview samples of your work from methods classes and student teaching in a portfolio format. A videotape or photographs of your teaching may be worthwhile to leave for later viewing, along with samples of children's work from classes you have taught.

—Some popular questions that arise during interviews are:

> What do you feel you can contribute to our school system?
>
> What would you say is your greatest strength in regard to the teaching profession?
>
> Do you expect discipline to be a problem? A simple "Yes" or "No" response would be inadequate.
>
> Explain how you would manage discipline in your classroom.
>
> Why should you be selected over the other 100 applicants for this position? Use your creative talents in your response.
>
> Are you conversant with the new programs in science (or mathematics or any other program)? Respond honestly. Do not attempt to bluff your way through this. A little prior research would help here.
>
> What are your educational goals? Don't go into too much detail. The interviewer might admire any lofty goals you express, but he or she probably is looking for stability, for someone who will stay in the position for a number of years.

Interviewing for a teaching position is a challenge. It would be rare if one interview netted you the position of your choice. One learns from interviews. Every interview will contribute to your skill and poise. Practice makes perfect. Don't get discouraged. There is a position waiting somewhere for you. It is a matter of planning, preparing, and executing your plan. Follow each interview with a thank-you letter expressing continued consideration of the position. Attention to small details pays large dividends. Follow up on all interviews to ascertain the status of the position and your continued consideration for it. For those positions that you do not receive offers, ask the administration to critique your performance so you will do a better job at your next interview.

MAINTAINING ONE'S TEACHING POSITION

Maintaining and retaining one's teaching position is based on many things. Some of these are:

Personality. How well do you get along with the administrators, faculty members, parents, and students? Teaching is a people-oriented profession, and warm, friendly, cooperative qualities are important.

Attitude. It can be like an antenna, broadcasting much about one's inner feelings. Be positive. Think up. Agree. Take part. "Yes, I will. I would be most pleased to do that. Thank you for asking me." Attitudes show, and people gravitate toward people with a pleasant attitude.

Acceptance of Responsibility. You are the responsible person. You are in charge. The class is assigned to you; they are your responsibility. You are in charge of the learning that takes place inside the classroom. The class mirrors your actions; and their actions are, in part, a reflection of you. You will get the respect you deserve. If you ask for respect and cultivate the process of acquiring it, it will come. Respect has to be earned, and teachers earn it in different ways; it does not come with the teaching contract. Embrace challenges that promote leadership experiences.

Personal Health and Hygiene. Teaching is a rigorous profession. It calls for a great deal of stamina and vigor. At times your throat will go dry, your feet will hurt, and your head will ache from the daily clamor and din of children. Like their students, teachers need plenty of rest.

Wardrobe. Outside of work, removed from the school, students, and the job, you can, if you so desire, smoke cigars, drive a Harley, and wear leather jackets and chains. But, as a teacher of children, common sense must always prevail. You are their model. The school may have a list of what is unacceptable. Some schools do not advocate teaching in jeans. Dress appropriately; wear comfortable, acceptable, unincitable clothes, and comfortable shoes. The children will mimic you and your demeanor. They wish to please you.

Continued Learning. Teaching is an eternal learning adventure. Teachers are rewarded financially and otherwise for their continued pursuit of learning. Early in your career map out a plan of additional learning and enroll in the appropriate courses. Time passes and, before you know it, you will have achieved your goal.

Work. Willing workers win out. Workers who are smart are noticed. Don't be satisfied with the minimum; reach out for the maximum. Work pays off. Opportunities open for those who have their arms outstretched.

Duty. Lunch, bus, hall, playground, and rest room . . . What do all of these words have in common? Duty. As a teacher, you will be expected to stand guard over the troops as they enter and exit the building, wait in line for lunch, and charge up and down the slide. You may be searching for cigarettes or drugs behind the stools in the rest room or quieting the masses in the lunchroom. It is all in the line of duty. Make the best of it. Take a positive approach. See how many students you can welcome with a warm smile each day. Create word games students can play as they wait in line for lunch. Talk to the children on the playground who have no friends and get them involved. Be glad you found the drugs so more students will not try them. Open drink bottles for the younger students in the lunchroom and cut apples for the students with braces. Remember that with the right attitude you can make a difference for the children you serve: ALL of the children in your school.

AGE-LEVEL PROFILES: WHAT DO CHILDREN LOOK LIKE AT THE . . .

No two children are alike. Yet, they are alike in many ways. Despite their similarities and differences, some empirical summations about their physical, behavioral, and unique requirements have been observed in different age groups.

Preschool Level

Preschool children (below five years of age) may be described as children with a complete set of teeth and as toilet trained, individuals who, although they may sleep 12 hours per night, fatigue easily and require frequent rest periods during the day. Generally they have unevenly developed motor skills. Large-muscle coordination is good. Eye-hand coordination and small-muscle coordination are still not fully developed. They make a quantum leap in language development. They move from a vocabulary of a few words to one of several thousand words, and they are renowned for asking many, many questions.

Preschool children are learning to adjust to the environment and the world around them. They are beginning to learn how to accept directions and instructions. They are usually unhappy about all of this and occasionally exhibit some degree of reluctance to instruction, reacting accordingly. But this passes quickly, for they covet adult acceptance of their behavior. They are great imitators and enjoy mimicking personalities, languages, and manners. They have a built-in supercharger that keeps them constantly active, generating countless questions, and always wanting to know everything about their surroundings. They possess an innate curiosity. They can sustain long periods of subdued activities. As they tire, they become irritable and somewhat disgruntled.

Children in this age group crave security. They are always concerned with things around them and how they affect them directly. They want to know who will take care of them, feed them, and protect them. They engender a lot of "me-ism." They are self-centered and need constant assurance of affection and love from parents. Preschool children need constant guidance and require patterns of behavior to follow. They operate best when things are kept simple, clear, and routine. They perform best when choices provided are direct and kept to a minimum. They become easily confused when asked to make selections from a large number of alternatives.

Five-Year-Old Level

At the five-year-old level, body growth slows a bit. Hands and feet grow larger, catching up to the rest of the body. Small-muscle coordination still lags behind large-muscle coordination. Most five-year-old children are apt to be farsighted. Usually vision is not quite ready to handle reading skills. They are active with short, but increasing, attention spans. Girls' physical maturity exceeds that of boys' by about one year.

Five-year-olds are emerging individually, and lifelong traits are becoming pronounced. These children are stable and wish to assume some measure of responsibility. Five-year-old children handle criticism reasonably well. They desire group activities and wish to be recognized as a sociable member of the group.

As with preschool children, five-year-olds need assurance of love and acceptance. They are anxious to take on tasks and develop their own capabilities. They observe and they want to do. Continued guidance with five-year-old children is a must.

Six-Year-Old Level

Six-year-old children possess better large-muscle development. In fact, they are somewhat inept at activities requiring the use of small muscles. They, like their five-year-old counterparts, need 11–12 hours of sleep nightly, they possess immature eye development; and they can only remain in high activity for short periods of time. They fatigue easily even though they have an insatiable desire to learn.

Six-year-olds want to participate actively in group activities. Individually they provide spontaneous actions. They enjoy dramatizing and acting out events. Six-year-olds are aggressively competitive and wish to be first in all actions. Despite this strong desire, they have short periods of interest and exhibit poor decision-making skills.

Six-year-old children need and want encouragement, praise, and acknowledgment from adults. They have begun to select best friends, pals, or buddies. They revel in acceptance by others. They require supervision, but they desire to proceed with minimum interference. They are reaching out for responsibilities but shun multiple decision-making situations. They shun pressures associated with various tasks.

Seven-Year-Old Level

Seven-year-olds are gaining on small-muscle and eye-hand coordination mastery, but they are not there yet. Their eyes are still not ready for sustained close work. They can be identified by missing teeth, as permanent molars push their way in. They are gaining weight, and their growth is strong and steady.

Seven-year-old children are anxious to assume responsibility. They seek the approval of adults. They are beginning to focus on certain aspects of learning, acquiring simple understandings of time and the values of different forms of money. They possess great energies that dissipate rapidly. They are sensitive to how they are perceived by other children and by adults. They appear confused in that while differentiating right from wrong, they may take possession of things that are not theirs. They tend to exaggerate and tell fantastic tales. A gap begins to exist in interest and play between boys and girls.

At this stage they are still perceptually oriented. They are becoming more aware of details, a quality that enables them to begin classification into subgroups. These children can also measure in relative arbitrary measures. They require much encouragement and numerous opportunities for expressing independence.

Eight-Year-Old Level

At the eight-year-old level, things are starting to come together. Large and small muscles are becoming more developed. Manipulative skills are increasing. Vision is ready for close and distance use. Some nearsightedness may begin to be observed. Increased attention span is acquired. Poor posture may become more obvious, and attention to this may need to be provided.

Eight-year-old children are gregarious individuals. They are friendly, easy to communicate with, eager, and enthusiastic. While developing a greater capacity for self-evaluation and an awareness of individual differences, they are sensitive to criticism. Eight-year-olds are beginning to develop different allegiances. They develop a loyalty to other children, usually those of the same sex. Best friends and even the formation of cliques or gangs become discernible. They are responsive to group activities. The great spontaneity and enthusiasm for life that eight-year-olds possess make them prime candidates for rushing into things and situations. They seem prone to accidents.

Eight-year-old children are beginning to develop a mental reversing process. Their judgment is based on perception. They can distinguish between observations and inferences to explain phenomena and make predictions based on past observations.

Nine- and Ten-Year-Old Level

Physically this group is fast advancing on preadolescence. Their eyes are almost adult size and their eye-hand coordination is advanced enough for small, craft-type work. Their eyes are subject to less strain associated with small details. The lungs, digestive, and circulatory systems are now mature. Their hearts, however, are subject to stress and strain. The growth of females still exceeds that of males.

Within this group wide discrepancies are noted, particularly in reading. Individual differences are becoming pronounced. Individuals are becoming aware of their placement relative to the abilities of other members of the class. They are becoming aware of who the owls are and who the mice are, both in the class and in the school. They are beginning to identify their niche within the hierarchy of things. Nonetheless, they all strive for individual perfection. They all wish to succeed, but they lose this desire if pressured or discouraged. For some members of this age level there is a definite slump period. Some educators have referred to this as the fourth-grade slump. It appears that to some, the novelty of attending school, being away from parental guidance, intermixing and making friends, and so on, is beginning to wear thin. They recognize the daily routine of school as repetitious, somewhat boring, and in a sense a form of penance. They may, for the first time, be finding their operative level within the system and they may not be pleased with what they see, while those in the upper echelon of the class seem to maintain their drive, enthusiasm, and hunger for the classroom environment. Nine- and ten-year-old children offer loyalty to the teacher, the school, the community, and the country. They enjoy open discussions. They desire adult approval, but are critical and outspoken toward adults. They usually are decisive. They are dependable and responsible individuals who often plan their own work and wish to carry it out independently. They have a strong feel for what is right and wrong, and they will argue vehemently about what is supposedly fair.

This group wishes to learn without great pressures. They read widely. They invite definite responsibilities. This age level can work with two or more variables. They develop the capability to hypothesize requiring abstract thought.

Preadolescent Youth

This is a period in which children's lives are marked by frequent stalls, starts, and quantum leaps in body growth. It can be a confusing time for these individuals. It follows a "growth-resting" plateau, then rapid growth in both height and weight, not necessarily at the same rate and time—and not the same for everyone. Growth in height generally precedes weight increases. Girls continue to lead the boys in maturity by as much as two years. They are taller and heavier. The preadolescent group is distinguished by gargantuan and capricious appetites, rapid muscle growth, maturing reproductive organs, and uneven growth of different parts of the body. These anomalies take place at or about 9 to 13 years of age.

Accompanying these differences in growth are a level of self-consciousness, a feeling of being out of sorts, clumsiness or awkwardness, a sense of restlessness, and low energy. These feelings are usually a direct result of the rapid and uneven growth. These effects are also reflected in preadolescents by moodiness, rebelliousness, and uncooperativeness. The maturing of reproductive organs takes place at this time. Flirtatious interactions between the boy and girl groups are more obvious—teasing, displays of affection or disaffection, and occasionally even antagonism toward each other. A general awareness of differences between the groups becomes paramount in choosing sides, selecting partners, and so on. Machoism and muscle displays by the boys become more common. A wide range of individual differences in maturity exist. Boys, more than girls, continue to seek membership in social groups and are more loyal to the groups than girls are. Opinions of groups seem to be preferred to those of adults. Peer pressures are becoming more and more important.

The preadolescent requires tolerance and understanding by adults of what is transpiring within them physically and emotionally. Schools should plan to accommodate the needs of those who are approaching puberty. Sometimes this calls for changes in recreation programs and daily schedules to accommodate this concern. This emerging group still needs many of the supports provided for younger children. They still need affection and tolerance toward their new status. They still need to belong. With these changes they are expecting greater opportunities for supervised independence and, at some later date, unsupervised independence. Pressure, talking down to them, ridicule, and so on are not well received by this group.

Adolescent Youth

This group is marked by more growth, more weight gain, large appetite for food, rapid heart growth, and completed skeletal development. Sometimes these rapid changes result in a period of glandular imbalance. In this growth period, sexual maturity and its associated physical and emotional changes can also be observed.

The adolescent group is often described as the "know-it-all" group. They are somewhat emotionally insecure and often go to extremes to prove a point. Their prime concern is acceptance by the social group. Some of these social groups grow into strong cliques. Among the greatest fears of this group are rejection, ridicule for being different, or being unpopular. They are caught between a regression to some unsavory habits of their younger years, such as hair pulling, nail biting, leg twitching, or impudence, and a strong desire to show independence by cutting themselves off from the family. Girls, with their advanced maturity, are more interested in boys than boys are interested in them. Both males and females of this group have a noticeable interest in physical attractiveness.

Adolescents have a strong need for assurance. They vacillate from dependence to independence; and they need to have experiences that do not close doors as they engage in this vacillation. Gentle adult support and guidance offered in a nonthreatening environment that promotes the adolescent's desire for freedom is invaluable. They crave acceptance by others of their own age. They wish to belong. They wish to champion something constructive. They have a strong desire to contribute to society in a cause, an idea, or an issue. This group needs to be apprised of social concerns such as drugs, sex, suicide, and AIDS.

TEACHING AT THE GRADE LEVEL OF YOUR CHOICE— MATCH OR MISMATCH

Teachers often have a love affair with the grade level at which they completed their student teaching experience. In fact, studies show that most student teachers end up teaching no more than one grade level above or below the grade at which they student taught. Teachers get attached to it and, upon graduation, they usually seek and find a teaching position at the same grade level. The grade level at which a new teacher starts usually remains the same throughout the major portion of his or her teaching career.

Teachers identify with certain age groups of children. Some prefer working with the lower age levels. They like the laughter and the noises little children make. They like the exuberance, the uninhibited manner, and the enthusiasm of little children, and they like the many nuances that emanate from unbridled innocence. By contrast, other teachers enjoy working with older children, interacting with more mature minds and personalities. They also love their subject discipline, be it English, history, science, or mathematics. Elementary/middle school teachers, when asked what they teach, respond, "Children!" Subject discipline classroom teachers respond to the same question by stating, "Mathematics" (or some other discipline). Every grade level has its pluses and minuses. Individuals seek and find a grade level that complements their strengths, weaknesses, likes, dislikes, and personal goals, plus the physical, social, and unique characteristics of the children they are interested in teaching. Creative teachers are flexible and are willing to teach at different grade levels.

POINTS TO PONDER

How flexible will you be in order to obtain your first teaching position? After 5 years of teaching? After 20 years of teaching? Explain your answer.

THE FIRST DAY

Even for senior staff members, the first day of school is always an adventure. New books, new supplies, and new students all add to the excitement. All teachers privately ponder the arrival of those students who become "theirs" for one year.

Teachers usually are concerned about the class they inherit; the children, in turn, are concerned about the teacher they inherit. It works both ways. It is in your favor that regardless of your personality, intelligence, and so on, the children you are assigned accept and defend you loyally to the end. Good or bad, you belong to them (at least for a year) and, no matter what, they desperately want to please you. This is a plus; they are on your side.

Some Cautions for the Day

Allow yourself appropriate lead time before the first day arrives. Plan the first three weeks well in advance. The more prepared you are, the more relaxed and resilient you will be. It is hard to know if it will take the students 2 or 30 minutes to complete an activity. Be prepared. In teaching, there are few substitutes for good organization and planning. Plan sufficient instruction in detail. This instruction should be supported by appropriate ancillary activities, some of which extend over a week, a month, or over the entire year. Not all learning should be regulated by uniform periods of time.

Be prepared to involve the children the first day in some exciting lesson. Do not spend the entire day with so-called housekeeping chores or clerical tasks such as passing out books, paper, or instructional notes. Inasmuch as the first day can be your best shot at setting the tone for the entire year, pick a winning lesson and kick it off with gusto. Do not make it too hard, too involved, or too long. A short, high-interest lesson coupled with some exciting hands-on involvement to set the stage for an action-filled year will do the trick. Revel in the "oohs" and "ahs" and prepare yourself for an exciting year-long engagement with children.

Start the year off by presenting a firm image of yourself. You can always lighten up as the year winds down. If you start loose and try later to tighten up a bit, you may find it difficult to recapture lost ground. Practice projecting your voice. Can you be heard throughout the room? Could you muster the troops in case of an impending disaster? Can you shatter the glasses in the lunchroom from a distance of 100 yards? Practice several voices; different occasions require different voices. Practice numerous nonverbal clues such as a furrowed brow, a quizzical posture that communicates that nonverbal statement, "Who did that?" or "What are you doing?" Practice several body stances that can be incorporated into your "projecting" gestalt. Among these should be the friendly stance, the "I'm pleased" stance, and the "I like you" stance. Develop your "you." Your voice, your stance, your stature can command much. These can become your most powerful tools for promoting learning and maintaining discipline. Practice these until you feel you can communicate the intended messages when the occasion requires them. Command respect. This is an earned commodity. Usually teachers receive the respect they deserve and demand.

Establish a few essential ground rules, but don't overdo it. A few rules well observed and practiced are better than many rules unobserved and rarely practiced. Rules of behavior that emanate from the children in your class are preferable to those initiated by the teacher. Remember that a rule unenforced is not a rule at all. If you establish rules and fail to implement them and carry them out, future rules are destined for the same fate. Consider these examples: Everyone is responsible for his or her own behavior. Equipment is to be checked out, used correctly, then cleaned and stored in its proper place. A few enforced rules can provide strong classroom guidelines establishing the parameters of action by children. Lack of rules can be confusing to children. They will wonder how far they can go.

Do not allow yourself to get into arguments with the children over such impatient reactions as, "Do we have to do this?" Provide the students with your rationale, explaining the necessity for what is to be done, and then ask them to do it. You are in charge. You know it, they know it, and they know you know it.

Be confident. Don't worry about making mistakes; everyone makes a good share of them. Not every lesson turns out exactly as it is supposed to. When teaching science, not every mothball placed in baking soda and vinegar rises and sinks, and so it goes. Be flexible. In teaching, the unexpected should be the expected. A seemingly simple assignment, such as planting seeds in a tumbler garden, can have a wide range of results—from the growth of a healthy plant to the development of a vigorous mold. Unexpected results raise the question "How come?" and sometimes generate more interest than anticipated results. Make use of them. Sometimes what is uncovered is as important or perhaps more important than what was intended to be covered. Resiliency is your buffer for maintaining your equilibrium. You must be like a reed in the wind: bending, rebounding, but not breaking.

Do not be overly concerned with criticism. No other profession is as susceptible to criticism as teaching. Listen to criticism. Discern what may be constructive in it. Cast aside the trivial and work on the constructive with this goal in mind: to become a better teacher every day in every way.

Take some calculated risks. Try those teaching innovations you have been wondering about. (Do they really work?) Grouping, independent work, cooperative learning, the use of numerous divergent questions, open-ended experiments in science, the use of interest centers are all exciting possibilities for improving and enlivening instruction. Try some of them. Remember: little risk, little progress.

Don't waste time. The most precious thing students bring to your class is time. It should not be squandered. If you waste 5 minutes an hour in a 6-hour day, 5 days a week, 180 school days a year, you waste 75 hours a year or about 12 6-hour teaching days per individual per year.

Work at staying healthy. Remember, you are probably the oldest (as well as the dearest) thing in the classroom. Protect your health from the continuing onslaught of typical classroom illness by getting lots of rest. Enthusiasm and vitality are two of the most important ingredients in good teaching. Nourish them continuously, and they will flourish. Creative teachers:

—Give positive recognition.

—Assure each student some success.

—Involve students in making choices and setting rules for acceptable behavior.

—Involve students in helping each other.

—Plan with students.

—Make the classroom a special place.

—Encourage student-constructed materials.

—Encourage independent problem solving.

—Provide activities to help each child take pride in his or her contributions.

—Develop freedom with responsibility.

—Involve parents, principals, and anyone else who will help.

—Assign homework with choices.

—Emphasize mastery of skills.

—Spice teaching with humor.

—Show enthusiasm.

—Work hard!

Strive for sufficient control to achieve your objectives. Control should not be an end in itself, but it is needed to maximize learning for the children the school serves. Control can be elusive. It is delicate and fragile. You can have it one moment and lose it the next. It takes nurturing to establish it and to maintain it until it becomes self-sustaining. Control is necessary for the natural order of events vital for learning to take place. Chaos is not conducive to learning. Control is the tranquility that comes from order. Creative teachers provide the initial control guidelines, which diminish as children master the skills and attitudes to function independently. Personal inner controls plus peer pressure should eventually replace teacher control. The timing of this transition is your decision.

DISCIPLINE AS A PART OF CLASSROOM MANAGEMENT

Beginning teachers seem to agree that establishing and maintaining order in the classroom is both an awesome responsibility and a challenging task. In our conversations with teachers and prospective teachers, we notice that the word discipline means different things. It is, perhaps, most frequently used to mean "the degree of control or order that is found in a classroom." To some, it is the set of techniques used to bring about that order. In some contexts, it can mean "self-control"—the extent to which an individual controls personal activities. We also note that the word discipline is commonly used to mean "punishment."

Creative teachers know that along with the tasks of preparing lessons and devising suitable teaching methods, they must create and maintain a climate for learning. The optimum environment for learning is one in which teachers and students are all actively involved in a learning process relatively free from interruptions.

Many teachers point out that a bewildering variety of events can trigger disruptions that bring learning activities to a halt—anything from an announcement made over the loud speaker to a student's discovery of a fly or a bee that continues to buzz around the desks. More generally, disorders occur at the beginning and at the end of something (and sometimes in between). Interruptions can occur at the beginning of the school day, the class period, the week, the holiday or vacation period, the lunch period, and, of course, during preparations for any class. Invariably disturbances accompany landmark events such as report-card day, awards day, fire drills, substitute teachers, an accident, and so on. As a matter of fact, whenever students get in line to go anywhere—music, physical education, art, computer lab, recess, lunch, or to the rest room—the opportunity exists for a little turmoil and an increase in the noise level. Disturbances such as these are considered normal, and so are the children who cause them.

The number and duration of the interruptions you allow is related to your personality, philosophy, and tolerance. Some teachers permit more interruptions and for longer periods of time than others. Your tolerance for interruptions will vary. What you may view as a discipline problem one day might cause you to chuckle on another day. Your reactions will depend on many things—your health, how well rested you are, or the announcement by the principal that your pay raise was approved. Normal interruptions should be viewed for what they are. They should be tolerated but never encouraged. Above all, they should be viewed with common sense. It helps if you are consistent in handling these disorders. Children become confused by teachers' inconsistency in reacting to disorderly behavior.

An observant teacher can sense the climate. At times it is helpful to have a class discussion about problems that are occurring in the classroom, rest room, hallway, bus, or playground. Allowing students to talk about the problems and brainstorm various solutions helps the class to deal with related issues and makes everyone more aware of his/her responsibility in maintaining discipline. The discussion may also make the teacher more aware of the feelings of the students and give him or her insight for enhancing the self-concept of each child.

Until now we have been talking about the minor disruptions that occur on a day-to-day basis. It is possible you may face more serious problems such as cheating, lying, stealing, chronic misbehavior, persistent absenteeism, physical aggression, open hostility, destructiveness, drug use, alcohol abuse, and sexual offenses. Such problems are of major concern to teachers and other school officials and should be handled by trained personnel such as the school psychologist, counselor, social worker, or principal. Some discipline problems may be related to physical disorders that can be controlled by diet and/or medication. Contact the school nurse to assist with these cases.

Parents are also important players on the discipline team. They want—and need—to know what is happening. Parents should be involved. Give them a call at home or, if necessary, at work. Have a conference to discuss the child's problems and possible solutions. Keep the parents informed of progress. Teamwork is important.

Preventing and Defusing Behavior Problems

Operate on the assumption that it is easier to give up something than to recapture it. Start the year being firm and, if warranted, loosen up as the year progresses. The reverse procedure is much more difficult.

Establish the ground rules for behavior you will and will not accept. Be sure the ground rules are reasonable and that they can be met. Do not threaten. React expeditiously and confidently. You are in charge. Let the children know it. Let them know that you know they know. Send a copy of your rules home to the parents before discipline problems occur.

Avoid overfamiliarity with students. Teachers want all their students to love them. This is not always possible; for many of them to like you should be sufficient. Your assignment is to teach and to be respected in the process. Good teachers usually get the love and respect they deserve.

Do not abuse your authority as the disciplinarian. Be firm, but be gentle. Ridicule and embarrassment add fuel to the fire of behavior problems. Fairness, discreet correction, consistency, and impartiality are absolute necessities.

Check with the principal to make sure your discipline measures are compatible with school policy. Ask the principal what is expected of teachers in maintaining appropriate behavior. Also determine how far the principal or other administrators will go in supporting your efforts in classroom discipline.

The most valuable assets you have for maintaining control are your vitality, your enthusiasm, and your voice. Start your lessons with vigor and enthusiasm. Don't waste time. Convey the idea that what is going on is vital and necessary in the learning process of each individual. Develop a voice that is pleasant to listen to, one that commands attention. Cultivate variations in the way you use your voice that permit you to communicate in many different ways—from whispering a ghostly Halloween story to marshalling the class for a mass exit to avoid an oncoming catastrophe.

Establish a set of classroom signals for gaining attention of the entire group, especially if the class is engaged in an activity. It may be holding up your hand and having each student do the same or flipping off the lights for a few seconds. Once in control you can give further directions in a positive and constructive manner.

Alternate your approaches. Sometimes direct your remarks to the class: "Someone is not paying attention!" This can get all the children thinking, "Does the teacher mean me?" If this approach does not work, be direct and identify the individuals. More serious disturbances dictate use of the latter method. Never punish the entire class for the misbehavior of one individual or a small group.

Always strive to teach as if you were being considered for the school's congeniality award. Then, when you are forced to present a firm posture, it will have more impact.

Do not be afraid to call parents. They want to be informed about their child's behavior. Often the same behaviors are happening at home. You can work as a team in the interest of the child. Make it a habit to call parents about good behavior too! It will make their day.

Your role is to teach. Disciplinary actions must be minimized because they hinder the learning process. Through practice you will develop your own style of handling disruptions. As you develop your repertoire of disciplinary actions, children should grow in self-discipline. Opportunities need to be provided to nurture self-discipline or peer-group discipline. Often it is easier and safer to hold onto the reins of discipline than risk losing control by transferring them, but the children's mastery of self-discipline is well worth the risk.

Many behavior problems can be avoided if lessons are well planned and interesting. As often as possible lessons should exhibit a balance of exposition and student involvement and should be devoid of catch-up and wait time. Nebulous assignments, unclear communication of the objectives of the lesson, repetitive teaching methods, the onslaught of volumes of ditto sheets, and failure to provide for individual differences are pitfalls that creative teachers avoid. Teachers should ask themselves the following questions before beginning a lesson:

1. What are the most effective ways of organizing my classroom for laboratory work, discussion, and demonstrations?
2. What are some different ways of presenting a lesson to meet the needs of all the students?
3. How can I phrase my questions more effectively?
4. How much should I guide children?
5. What are some effective ways of storing and distributing materials?
6. Are my activities motivational and interesting?

It is also important to focus on the positive. Get in the habit of catching students doing something right. About every 15 or 20 minutes privately offer some words of encouragement to a student. You can comment on the way a student is paying attention, the detail that has been given to an assignment, a neat desk, a smile, a caring attitude. There are always positive things happening in the classroom; it just takes a special teacher to emphasize them. For a visual cue, put the word "positive" somewhere in your room. It will act as a powerful reminder.

POINTS TO PONDER

Studies show that teachers who treat students as individuals have the best discipline. Why don't more teachers use this technique?

Many teachers involve their children in the development of the rules for their class. Develop a plan to accomplish this in your classroom. Who should approve your plan? How will you inform the parents? How will your discipline plan be reinforced?

In Charge and In Control

In the process of acquiring creative freedom and independence in learning, control seems antithetical. Nonetheless, in order for children to acquire these attributes, they need to start the learning process within a structured environment where controls are obvious and exercised. Chaos does not engender a creative mind. Creativity, initially, is anchored in controlled learning situations that enable children to master the skills and attitudes they need to function independently. A suitable analogy would be the creative act of painting using oils. It would be preferable to exercise control and instruct children in some fundamental skills associated with oil painting—arranging the paints on a palette; mixing the paints to achieve certain tones and hues; gaining some notion of techniques for filling the canvas such as balance, spatial relationships, and harmony; preparing the canvas for the paint, and cleaning the brushes and other painting instruments. By contrast, simply to have turned children loose without any prior instruction in oil painting would have been an invitation to disaster. Controls are easier to remove than chaos.

Setting the stage through the use of controls provides children with confidence, enabling them to move forward on their own. If they receive some instruction in the basic skills and techniques and some directional guidance, they would have some feel for the expectations and they would feel more comfortable with the new undertaking. If, after a sufficient trial run, visible clues emanating from the students lead you to believe they are not quite ready, back off and reinforce your earlier instructions until you feel they can navigate on their own. Waning support, over time, insures growth in independent creative action. Control is not an end in itself, but it is a necessary ingredient for the learning process.

WORKING WITH THE INTELLECTUALLY GIFTED

For years educators believed that one need not worry about gifted children. It was thought that they could and would take care of themselves. The classic statement has always been, "They'll learn in spite of us." Evidence tells us something different, however: Gifted children may be the most neglected students in the schools today.

Definitions of gifted vary. Earlier in this century we linked the definition solely to intelligence quotient (IQ), particularly as measured by the *Stanford-Binet Intelligence Scale.* Those children whose scores on this test placed them in the top 1 or 2 percent were declared to be gifted. Today students are selected using multiple criteria such as IQ scores, achievement scores, writing samples, products, portfolios, and teacher, parent, and student nominations. A wider range of students may be identified to include the top 15 percent, depending on the type of educational program being offered.

The definition currently being used was given by Sidney Marland (1972), the former United States commissioner of education.

> Gifted and talented children are those . . . who by virtue of outstanding abilities are capable of high performance. These . . . children . . . require differentiated educational programs and/or services beyond those normally provided by the regular school program in order to realize their (potential) contribution to self and society.

Children capable of high performance include those with demonstrated achievement and/or potential ability in any of the following areas:

general intellectual ability

specific academic aptitude

creative or productive thinking

leadership ability

visual and performing arts

psychomotor ability

This definition is an attempt to recognize children who possess a variety of talents. "Talented" generally refers to a specific dimension of skill; for example, in music or art. In most gifted children a strong relationship is found between their giftedness and talented performance. Even though we acknowledge that superior intelligence is only one factor in determining an individual's ultimate success, achievement, or contribution to society, it still remains a basic attribute of the gifted.

It is possible to list some characteristics of the intellectually gifted:

an outstanding memory

an early attraction to problems (Gifted children are concerned with the why of everything.)

an early concern with one's own thoughts and feelings, and an ability to analyze situations

a fascination with reading (An early interest in books often stimulates gifted children to teach themselves to read long before they go to school.)

an unusually precocious talent in art and music

a tendency to seek out and associate with older children and adults rather than with children their own age

The direction a gifted intellect takes depends on many factors, including experience, motivation, interest, emotional stability, mentors, parental urging, and even chance. In the classroom many gifted children seem to appreciate almost any change from the routine that has come to characterize schooling. Gifted children seem to thrive on acceleration and enrichment and show no sign of serious maladjustment because of it. It is important to realize that meeting the needs of gifted students is not giving them more of the same. It is pretesting the students to find out what they already know and developing differentiated activities that will challenge them.

Gifted children, because of their early maturity in reading, are interested in a variety of topics. The ability of gifted children to read, coupled with their attraction to problem-solving situations (wherein they can demonstrate their concern for humane resolutions of today's problems) makes the study of history and science popular with them. They delve into research on controversial issues, such as genetic engineering, euthanasia, or toxic wastes, and relish taking part in simulations on the pioneer movement, the stock market, or terrorism. Gifted students are intrigued with mental math, tessellations, probability, and solving complex math problems. Get them involved with on-line data retrieval, telecommunications, and hypermedia. Many gifted students enjoy public speaking and should be encouraged to practice this skill through meaningful oral presentations, debates, speeches, and newscasts. Foreign languages should be available for gifted students in schools beginning in first grade, even if a parent or paraprofessional provides the instruction. Gifted students have the ability to absorb foreign languages and like learning about different cultures.

Beware: Gifted students may not be talented in all areas. They may have terrible handwriting or they may be poor spellers. Encourage them to use word processors with built-in dictionaries. Find ways to unleash their talents.

Gifted children need programs specifically designed for them. Being gifted is, in a manner of speaking, a handicap. Gifted children need an environment for learning as special as any we create for other handicapped children. Anxious to address themselves directly to the problem at hand, they express disdain for the slow-paced accumulation of discrete facts or the "bits and pieces" of average programs. Gifted children want to be immersed in a problem and engrossed in the pursuit of the larger aspects of the problem. You can emphasize the concepts and basic principles of the subject matter for gifted children. You can also lead them to explore how information is derived instead of concentrating only on what the information is. Gifted children enjoy involvement in special projects that allow for independent work. They also need to interact in groups with other gifted children who have similar interests.

POINTS TO PONDER

Gifted children are children with special needs. How will you identify the gifted children in your classroom? What differentiated activities will you provide for them?

WORKING WITH THE EXCEPTIONAL CHILD IN A MAINSTREAMED SETTING

Nothing is so unequal as the equal treatment of all children.

Anonymous

Most of us ask, who are the exceptional children? Numerous attempts have been made to define the term. Most simply, we could say that *exceptional children* are those who require special educational services if they are to realize their full potential. They exhibit some characteristics educators should know about when faced with the task of identifying them. To understand who these children are, the following groupings may be helpful:

- those with mental deviations, including children who are (a) intellectually superior or (b) slow in learning—mentally retarded

- those with sensory handicaps, including children with (a) auditory impairments or (b) visual impairments
- those with communication disorders, including children with (a) learning disabilities or (b) speech and language impairments
- those with behavior disorders, including children with (a) emotional disturbance or (b) social maladjustment
- those with multiple and severe handicaps, including children with various combinations of impairments: cerebral palsy and mental retardation, deafness and blindness, as well as severe forms of physical and intellectual disabilities.

In the past, educational theory and practice supported placement of children needing special educational services in special classrooms, excluding them from the mainstream. They were taught by special educators, and neither the children nor their teachers were involved with the regular classroom teachers. Such placement was based on the belief that the educational needs of these children required special methods, smaller classes, and different curricula.

Social considerations, such as the desirability of insulating the handicapped child from the potentially negative reactions of other children, added support to the advocates of the separate special-classroom approach. Children with severe handicaps were often excluded from public schools because of the lack of appropriate programs or the presumption that they could not learn there. Changing theory and practice in special education have resulted from four powerful forces: educators themselves, parents and other child advocates, the courts, and the policy and legislation of state and federal governments.

Over the past decade, evaluative research and model educational programs have demonstrated that many past policies and practices were not appropriate. This awareness dramatically culminated in far-reaching federal legislation. In 1975, Public Law 94-142 was passed and signed into law. This landmark legislation, known as the Education for All Handicapped Children Act, contains the mandatory provision that every school system in the nation must provide a free, appropriate public education for every child between the ages of 3 and 21. A unique feature of the law is the emphasis on the regular classroom as the preferred instructional base for all children. A new philosophy or approach to educational programming for handicapped children was clearly set forth, and the principle of the least restrictive environment became part of American education.

As states began implementing the least-restrictive-environment principle, the term *mainstreaming* quickly entered our vocabulary. In practice, mainstreaming means the instructional and social integration of exceptional children with other children. Several significant criteria guide mainstreaming. When the educational needs of the handicapped child can best be served through placement with nonhandicapped children, the regular classroom will be the least restrictive environment. Primary instructional responsibility, then, lies with the regular teacher. When the handicaps are severe, however, assignment is made to special classes or separate programs.

Another section of PL 94-142 that has great implications for creative teaching requires that an Individualized Education Program (IEP) (see Figure 3.1) be developed and maintained for each handicapped child. An IEP must include:

a statement of the child's present level of educational performance;

a statement of annual goals, including short-term instructional objectives;

a statement of the specific special education and related services to be provided to the child and the extent to which the child will be able to participate in regular educational programs;

the projected dates for initiation of services and the anticipated duration of the services;

appropriate objective criteria and evaluation procedures (such as the evaluation models for the three domains of learning) and schedules for determining, on at least an annual basis, whether the short-term instructional objectives are being achieved.

The law is clear in requiring that an IEP be developed for every handicapped child at the beginning of the school year and that it be reviewed annually. Once a child has been identified as handicapped, a conference must be held within 30 days for the purpose of developing the IEP.

The IEP conference must include a number of participants: a representative of the public agency who is qualified to provide or supervise special education, the child's teacher, one or both of the parents, the child when appropriate and, at the discretion of the parent or agency, other individuals.

The IEP represents the primary vehicle for assuring quality education for the handicapped. It provides a base for assessing the child's level of performance and for providing an effective educational program.

Since creative teachers emphasize skill instruction, problem solving, and individualization for all children, they are able to include handicapped children in their programs. Creative teachers use activities that emphasize the senses of sight and touch for the hearing impaired, for example.

In the past, unfortunately, most handicapped students were barred from pursuing certain careers because they were not exposed to problem-solving and skill activities in the elementary grades. Creative teachers are beginning to rectify this situation because of their belief that *all* children should learn all subjects and that this need is especially acute for the handicapped child.

The general effect of PL 94-142 will be increased recognition of the importance of good creative teaching. Instruction for all students will become more individualized, more specialized. Thus, while all students will be educated in the mainstream, that stream will be broader and deeper than in the past, resulting in more educational opportunities for all children.

In an article entitled, "Effective Mainstreaming Strategies for Mildly Handicapped Students" (Scruggs and Mastropieri, in press), specific strategies are suggested for effective instruction of mildly handicapped students. These include:

- *Modify the rate and presentation of the curriculum.* Slow the rate of presentation and include more visual organizers.

Figure 3.1 Sample individual education program

SAMPLE INDIVIDUAL EDUCATION PROGRAM

Student _____ Date _____ Teacher (s) _____

School _____ Program _____

1. Present level of performance—academic and nonacademic (List test given and observations made to indicate levels.

_____

Educational strengths: Educational weaknesses:

2. Placement decisions
_____

Educational programs and services	Person responsible	Initiation	Ending date	Percent of time

_____

3. Long-term objectives: _____
_____
_____

- *Provide additional time to learn.* The teacher, aide, peer, mentor, parents, and special-education teacher can all assist in providing additional learning time.
- *Use effective teaching strategies.* They include prespecified objectives, systematic presentations, questions related to the instructional objectives, guided and independent practice activities, and direct monitoring of student progress.
- *Allow sufficient time for responding.* These students may need additional time to respond to a question. Teachers need to practice sufficient waiting time after asking a question before eliciting responses from students.
- *Assist students with listening skills.* Help students recognize and identify when listening is an important consideration for them.
- *Reinforce positive classroom behavior.* Specific behavior expected

Figure 3.1 *(continued)*

Activities and materials used		Evaluation	
Date begun		Date	Results
Committee members present; parents must sign and date	Dates of meetings	Recommendations for specific procedures/techniques, materials, learning styles	

should be communicated to the students and should be rewarded when it is observed.

- *Teach social skills.* Work with the special education teacher to help the students gain the social skill development desired.
- *Employ parents and other adults as tutors.* Parents and other adults can be very useful in helping students gain additional learning time that may be necessary.
- *De-emphasize textbook approaches where appropriate.* By moving the classroom learning environment from textbook centered to direct experiences, teachers can more easily include students with basic skills deficits.
- *Teach specific study and test-taking skills.* Teachers need to teach students how to study and prepare for tests that will be administered.

Figure 3.2 Ian Hudson story

Ian Hudson's aide keeps a list of which pupils have pushed his chair. Today it's Amber Mullendore's turn.

Ian watches letters form from his own hand under the guidance of his classroom aide.

Froedge pushes Ian through a square dance routine in gym class. His partner for the exercise is Stephanie Rice.

A POET INSIDE

There's far more to 7-year-old second-grader Ian Hudson than his handicap

By NELSON PRICE
The Indianapolis News

CRAWFORDSVILLE, Ind. — There is at least one difference between Ian Hudson and the poet whose life was the basis for the movie "My Left Foot."

But first, some similarities.

Like the late Irish poet Christy Brown, 7-year-old Ian has cerebral palsy.

The blond, blue-eyed boy also has an impish sense of humor, demonstrated by his venturing out last Halloween as a toga-clad, shield-toting Ben Hur. (Ian's "stander," a wheeled device to which his legs are strapped so he can remain upright, became his chariot.)

Ian also is a poet. His writings include a poem about the Persian Gulf war.

And like Brown, his is an extroverted spirit trapped in a body with minimal muscle control or vocal ability.

Which brings up the difference.

"Ian doesn't even have the capacity with his foot that Christy Brown had," noted his mother, Helen Hudson. A former college professor, she teaches American literature at Crawfordsville High School.

Her son, a second-grader in the gifted and talented program at Laura Hose Elementary School, communicates by lunging his torso — or flopping his arm, often with the help of an adult — on a desk-sized mat with letters of the alphabet.

Using that technique, he "speaks," spelling out every word.

Tests indicate Ian may be a genius. Yet the intellectual abilities of the straight-A student — whose vocabulary has been assessed at a senior high school level — were a mystery for years.

That's because, with Ian unable to communicate, examiners had no way to measure his intelligence.

The breakthrough came when Marilyn Webb, a psychometrist for Crawfordsville Community Schools, noticed a flicker of deliberate movement. She realized that Ian, then 5, periodically had enough control of one hand to indicate a response to multiple-choice questions.

This is his second year in Margaret Zimmerman's gifted and talented class.

He is the only handicapped child in the class of

Classmate Drew Twarek (above) helps Ian with a computer program. At the end of the day (left), little sister Alix leads the way as mom Helen Hudson walks Ian through the school hall.

20. But because of Ian's advanced abilities, particularly in his favorite subjects of math and science, classmates often ask their peer to help them with homework.

"His presence is a terrific influence," said Ginny Froedge, a classroom aide assigned exclusively to Ian. "It gives these gifted kids a whole new concept about what 'perfect' means."

Ian's family includes his father, Marc, an English professor at Wabash College.

POET: No patronizing

and his sister, Alix, 18 months old. Marc Hudson has written several books of poetry, which may explain Ian's fondness for verse.

Ian attends school three full days and two mornings weekly. He spends his two free afternoons in forms of physical therapy, including horseback riding and underwater swimming.

Exercises are designed to strengthen his lungs and reflexes since, in Mrs. Hudson's words, "This is a kid who has never had a chance to run the 100-yard dash." Plans for next year are for Ian to attend school full time.

Asked about career goals, Ian grinned and spelled out:

"P-R-O-F-E-S-S-O-R."

Elaborating, with Froedge helping him select letters, the boy indicated he would like to teach math to college students.

Watching from a few paces away, Zimmerman conceded she was panic-stricken when she learned a boy with cerebral palsy and severe physical limitations would be among her pupils.

"I didn't find out until five days before school started," she said. "I had already had all the start-of-school contacts with families of the other students, so I would not be talking to them to let them know.

"Ian came 15 minutes late the first day. Before he arrived, I told the class Ian would be with us. He showed up with a family friend, who explained about Ian.

"Just by sheer luck, he sat in a group of desks next to a little boy named Aaron who felt at ease with him. Right off, Aaron pushed his chair at recess. That made all the other kids relax."

Froedge now keeps a list of which classmates have pushed Ian's wheelchair. She rotates the task because of the overwhelming number of requests to help the popular, vivacious boy.

Sometimes, when convenience or speed in maneuvering is important, the aide carries Ian.

He participates in all activities, including gym class. Last week Ian square danced with his peers, twirling about in his wheelchair.

"He is constantly being invited out to play at home and is included in birthday parties," Zimmerman reported.

"One mother wanted her son to let Ian win at computer chess. The boy refused,

---

'The prognosis was grim. We were told there was no guarantee he would live. . . Two years ago this would have been beyond my dreams.'

— Helen Hudson
Ian Hudson's mother

---

which I think is terrific. There is no patronizing."

The only adjustment problem, she added, surfaced about six weeks after Ian's arrival.

"At the first parent-teacher conferences, I learned some of the kids were coming home and sobbing because they felt so badly about Ian," Zimmerman said. "I didn't know this was happening because they weren't crying at school.

"The next day we talked about the fact that, yes, it was sad this would happen to Ian. It's sad this could happen to anybody. But we also needed to look at all the positives about Ian — that he is here with us in school, that he has so many friends, that he is so bright and creative.

"I also pointed out that Ian isn't sad. He comes in every morning just beaming."

According to Mrs. Hudson, her son's cerebral palsy is the result of an accident involving oxygen deprivation during Ian's birth in Washington state.

"The prognosis was grim," she said. "We were told there was no guarantee he would live."

Mrs. Hudson, who shares her son's sunny disposition, called his presence in a classroom for gifted children a miracle.

"Two years ago," she explained, "this would have been beyond my dreams."

But family members always sensed Ian possessed remarkable capabilities. "From the very beginning, he watched things," Mrs. Hudson recalled. "His eyes would follow objects. He was alert and inquisitive. I just *knew* there was something going on inside."

After examining Ian at age 2, a New York specialist in cerebral palsy told the Hudsons: "Your son does not miss a beat."

Friends gave the family boxes of toys, including magnetic letters. One afternoon when Ian was 3, Mrs. Hudson sprawled on the carpet with Ian and spelled out "frog" and "cow."

"I said, 'Ian, which is green?' He rolled out of my arms and onto 'frog.' I said, 'Which moos?' He indicated 'cow.'

"This hinted to us that Ian had been reading while he was on our laps. Marc and I started spreading the Sunday New York Times on the floor. Marc would say, 'Where is a headline that says 'blank,' Ian?' He would 'point' for us. He was always exactly right."

Mrs. Hudson reported one of her son's biggest frustrations is that he needs someone to feed him. And that he is unable to read alone because he cannot turn pages.

Ian has finished several C.S. Lewis fantasy novels and just completed Robert Louis Stevenson's "Treasure Island."

"He doesn't like TV," Mrs. Hudson reported. "He recognized very early that

TV is an easy way to 'park' him. The exception is (TV personality) Mr. Rogers. He says Mr. Rogers is a very wise man. Ian liked what he told children about the war."

After the stay in Washington, the Hudsons moved to Wisconsin, where Mrs. Hudson, an expert in Icelandic folklore, was on the faculty at a college. The family moved in 1988 to Crawfordsville, where Alix was born.

Ian indicated he enjoys his young sister. Indeed, after being apart for a morning, the two shared a long, warm hug.

"It takes one full parent to manipulate Ian, and that sometimes upsets Alix," Mrs. Hudson confided. "She gets a little jealous."

The family subscribes to Car & Driver magazine because Ian is fascinated with automobiles. He also wants a golden retriever.

"The point about Ian's story is that there are always possibilities," Zimmerman said. "With enough support, it is perfectly possible to integrate a child like Ian into a regular classroom.

"You couldn't find any less experienced person than me to deal with this. If I can do it, anyone can."

Zimmerman selected Froedge, the energetic mother of three sons, as Ian's aide. "I knew she would get him in the middle of whatever was going on in the classroom."

Like the salaries of other aides for handicapped students, Froedge's comes from the school district.

A speech therapist at Methodist Hospital has told the Hudsons that, by age 16, Ian may be able to vocalize so strangers can understand him. Now he can make a limited range of sounds, which usually are indecipherable even to his parents.

In private "conversations" with his mother by using the alphabet-thrusting technique, Ian occasionally expresses exasperation.

Some frustrations concern adult acquaintances who talk about him in his presence as if he were invisible. He also is bothered by those who, even after learning he is the top student in a gifted program, treat him as though he were much younger than 7.

"That is always a problem with a kid in (a parent's) arms, with a tray in front of him or in a chair," Mrs. Hudson noted. "Those are all barriers."

Asked to offer advice for other parents, Mrs. Hudson warned against dwelling on a child's limitations.

She paused and watched as her son, clad in jeans, a blue sweatshirt and sneakers with chartreuse laces, spelled out his thoughts despite limp arms and legs.

"I think of my child as the kid with blue eyes."

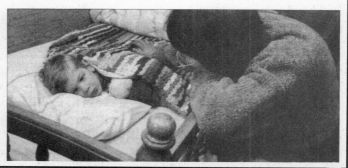

Ian and his dad, Marc Hudson, (near right photo) laugh over a friendly competition with slot cars. Then mom Helen (far right) tucks Ian in for the night.

My Song

Poems are nicer than letters
Because they have a song in them.
My gift to you is the tune I write here.
Listen quietly for my voice—
I may quit speaking at any moment
But I can never stop singing.

Ian Hudson

Pilgrims in the Night

Domes of the cathedral gleam in the moonlight,
Questing pilgrims, hoods pulled low,
Pass my cozy bed.
Where in the wide world
Might they be going?

Ian Hudson

Christmas Poem

*S*anta Claus brings joys to girls and boys.
*A*ntlers gleam in the light. What a lovely sight.
*N*ight of wonders and delight.
*T*he star of Christmas shines above.
*A*ll the world wrapped in love.

Ian Hudson

Source: Ian Hudson. *Second Grade Poet.*
By Permission—*The Indianapolis News*, February 12, 1991, pp. C–1.6.

POINTS TO PONDER

If the individual education of each child is special, why isn't the individual education of each teacher special?

WORKING IN A MULTICULTURAL ENVIRONMENT

By the year 2020, the United States will have nearly 300 million people. Of those, 38 million will be African Americans and 46 million will be Hispanic Americans. Today's typical fifth-grade class that will be graduating in the twenty-first century would find 24 percent born in poverty, 14 percent born with a handicap, and 40 percent representing ethnic, racial, and/or linguistic differences from the white majority. There are more than 30 million people in the United States whose first language is not English. At the same time, approximately 95 percent of the preservice elementary teachers in college today are white females of European ancestry. As a result, preservice teachers must be prepared to work in a multicultural environment.

Recognizing the importance of education for *all,* creative teachers insure that cultural diversity is recognized and celebrated through their actions and selection of teaching materials. They understand the importance of providing integral curriculum materials and opportunities for Asian Americans, African Americans, Hispanic Americans, Native Americans, and other cultures with respect to their histories and achievements. They help youngsters of European ancestry understand the contributions of all cultures to the social and economic development of the United States.

Creative teachers recognize that add-ons to social studies units such as Multicultural Day or Black History Month are superficial and nonproductive simplistic activities. They celebrate multicultural learning all day, every day as an integral part of the learning process.

Creative teachers help children share cultural experiences with each other through writings, stories, poetry, art, and other activities. They help children understand the messages about ethnic diversity received from television, movies, parents, siblings, or peers.

All children can become victims of ethnic prejudice and misunderstanding. The following segment from *Facing Racism In Education* (Hidalgo, McDowell, and Siddle 1990) is very revealing. Could this ever happen to you?

> Leslie was a bright child, somewhat mischievous, yet usually sensitive to the feelings of others. She looked seriously at me and shrugged her shoulders. She obviously knew she was in trouble but didn't seem to understand why. "Did you know you were hurting my feelings?" I asked. She shook her head no. "People do that to make fun of those like me," I told her. "They make fun of Asian-Americans and the shape of their eyes."
>
> Leslie, who was almost seven, was unaware of the message she was giving, although she realized her behavior was "bad." A tear ran down her silent face. We gave each other a big hug and she said she was sorry. I called a class meeting and we discussed how prejudice was hurtful to others and to ourselves. Some of the children were sensitive about wearing glasses; others had been teased about being short. I was able to use their personal experiences to discuss the feelings of minority Americans and how we cringe at stereotypes and ethnic slurs.
>
> Rodney and Leslie, two first graders, had lived their entire lives in a typical small American town. Few members of ethnic minorities resided in the area. These two children had had no personal contact with members of ethnic minority communities until I became their teacher. The messages they had internalized about ethnic minority peoples might have come from television, movies, parents, siblings, or peers. Our responsibility to our students is compelling; the misunderstandings children develop about others can affect their adult attitudes and behaviors, and help them understand how they could act unfairly towards an individual or a group of people they did not know.
>
> All children can become victims of ethnic prejudice. It can manifest itself

in the creation of a "we" and "they" orientation. Individuals who the children consider to be outsiders may be labeled "strange," "wrong," or "inferior." For minority children, negative perceptions of their ethnic groups can evolve into self-degrading feelings, especially if these messages are reinforced in their school and society. One example of the in-and-out-group affiliation is name calling.

Sometimes White children can find themselves similarly stigmatized. I remember a painful incident that occurred when I was teaching first grade in a 97 percent minority school in the Central area of Seattle. I had 22 first graders in my class: 19 Black Americans, 2 Native Americans, and 1 White American. One day during art class, as I was circulating around the room helping students cut out materials for their unit on dinosaurs. I heard a voice yell. "I'm not White. I'm Black." Peter, a small, active, blond-haired child, had his foot on a chair steadying himself, ready to throw a pair of scissors at another student. "Peter, get down off that chair NOW!" I said sternly. Luckily, Peter did get down, and I quickly grabbed the scissors from him. Tears poured down his face as he attempted to tell the class. "I'm Black. I'm Black. I'm Black." I heard murmuring around the room. "You're White. You're a honky."

Peter was White, yet he identified strongly with his Black peers. All his friends were Black, and he had grown up in the Black community. Later, I discovered Peter and a classmate had been arguing over the scissors. His Black classmate knew Peter wanted to feel a part of the group and knew that making him feel like an outsider would sting. Ethnic slurs can be used to hurt or control any person, including majority children.

POINTS TO PONDER

What would you do in this situation? How would you help these children understand these situations and rectify these problems?

FIELD TRIPPING

Someone once said, "There aren't many wondrous events in a lifetime, but a few will suffice." If properly planned, a field trip can be classified as a wondrous event. Proper planning and attention to some basic concerns can insure success.

Why Take Them?

A field trip means many things to many people. For some, it may be a quiet walk to view autumn leaves that fringe the school yard. For others, it may be a three-day trip to the Royal Gorge. Regardless of the type, extent, or duration, most field trips have many similarities. One important consideration always has to be: Why take field trips? This question has a variety of answers.

It is your turn. Everyone in the school system has visited the ice cream factory, the post office, the zoo, the local bakery, the local newspaper, and the police station. Your students are asking, "When are we going someplace?" But just going someplace is not sufficient. Your field trip should serve a purpose. Perhaps it is to collect some rock-forming minerals to reinforce your current science instruction or to observe dinosaur models at a museum, or maybe you will go to a local theater to see "behind the scenes" because you are getting ready to do a class play. The major purpose is to give students the kind of firsthand experience not obtainable in the classroom.

On a field trip, you see your students in a new setting. This is usually reflected in a set of behaviors different from those in your classroom. The students see you in a new setting. You look and perhaps act differently when viewed in the field by children.

Some Precautions

If possible make a dry run of the field trip with a select group of students. Observe their reactions as they peruse the site. Your ability to interpret a wrinkled nose, an impish glint in the eye, or a twitching ear will enable you to forecast your whole class's reactions. Step back and view the field trip with a critical eye. Think of it under the worst possible conditions and let that dictate the kind of equipment, clothing, and other things you should have your students bring. Take slides of the area, including landmarks, trail signs, places to see, things to do, things not to do, drinking fountains, and items to be observed or collected. If possible bring back actual samples of collectible items. Show the slides to the children prior to the actual visit. These slides and later shots of the group are very useful in the debriefing discussions that follow field trips.

In preparing for a field trip, write a letter to the parents detailing the trip. Include a schedule of events, information about lunch, snacks, and the cost of the field trip. Have each parent sign a permission slip. For your convenience, have the parent list any medical problems, medications, dietary needs, and the family doctor's name and phone number. In an emergency, you will be prepared. Have a phone tree organized, so if you are delayed parents can be informed quickly. Make arrangements well in advance if you are planning to go to a commercial area. Double-check to make sure the bus has been scheduled. Arrive with your confirming letter substantiating the arrangement. Have a name to ask for in case all does not go well.

Common complaints of field trippers are: They can't see. They can't hear. They can't keep up with the traffic. Solutions can be found for these problems. Distributing maps that have labels of the field-trip stops as well as printed details of what to see at each stop can eliminate some of the complaints. Dividing the class into smaller groups led by informed adults who can monitor the movement and instruction is also helpful. Including on the map the location of rest rooms, eating facilities (type and price range), and recreation areas will eliminate other complaints.

Even if you can squeeze everyone on the bus, it is a good idea to have at least one parent driving a backup car behind the bus. Many emergencies or "early-return-homers" can be handled more readily using this backup system.

Bring emergency, compact, lightweight, highly nutritious food such as granola bars, trail mix, or peanut butter crackers; a few basic medical supplies such as Band-Aids, insect repellent, and sunscreen; cameras; containers to collect things; plastic garbage bags; tissues; safety pins; a can or bottle opener; and extra money.

Spell out the rules of conduct. Don't deviate from your prescribed trip behavior. Remember, you are not responsible for minding the lunches, nor are you the keeper of purses, wallets, cameras, or contact lenses. Never allow children into public rest rooms alone. Send them in groups of three or four. Wear comfortable, loose-fitting clothes. Good stout shoes are a must. Have an emergency plan. Inform the children of the time and place for departure. Alert the group to a recall signal. One blast on the whistle means the group has five minutes to assemble at the bus, two blasts—three minutes; and three blasts—stragglers are on their own, and the bus is leaving without them. Have children buddy up. Keep a head count. You should not return with fewer or more students than you started with.

Bring a list of telephone numbers with you. This list should include each student's home phone, the principal's number, and the number of the nearest state police station. When there are problems everyone needs to be informed. If the trip extends beyond the normal day, arrange to have the children dropped off at their homes or at school. It helps to have a phone handy if students need to call. Arrange a time for parents to pick up their children. Never leave until all children are on their way home.

Reasons Why Some Field Trips Fail

Adequate preplanning is not carried out—administrative approval, parental approval, site approval, transportation, familiarization with the route, parking, facilities, equipment, prior discussion of the trip.

The teacher is unenthusiastic. (The teacher's attitude sets the tone for the field trip.)

The students may have been there before.

The students may have been forewarned about the kind of field trips you undertake.

The students may not have had a part in planning and selecting of the field trip area.

The objectives of the field trip may be beyond or below the level of achievement of the students.

The field trip is taken merely to discharge a duty.

It is a "look-see, don't touch, nothing to do" field trip.

The field trip is overstructured. Everyone is too busy collecting, inspecting, cataloging, and filling out worksheets. No free time is allotted for individual exploration and investigation.

The cost of transportation and meals is excessive. Too much pocket money is required.

An undisciplined student can spoil the trip for most students.

There is not enough adult supervision.

The trip is too time-consuming. This investment is not worth the return.

Not enough time was allocated for lunch or necessary rest-room breaks.

Reasons Why Some Field Trips Succeed

Careful and meticulous but flexible planning is done by the students and the teacher.

The teacher and bus driver know the exact location of the field trip and where to park the bus. (Remember to send the bus driver a thank-you note.)

Enthusiasm is exhibited by the teacher. (Enthusiasm is infectious.)

A variety of field trips are initiated. (Micro- as well as macro-field trips are possible.)

Involvement of parents enhances the chances of success. (Field tripping is not necessarily a do-it-yourself endeavor.)

Pleasurable experiences are programmed into the trip: photos of students involved in various activities; surprise treats (a treasure hunt, or hot chocolate at the end of the trail).

Teachers forget they are teachers and join the ranks.

The field trip has a purpose.

A review of the results of the field trip is made to reinforce achievement of the objectives, and a review of slides is made; both reviews lay the groundwork for the next field trip.

POINTS TO PONDER

Design a field trip for your class without leaving the classroom.

Prepare a set of activity cards that will allow each student to investigate an individual problem on a field trip.

Prepare a list of reasons why we shouldn't take field trips. Next, prepare a list of ways to overcome the problems listed.

USING INFORMAL LEARNING CENTERS, MUSEUMS, AND RESOURCE PEOPLE

Informal learning centers and museums, in general, provide a whole new field of self-motivating experiences in learning because they offer exhibits that appeal to the senses, emotions, and intellect. They are among the most rapidly developing institutions of learning today. Science museums have more visitors than any other single type of museum. Visitors come to informal learning centers not only to learn facts, but to experience new and interesting phenomena. Most informal learning centers use self-selected experiences that foster the development of logical thinking for various age groups. In addition, the museum is one of the few places left where the family can go as a unit.

The informal learning center and museum usually provide experiences that are not available elsewhere. These experiences permit people to keep abreast of new developments in science and technology. Furthermore, these institutions present information on current issues objectively. Their goal is to present enough facts to enable people to make intelligent decisions independently.

Creative teachers should visit a museum or informal learning center long before they plan to take their classes. By doing so, they can decide what aspects of the tour they want to emphasize, how they will introduce the tour to children, what arrangements to make for a tour guide (docent), if desired, and what follow-up activities to use after the museum visit. If a class visit is impossible, teachers can prepare a presentation with materials such as slides, tapes, photographs, and brochures to share with their classes. Appendix II will serve as an excellent place to begin your museum contacts.

Most museums respond to the wishes of the classroom teacher. Creative teachers request inquiry tours with docents trained in inquiry techniques. Inquiry tours have the following characteristics:

1. They allow the students rather than the docent to draw conclusions.
2. Docents are not afraid to say "I don't know" when presented with questions they cannot or choose not to answer.
3. They make students feel that their observations are good and that they should elaborate on them.
4. The docent is not too quick to give the answers to questions. The answers are allowed to evolve from the questions and discussion.
5. They allow for creative discussion by using open-ended and higher-level questions.
6. Docents are not too eager to tell all that they know about an exhibit or object; rather, they encourage students' thoughts and questions.

Resource people can provide excellent input into the creative classroom. Every classroom has children whose parents and acquaintances have interests, hobbies, or occupations that may interest the students. Creative teachers capitalize on this by finding out what talents are available through parent-teacher meetings and questionnaires parents and children complete. Preparation and planning are important. It is up to the teacher to insure that a resource person is able to communicate with the children at their level.

POINTS TO PONDER

Why do most museum tours concentrate on giving information rather than on responding to children's interests?

SELECTING BOOKS FOR CLASSROOM AND LIBRARY

How are books selected for the classroom or the school library? Some states have statewide textbook adoptions, while in others books are purchased at the local level with no state restrictions or limitations. States that have a statewide adoption program usually buy books in cycles—books for each subject are adopted for a six-year period. A textbook series adopted in 1994, for example, would not be changed until 2000. Other states allow individual school districts to adopt books as needed.

How should a textbook be selected? Should the selection be based upon the content, the size of the type, colored pictures, good binding, teacher guides, or supplementary material?

Creative teachers first select a textbook or program that emphasizes the thinking abilities of children and is action oriented. Second, they look at the content to find out if it is suitable and corresponds to state or local guidelines. Third, they examine the layout or format of the book to determine if it is compatible with appropriate pedagogical practices.

Some questions to ask include:

1. Is the content presented at the appropriate reading level for the students in your class? Are challenging activities provided for high-ability students and supplemental materials available for motivating all levels of learners?
2. Do the materials promote a positive attitude toward the discipline?
3. Do the materials lend themselves to the development of statements of problems for children to solve? Are children given opportunities to observe and compare, build systems of classification, reinforce skills, analyze data, use instruments, make measurements, write original ideas, conduct experiments, evaluate evidence, work cooperatively, draw conclusions, think creatively, and invent a model or theory?
4. It is difficult to forecast precisely what content the child needs to know. Therefore, a program should emphasize research skills as well as critical- and creative-thinking skills that will allow the child to pursue knowledge in later life.
5. Are the materials concept-oriented to allow for integration with other subjects such as science, language arts, mathematics, social studies, art, and music?
6. Are computer programs available to enrich and to reinforce the content?

Many schools have committees of teachers, parents, and administrators who make the final decision about textbook adoption. If you want some say over what material is presented to students, volunteer to be an active member on a textbook adoption committee. You will have the opportunity to review and evaluate textbooks and attend publisher-sponsored sessions to gain more information about each series. Most important, you will be part of the decision-making team. You will have an impact on education in your school district for the next six-year period.

Whenever possible, the creative teacher assists the school librarian or media specialist with the selection of children's books and other learning materials to add to the school media center. Monthly reviews of most new children's books as well as a selection of the best books for each year are published in various teacher magazines and library journals.

Keep your eyes open as you browse through bookstores and go to conferences. Select a wide variety of books to enhance various content areas: reference books, fiction, biographies, and illustrated nonfiction books. Computer magazines are wonderful for making software comparisons. Be aware, however, that most of these magazines make their money from the same software companies running ads in their magazines, so read the reviews very carefully. They are seldom very critical. Some states have preview centers where you can preview books or look at software before you purchase them. Take advantage of these opportunities. What about asking the students? They may be the best evaluators. Students will quickly tell you what is motivating and appealing. In a creative learning atmosphere, children are free to make recommendations and to evaluate critically the selection and use of materials.

POINTS TO PONDER

Why do most textbook evaluation forms concentrate on the physical aspects of the book rather than on the questions in the preceding list?

Why should parents and students be included on the textbook adoption committee?

HOW TO ORDER AND OBTAIN MATERIALS AND EQUIPMENT

Some elementary-school teachers live within walking distance of the schools in which they teach, yet few teachers are ever observed walking to work. The reason is that teachers daily carry books, bags, or boxes filled with educational paraphernalia they need in their schools. The bags and boxes may be filled with anything from boxes of straight pins or soda straws to corks, rubber cement, flour, aluminum trays, coat hangers, wire, newspapers, panty hose, and so forth. Nothing is sacred. If it is needed and if it is available, it is carried in. Textbooks often contain only pertinent poems, short stories, or references supporting ongoing lessons. Elementary-school teachers need paraphernalia to augment the day-to-day job of teaching. Some teachers call this material "junque," and it is. But it is necessary junque if teachers subscribe to the notion of hands-on instruction, which invariably requires sufficient and diverse materials and equipment. Placing sufficient materials and equipment into the hands of children is essential. Sometimes this mix is one set of paraphernalia for each child, sometimes one set for every two children (or three, four, or more) depending on the availability of the material and equipment; cost (if any); safety considerations during usage; storage facilities for these materials; and the strength, energy, and resourcefulness of the teacher.

Each area of the curriculum has discrete requirements for materials and equipment. In science, elementary-school teachers substitute common household items such as mayonnaise jars, aluminum pie plates, medicine bottles, and eyedroppers for commercially produced equipment. Some items, like magnets, timers, magnifying glasses, glass tubing, and stoppers, must be purchased periodically from commercial sources. Art, music, health, mathematics, language arts, and social studies also require materials and equipment. Chalk is no longer the dominant teaching tool. Manipulatives, computer programs, simulations, videos, and learning games are used to reinforce skills and actively involve students in the learning process. Appendix V will serve as a beginning source of supplies and equipment for the creative teaching experience.

Before requesting catalogs and prices from various distributors, check with middle-, junior high-, or high-school teachers in the district. Usually one or more of these individuals will have catalogs and price lists available. They may have subject-specific catalogs that contain valuable material. They may also be able to tell you if the school district already has the equipment at another location. School media specialists also have catalogs relating to audiovisual media, computers, and reference materials. Principals usually have catalogs for basic school supplies such as bulletin-board trim, globes, playground equipment, and art supplies. Before ordering materials and equipment, compare quality and prices in the catalogs of different supply and equipment companies. Also check the shipping costs.

POINTS TO PONDER

Find out where in your area you can obtain materials needed for your classroom and prepare your own materials list. Try businesses, industries, other schools, colleges, and universities. Prepare a list of common household items that you could recycle and use in your creative-teaching program.

ACQUIRING, ORGANIZING, STORING, AND DISTRIBUTING EQUIPMENT AND SUPPLIES

What To Get and Where To Get It

It is a sinking feeling to walk into a classroom with all the joy and enthusiasm of being the best teacher in the world and find the cabinets empty. Creative teaching takes a multitude of supplies. Yarn, tape, poster board, magnifying lenses, microscopes, calculators, geometric shapes, math manipulatives, geoboards, measuring devices (rulers, thermometers, graduated cylinders, timers, stopwatches, balances, protractors, teaspoons), hot plates, candles, matches, kitchen chemicals (salt, sugar, baking soda, vinegar, food coloring), paint, clay, glue, aluminum foil, plastic bags, eyedroppers, safety glasses, magnets, corks, string, glassware, globes, maps, games, puzzles, and batteries are all essential for the creative teacher who believes it is important to get the students actively involved in the learning process.

Some materials may be provided by the school, but creative teachers are always on the lookout for useful materials. A good way to locate materials is to send a list of needed supplies home with the students. Many times parents have extra materials around the house such as containers, magazines, tools, books, audiovisual equipment, and games they are pleased to donate. A box of baby-food jars may be just what is needed to have a creative art lesson or a hands-on science experiment. A used typewriter or word processor may be the piece of equipment necessary to start a classroom newspaper or publishing center. Old magazines can be used for learning games or creative-writing sessions. Yard sales are good places to find inexpensive books, yarn, fabric, games, marbles, tools, and kitchen utensils.

While scrounging for materials, it is wise to plan and organize a basic tool box. Screwdrivers, pliers, a wire cutter, wrenches, a flashlight, a hammer, tin snips, and a staple gun are extremely handy to have. Include an assortment of screws, nails, nuts and bolts, staples, and wire. A tool box will save you hours of hunting for the school custodian. It will also make you the most popular teacher at your end of the hall.

Parents and yard sales can provide many of the simple, basic materials, but there are always new materials or expensive equipment items that are essential for enhancing your teaching. Therefore, it is important to tell your principal that you have a "wish list" on file. The desired items should be organized in order of priority with order forms, catalog numbers, and prices. In education there is either feast or famine. Money is budgeted into different accounts and some money is kept in reserve for emergencies. At certain times of the year the money has to be spent or it may be liquidated. This is when the "wish list" comes in handy. If the principal or department head is aware that you need a microscope, set of magnets, bookcase, calculator, tape player, video camera, or computer program, your request may be filled.

Remember, if you do not ASK, you will not GET. Always ask politely and professionally. If you make good use of equipment and materials, you may be more likely to receive additional equipment and materials when needed.

Getting Organized

The next step, organizing this equipment and material, is crucial. All that you have acquired is useless if it is not organized so it is readily available. Frequently used items should be stored in durable, labeled boxes or containers, and located in areas that are accessible to students. Items that are used for once-a-year units can reside in the hard-to-reach top shelves and cubby holes. Keep your eyes open for boxes and containers. Often preview books, sent for textbook adoption, come with wonderful creative containers. These containers can be covered with contact paper and color coded for various subject areas. Knowing that all of your math manipulatives are in red boxes, your spelling games in green ones, can be a great time saver.

Organization expedites creative teaching. Time is the most precious commodity that students have, and to waste it would be improper. The best-conceived lesson loses its effectiveness if it is confounded by delays and shortages of equipment. Discipline problems fester in the time between instruction and direct involvement. The longer the delay, the greater the inducement for students to engage in activities other than those you have planned. Organization is prime. It is part and parcel of good planning.

Places To Store Materials

You will need space for storage. An old guru once said, "Every graduating education major should get a sheepskin, keys to a warehouse, and a strong burro." While it may at times seem as though you need a warehouse (and occasionally a burro), lesser space will do. Using your investigative talents, ferret out all the nooks and crannies in your school. A closet or janitor's workroom will do. If your school is not so endowed, a corner of your classroom will suffice. Shelves would be ideal, but plastic milk crates, copy-paper boxes, or bricks and boards can be substituted for them. The only constraint on finding space is your desire to achieve the goal. Don't weaken. The end result is well worth the trouble.

Having discovered or created a storage area, you will need to decide what equipment and materials fall into the categories valuable/not valuable and storable/not storable. Valuable and dangerous items should be under lock and key. You will need a foolproof backup system for an extra key. (Many a fine lesson has gone awry for want of a key.) Large pieces of equipment—balances, for example—should be accessible in the classroom. Computers, microscopes, calculators, and timers should be common, visible pieces of equipment. Students should be encouraged to use them as frequently as they use the pencil sharpener.

Ways To Distribute Materials

Making the students responsible for getting materials and returning them to the proper places is the key to distributing materials. Chaos, you say! It could be—without an organized teacher behind the scenes. It takes the mastermind, a creative teacher, to select the right materials; to number the calculators so they are all returned; to have the timers and string in a convenient place; to keep all the paper supplies on the same shelf; to remember to purchase the balloons; to test the batteries; and to have extra protractors, compasses, and rulers handy.

Work centers also help in the distribution of materials. Tables or desks can be converted into centers, each with a set of materials and directions for experiments, writing labs, or problem-solving activities. Students can move to another center as they complete each activity. New activity centers can be added or replaced on a rotating basis that allow the teacher time to organize materials and develop new activities without being overwhelmed. As you pack away the center, remember to include an index card that lists all of the needed supplies. This will act as a valuable reminder when you pull out the center next year.

But how do you keep the centers fully equipped? Elicit the help of your class organizers—you know, the students who always have everything in place. As part of a classroom business or class jobs, "hire" these students to keep the centers supplied. When expendable items are running low, have the student write the needed items on a pad of paper that is located by the door. As the teacher leaves for the evening, the list is torn off the pad of paper and supplies can be purchased before the next day. Younger children can place samples of the needed items in a basket by the door.

You Can Do It—With a Little Help

Having read all of this information about the acquisition, organization, storage, and distribution of materials and equipment, you may say, "See? That's why I am reluctant to do activities!" This process does not have to be tedious. Again, the key is your ability to organize—parents, the students, the librarian, and, if possible, the principal. They can all help you to procure, clean, keep track of, and sustain your supplies and materials.

SAFETY AND CREATIVE TEACHING

Teaching well is teaching safely. No one wants to invite safety problems; to be forewarned is to be forearmed!

Some Cautions for Teachers

School safety is everyone's concern. Safety and the welfare of the children within a school is a number one priority. Schools are made as safe as they can be. Fire drills, tornado drills, earthquake drills, and general building-evacuation drills are held regularly to insure swift, safe, and automatic responses to impending safety concerns.

Reading, writing, and spelling are thought of as relatively safe areas of the curriculum. Accidents rarely occur while silently reading *Charlotte's Web*, writing "My Favorite Hobby is..." or spelling "antidisestablishmentarianism." Not that safety problems could not happen, but they rarely do. Nonetheless, creative teachers always anticipate problems and constantly keep alert for the unexpected. Eternal vigilance is success guaranteed. English, music, and social studies all have safety concerns, but again these are minimized by nature of the instructional passiveness associated with these subjects. If these passive instructional techniques were altered, a greater concern for safety would be engendered. Again, unless instructional strategies in mathematics, science, art, and social studies cause the students to be out of their seats and on their feet physically involved with hands-on activities, few red-flag safety problems will occur. Not that they couldn't, but they usually don't. The safety concerns in art and science instruction can be distinctly different, particularly if taught by a creative, hands-on, action-involved teacher. Then they involve the use of special equipment, physical involvements, and experimentation, and require that special concerns be considered to maintain "safe" art and science instruction. In the teaching of science and art, try all activities and demonstrations beforehand. If you have any doubts about safety, make revisions to eliminate the hazards.

In the act of teaching, train yourself to be aware of those things that can be hazardous to children, to yourself, and to your colleagues. Several cardinal rules for dealing with safety are: never leave children unattended, never administer first aid (this is best done by a school nurse or someone who has been trained in first aid), and be constantly alert to potential dangers. Search out dangers and remove them. Always exercise prudent judgment. Litigation is a growing concern within the teaching profession. You will be challenged for safety violations that injure children. Therefore, always exercise common sense.

Safety concerns become magnified when certain conditions exist: large playground areas occupied by too many children and too few supervisors, too many children in too small a lunchroom area, playground equipment that is difficult to monitor, and physical education activities that involve fast-moving bodies and objects. If you are assigned responsibilities for safety and are placed in an untenable situation that exceeds what a normal teacher can adequately handle, you should go on record stating your concerns. Write a letter to the proper individual expressing your concerns for the children's safety. Keep a dated copy of this correspondence. If the situation does not change, write again. Retain a copy of this action. This would be prudent behavior on your part.

Other areas of concern that must be addressed are the problems of head lice and body-fluid emissions. Take all necessary precautions, alert the proper parties, and wear rubber gloves when dealing with problems. You must protect yourself and the children. Safety concerns when dealing with chemicals, cleaning fluids, and certain art materials must be observed. Oftentimes rubber gloves and/or special handling techniques to insure safety may be needed. It is always better to be safe than sorry.

Your school may have safety rules concerning the use of fire, wearing eye protection equipment, electricity, and so on. Always check with the principal or science supervisor before initiating any science activity that involves the use of an open flame, electricity, and other hazardous materials. When permission is granted, forge ahead, observing the appropriate safety precautions.

Not all hazards can be totally eliminated. In some activities—for example "Why does a burning match curl up?"—burning matches must be used. If hazards exist, provide the students with special instructions, highlighting the potential hazards and the precautions to be observed. This applies to items such as hot plates, propane tanks, soldering irons, electric wires, microprojectors, and audiovisual equipment. Many heated items retain heat long after use and, therefore, pose special problems in handling, removal, and storage. The heated items should all be allowed to cool thoroughly before being moved. While they cool, however, they need to be identified by signs that warn the children they are hot. Sometimes a small barricade is necessary to supplement this warning.

Constant supervision during science and art activities is a must, particularly when using equipment that might present safety problems. This supervision should take into account the number of pieces of equipment, the size of the class, and the length of time groups or individuals need to use the equipment to complete a task. Time constraints, as well as limited equipment, force children to rush. Rushing contributes to accidents. Limit the size of the groups to correspond to the available equipment. Never suggest that students extend the activity beyond the level to which you take it unless you review and approve the action. Unsupervised experimentation at home or in school can be hazardous. Remember that most accidents happen during lunch, recess, or physical education activities.

Everyone feels a bit foolish when an accident occurs. Students sometimes have accidents and suffer in absolute silence to avoid embarrassment. Insist that all accidents, no matter how small, be reported to you. Don't attempt to treat injuries; refer injured students to the nurse or to the principal.

Dull tools are more dangerous than sharp tools. The dull tool forces the user to apply force that can result in an accident. Be sure that all tools are in good condition and that students know how to use them.

Safety with Animals and Plants

Live animals in the classroom, while delightful, can be hazardous. The nice, gentle animal at home is not the same animal when it is besieged by 30 children vying for its attention and affection. Some precautions are in order.

All mammals should be inoculated for rabies prior to being brought into the classroom. (This requirement alone allows you a way out of agreeing to a child's request to bring in a pet aardvark.) Restrictions should be imposed on bringing to class wild animals such as snapping turtles, rabbits, wounded birds, or poisonous snakes.

When small animals are brought into the classroom, observe these simple rules: Provide clean, adequate living quarters free of contamination and secure enough to confine the animal. Plan for heat, light, water, food, and proper waste removal—even on weekends and holidays. Limit the handling of animals. Sanitary measures (washing hands after handling animals) must be practiced. Do not allow the animals to be teased. Any animal bite or scratch should be promptly reported and treated.

Plants, while seemingly harmless, must be viewed with some caution. Don't bring in poisonous plants. Don't allow children to eat or place portions of plants in their mouths or rub them on their bodies. Adverse reactions can occur.

Remember

All spinning objects are potentially dangerous.

All items under tension (rubber bands, springs) are potentially hazardous.

Heating a gas or liquid in a confined container is dangerous.

Always add acid to water, never the reverse.

All reagents should be properly labeled and stored in a cool, dry place (not the refrigerator). Combustibles should be stored in a locked metal container.

Only Pyrex or heat-treated glassware can be heated safely.

Bacterial cultures can contaminate unless sterilizing techniques are used.

Never leave children in an active classroom or playground unattended.

Knowing all this and always remembering to act prudently, enjoy yourself and teach creatively. We hope that, rather than turning you off to an activity-based classroom with all of these precautions, we have turned you on to creative teaching safety.

POINTS TO PONDER

Teacher A says, "I don't teach science because of all the safety hazards. I don't want to be sued." What is your response?

Addressing the concerns for safety in the classroom requires a suspicious mind. It requires one to be suspect of all things. For example, a sharp tool used in art, science, or social studies can become a safety concern. In the wrong place, in the wrong hands, in the wrong storage bin, sharp tools can present problems. Creative teachers analyze and anticipate safety problems before they happen. They train themselves to be alert to possibilities for danger. A puddle of water in the wrong place, an unmarked container with liquid in it, or a pencil left on the floor . . . almost anything can have the potential for an accident. Remove these. Creative teachers are prepared and get on with the job of teaching.

Never ask children to climb a ladder to hang decorations or projects. If something must be hung, don't let it be you. A teacher is a terrible thing to waste. You, the custodian, or another responsible adult should be the only person to climb a ladder in your classroom. Never permit children to climb chairs, desks, or counters for any reason. America is the land of litigation. All of these warnings do not mean you need to lead a cloistered existence, but you need to be well informed and well prepared. Success favors a prepared, informed teacher.

CONDUCT WITH CHILDREN

The teacher who the public wants and expects may not exist. Teachers are supposed to be perfect or nearly perfect. They are to be impeccable; they are to present a suitable demeanor at all times; they are to know *everything,* every current event, all historical data, every geographic area of the world, all major rivers, all mountain ranges of the world, and be able to distinguish a yellow-ducey warbler from a red-billed sapsucker at 150 yards. They are to use faultless grammar, have legible handwriting, never misspell a word, make mathematical computations in rapid order, and exhibit satisfactory to good art and musical skills.

While doing this, they are to be all things to all children. Teachers are truly amazing individuals. No wonder the world loves them so much.

Everyone is well aware of the many wonderful things that teachers do to and for children. These positive actions are well documented in the literature. What is not as well reported are the not-so-positive things that occur in the classroom. Creative teachers alert themselves to these events in an attempt to eradicate them. Some of these events are discussed below.

Treating Children Unequally

Most teachers believe they treat all children the same. Children would not agree. Teachers are sometimes unaware of the effects of their interactions with children and how their actions are perceived by children. Avoid rewarding those who instinctively please you and inadvertently neglecting those who displease you. Some children make it easy for you to like them. They invite your attention and affection. They do the right things, say the right things, and, in general, make your teaching day more enjoyable. Unconsciously they are rewarded by you for their actions. These rewards are administered in a wide variety of ways— a smile, a nod, a hand on the shoulder, and so on. They all convey the same message of affection. These actions reinforce the recipient, and repeated classroom interactions are thus engendered. Meanwhile the rest of the class feels somewhat alienated. Each child vies for your attention and affection, each in his or her own way. Often they have difficulty in communicating their actions. Children all desire much the same things: acceptance, a measure of belonging, and a portion of your affection. Those least-favored students probably need your recognition more than the top-favored children. However, they don't always know what to do to merit it. The skillful teacher makes every child feel that the teacher's existence in the classroom is just for that child. This accomplishment is not taught; it is acquired through continuous practice. It is not always easy to embrace each and every child's personality, but the results are usually well worth the effort.

Periodic evaluations from your students can keep you informed about how you are progressing. Invited evaluations are informative. Teachers are frequently surprised by what students say. Boys think you favor the girls. Girls think you favor the boys. Students will tell you what they think, but they are cautious. They request complete anonymity via unsigned evaluations, preferably collected after grades have been assigned. Ask for feedback. Consider the data and react accordingly. Keep working your magic.

Spreading Questions Among Only the Chosen Few

Avoid setting repetitive patterns of questioning. Vary your approach to asking or inviting questions of your students. Vary the pattern of student selection in your request for responses. Avoid the chosen few who always seem to have an answer, a comment, or a reaction. Teachers sometimes are too kind and wish to avoid embarrassing certain students who struggle for an answer when called upon.

Teachers, after a while, pass these students by. Alert the class to your desire to hear each child's voice at least once a day, every day, in response to questions. Don't harass children when waiting for responses. Don't nag them, but convince them that you value their contribution and if it takes a little time, the class (and you) should patiently wait for a response. Or you may wish to move on, stating that you will return, providing the individual more time to think of a response. Do not foster total class responses where the majority of the children leap up and down, moaning and groaning, waving their arms, and shouting, "Ooh! Ooh! Ooh! I know! I know" in rapid succession. For some children this is simply an aerobic exercise. The nonresponders may well know the answer, but they are reluctant to engage in class aerobics. Don't ask for a class response. Direct your questions to individuals. Spread your questions throughout the entire audience. Change the level of questions, or reword questions to suit a specific individual. Be creative, and think of new ways to involve everyone. Allow the children to formulate the questions, to ask the questions, and to call on various students (perhaps based on a previously established criteria) so everyone gets involved. Improve your waiting time. Not all children are swift thinkers. Some take time to weigh responses. They simply need more time than most teachers allow them. Teachers, again, become more uncomfortable than the deliberating children and they become anxious to move on. Be patient, and provide time to think. Be rewarded with good responses.

Projecting One's Personal Idiosyncrasies

Avoid projecting your own idiosyncrasies into the teaching art—especially those that might make children feel uncomfortable. For example, some children prefer to be called by their first name, some by a nickname. Teachers who call children by their last names only are often viewed with disfavor. Even Ms. or Mr. is uncomfortable for some children. Children prefer to be called by names they identify with themselves. Ask them. They will tell you. Avoid cute names that you might associate with some feature of the child. Some children might initially enjoy being called the Hulk, but with time it probably would wear thin. Some children do not enjoy kidding or chiding. They may tolerate a limited amount of it because of the teacher-dominated situation, but they may find no pleasure in it. Avoid references to certain children's personal characteristics such as foot size, weight, and height. Avoid complimentary comments about their attire, lunch sandwiches, or new shoes—unless, of course, you can manage to find something about which to compliment every member of the class. Not all children have the same opportunities for those things that evoke praise from the teacher. Rather than praise one child for a neat appearance, make a blanket statement such as, "Someone in the class looks especially nice today." All of the children will wonder who this individual is. Each child has an opportunity to say, "Could it be me? I wonder!" Perhaps everyone has been provided a chance to dream about a little praise. While the prior points discussed seem trivial and obvious, to children they sometimes appear monumental.

Neglecting the Niceties

Practice the same conduct you expect from children. "Thank you," "please," and "may I?" when used by you and when rewarded by you via some small nonverbal clue can reap benefits through reflected courtesies.

Use private moments away from the class to discuss behaviors with individuals you are concerned about. Do not mete out reprimands and punishments or embarrass children in front of the class or in front of other adults. If the problem is between you and a child, that is where it should remain. Variations in the problem can, of course, change the situation. Discussing behavioral problems before an audience is tantamount to a double sentence or punishment. Children appreciate the consideration of privacy.

Tittle-Tattle, Fiddle

Parents, teachers, administrators, and others desire, expect, and demand privacy. Children are not always provided the same rights. Children's problems, grades, parental and/or home problems, relationship to previous family members, attendance at the school, and so on are private matters to be discussed only with those who have a vested interest in the child's concerns. Careless statements are sometimes magnified and carried forth to where they do little or no good. Children are amusing, amazing, and amenable, but they are also vulnerable to circulated conversations that serve no purpose. Children have the right to privacy. Creative teachers respect this right and work toward insuring it.

Students entering school at the university level, on occasion, are asked how many outstanding teachers they may have had in all of their previous schooling. Invariably the number is one or two, rarely more. Given that a student may have had classes from 40 to 50 different instructors, this is a very small number. There is good reason: To be an outstanding teacher is a difficult task. When these same students were asked why these teachers were outstanding, the answers were, "Because the teacher liked me," "because the teacher helped me," "because the teacher made me feel special." The affective domain endears teachers to children. Children respond when they feel special. Creative teachers are special and they make children feel individually special.

BECOMING A LISTENER OF CHILDREN

Listening is an art, one that has not been perfected by human beings. It has been stated that the average listener can recall only 35 to 50 percent of what is said. In a matter of weeks this amount falls to 20 to 25 percent. Teachers talk and, hopefully, children listen. Children talk and, hopefully, teachers listen. A listener is a valued individual. We all desire to be located center stage and talking. Listening by contrast is a passive act, not as authoritative a role as speaking. It requires patience. High-powered, impatient people make poor listeners. They tend to act like they are listening, but their minds are racing ahead, anticipating their turn to speak. Hence, they do not listen well but merely wait their turn to speak.

Along with patience, listening skills can be enhanced by blocking out your interest in lieu of your children's interest. Be an intense listener. Think about what is being said and confine your thoughts to the speaker's message. Ask questions that resonate your concern. Maintain eye contact as much as possible. If uninterested, act interested. Listen for key words, phrases, concepts, or facts. Register these on your mental computer screen. Finally, don't feel that good listening is always a function of good speaking. Speaking and listening share responsibilities. The listener has the task of identifying the message, refining it, examining it, and reacting to it.

Children have much to tell us if only we would listen. Conversely, teachers have much to tell children if only children would listen. Teach them the techniques of good listening.

LESSON PLANNING—PLAN YOUR WORK AND WORK YOUR PLAN

Lesson plans are maps. They direct you toward your objectives. Lesson plans, well designed and interpreted, expedite learning. Lesson plans are constructed in a variety of complexities. Some are global, broadly based, and loosely descriptive. They outline where the learning is to go, how it is going to go, and how one would know that one has arrived at the stated objectives. This can be described and prescribed for the entire year. Subsets of these descriptions can be broken down to accommodate time constraints of one-half year, months, or weekly time concerns. These large-scale plans provide guideposts to insure that one "stays the course" in one's journey toward completing the stated objectives. One does not teach from these plans. These spell out the action for the day that moves children closer to the terminal goals and objectives for the year. Simply stated, teachers utilize broad plans and daily, detailed plans. Each complements the other, moving together to insure that children arrive intellectually, physically, and socially at the predetermined grade-level objectives.

Daily lesson plans are usually constructed several days in advance. Some teachers prefer to do these one week in advance. This allows them to view in perspective where they have been, are, and will be in one week's time. Daily lesson plans are the work-a-day timetable. Lesson plans delineate what will be done, for how long, and to what extent. They represent an estimate of what can be accomplished. Some characteristics of a good lesson plan are:

1. The lesson plan should represent a hypothetical plan of action with children. Things happen in class. Plans change. That is the way it is. One plans, revises, replans.
2. The objective of the lesson plan should be clear and realistic. Progress is difficult to predetermine. Interactions with children tell you how fast you can go. One cannot teach children faster than they can learn. Plan, pace. Pace, replan.
3. The planned actions of the lesson should match the time constraints. It is always better to be overprepared than underprepared. One's

self-concept deteriorates when one's materials expire but time does not. One is always more comfortable when one still has something to teach as the end-of-the-period bell rings.

4. Activities and involvement time are shared by the children and the teacher. Everyone is part of the act of learning.

5. Appropriate, provocative questions are provided, anticipated children's questions and problems are considered, and appropriate plans are made to accommodate these.

6. The lesson fits the sequence of what lessons have transpired and what lessons are still to be taught. Strive for a rhythm in the learning process.

7. Assignments emerging from the lesson are clear and realistic, matching the objectives.

8. The plan is flexible. If only a portion of the plan is covered, the unfinished portion is carried over to the next day. What one uncovers during the lesson may be as important and even more important than what was contained in the lesson plan.

9. Lesson plans are written not only for you and the children, but for any substitute teacher who may be called upon to fill in for you in cases of illness or other emergencies. Thus the lesson plan should stand on its own and be able to be interpreted by all. Thumbnail sketches of lesson plans that substitute for bonafide lesson plans do not serve the substitute teacher well.

KEEPING CURRENT IN EDUCATION

The creative teacher is concerned about keeping current. This means growing within the profession. Experience that is continuously supported by new encounters, considerations, trials, and challenges within the profession is preferred to repeating the *same* set of experiences over and over, year after year. Being current keeps one close to the cutting edge in one's profession. You deserve to know what's going on. There are several ways to keep current in education.

- Subscribe to educational journals. Monies spent on journals are well spent. There are literally hundreds of them. Each has its own worth. Each discipline, be it social studies, music, physical education, or art, has its own suite of journals. These generally range from something for the practitioner to something for the researcher. Most schools subscribe to one or more of these journals. They usually are housed in the library or the teachers' lounge. Make your input known. Principals and librarians like to please you. A review of any journal, be it in the area of reading, mathematics, or science, will yield a minimum of one new idea or activity per issue. Over time, reviewing such journals can yield a substantial number of ideas. Fresh ideas, viewpoints, editorials, research, advertisements, meeting announcements, and convention information keep you informed. An extensive list of journals can be found in Appendix I.

POINTS TO PONDER

Become a home subscriber to journals of your choice. Would you exchange approximately $2.95 for one, two, or more new ideas? Select at least three journals from Appendix I and ask for sample copies.

- Receive free educational materials from local, state, or federal government agencies (such as the Department of Energy), businesses, universities, and industries by writing and asking to be placed on their mailing lists.
- Scan newspapers and magazines for articles that would appeal to your students. This will quickly become a beneficial task. Articles must then be classified by topics; for example, tornadoes, earthquakes, pollution, success stories, economics, health, and social problems. These portfolios become very current topical references for children in your class. Even your most recent text cannot compete with your daily newspaper. Contact your local newspaper office; some newspapers put out publications pointing out how to utilize newspapers in the classroom. Some newspaper organizations even offer workshops explaining the advantages of teaching via daily newspapers.
- Attend local, state, regional, and national meetings of organizations such as the National Association for Gifted Children and the National Science Teachers Association to obtain new ideas and to search for new materials.
- Volunteer to test new materials in your classroom for a publisher, college, or university. Get involved with what is going on. Yes, it is work. Yes, it is time consuming. And, yes, it opens your mind to the fact that things are going on and you are part of them.
- Keep current. Enroll in workshops or college courses that apply directly to your interests. Then enroll in something that is 180 degrees from what you are interested in, something you know nothing about, but that would prove a real challenge. Who knows? You might open a door to something great!
- Become a participator rather than a spectator. Participate in the National Science Foundation (or similar government programs) institutes, seminars, and workshops (usually for credit, with your expenses paid by that agency). Contact the appropriate governmental agency for a list of schools you can contact.
- Go to Mongolia to study paleolithic nomads, visit the religious art of Bali (in Bali), or study survival strategies of the Anasazi Indians in New Mexico. Send for the University Research Expeditions Program (UREP), University of California, Berkeley, CA 94720.

- Participate in in-service programs at your school or volunteer to do a workshop for your school.
- Ask the children to bring in topics of interest to them. This diversity of interests stimulates the learning process.
- Invite parents into your classroom to discuss their areas of expertise. You just might discover a new hobby or interest.

Many government-sponsored workshops, conferences, and institutes are available for teachers each year. Often these programs allow teachers to obtain graduate credit at a nearby college or university. Tuition, travel, and meal allowances are paid for by the program. For information write to:

—U.S. Department of Education, Washington, DC 20550

—Office of Environmental Education, U.S. Department of Education, Washington, DC 20550

—U.S. Department of Energy, Washington, DC 20550

—The National Science Foundation, Washington, DC 20550

—Office of Metric Education, U.S. Department of Education, Washington, DC 20550

Each may send you a list of colleges and universities that you can write to directly for application information.

POINTS TO PONDER

How does a teacher keep from stagnating? How does one stay current? What is available? How do I take advantage of what is available to me? What kind of map can I make for myself to insure that I keep the "notion of motion" in my career alive?

MAINTAINING A POSITIVE APPROACH

Few things sustain themselves without an infusion of energy. Maintaining a positive approach toward teaching children, the continuous process of personal learning, the school, the administration, and the myriad of other concerns associated with the task of teaching require energy. Positive approaches to teaching can be best sustained when one's energy is maximized by good health. Without proper eating habits, adequate exercise, and sufficient rest, one's health suffers and one's energy level is reduced.

A positive approach is best maintained when one is satisfied with oneself and one's progress in achieving preset goals. Impossible goals and their continued elusiveness diminish a positive attitude. Goals should stretch you, but not break you. Always be realistic and grow with your expectations. Expect and plan for success. Be prepared if failures occur; work through them back to the successes. Stay relaxed, but keep improving your positive approach.

A positive approach can be maintained by constant vigilance. Safeguard the level you have already attained. Some additional suggestions are as follows:

Build on your receptive attitude. Become a receiver of positive thoughts as well as a transmitter. Avoid emphasis on negative criticism without being prepared to offer constructive, positive suggestions.

Conserve your energies. Prioritize your actions. Don't get bogged down in combating trivia.

Remain organized. Tranquility comes from order. Order frees you to do other things.

Remember great efforts bring great results. Persistence, intensity, and devotion to the achievement of a positive approach will bring rewards.

Eliminate destructive worry or anxieties. Eliminate fear and timidity. Raise your sights and think and act in a cavalier manner.

Take occasional risks. Don't make all of your choices safe ones.

Dream, then engineer your dreams down to reality.

Make yourself needed. Become essential to others.

Break away from the daily routine. Take time off to be alone to think and reflect about your present orientation and future directions.

BE YOURSELF!

RESEARCH SAYS . . .

Creative teachers must recognize that the term multicultural education means different things to different people. The only common meaning is that it refers to changes in education that are supposed to benefit people of color. Research shows that multicultural education consists of:

1. Teaching the culturally different (teaching children of color what white children are taught more successfully).
2. Human relations (helping children of color develop better self-concepts and friendships with white children).
3. Education that is multicultural and social reconstructionist (helping children of color learn to fight racism alongside white children).

While some research is available on the topic of multicultural education, there are virtually no studies available that address questions such as:

1. What is the role of the teacher in a multicultural classroom setting?
2. What types of curricular materials are most effective in a multicultural setting?

3. What is the impact on teachers and students when they work together in a multicultural setting?

Multicultural education is becoming an accepted and integral concept in the education community. Additional research studies need to be conducted in order to assist teachers and administrators in meeting the needs of all children.

PAUSE FOR A SUMMARY

Creative teachers frequently mention the following neglected areas in their preparation as teachers: the first day of school; how to order and obtain materials; acquiring, organizing, distributing, and storing materials; safety; field tripping; discipline as a part of classroom management; working with gifted children; mainstreaming; competency testing; using museums and resource people; selecting books and other instructional aids for the classroom and library; and keeping current. Remember:

> The first day of school can be one of the most important days for both the teacher and the students. Creative teachers prepare for the first day by incorporating exciting activities that involve students.

> Beginning teachers almost unanimously agree that the most difficult task of teaching is establishing and maintaining order in the classroom.

> Creative activities provide gifted children with challenge and intellectual stimulation.

> Creative teachers emphasize skill instruction (observing, inferring, classifying) with handicapped children in a mainstream environment.

> Creative teachers recognize that certain skills are needed for lifelong learning, and they assist each student in acquiring these skills.

> Creative teachers do not skirt the multicultural issues in their classrooms. They do not choose sides; they allow children to make choices so that when children face issues in real life, they will make wise judgments.

> Creative teachers use informal learning centers, museums, and resource people to provide self-motivating experiences in learning.

> Creative teachers select textbook series and/or programs that emphasize the thinking abilities of children and use action-oriented, hands-on activities.

REFERENCES

Aiello, B., ed. (1987). *Making It Work: Practical Ideas for Integrating Exceptional Children Into Regular Classes.* Reston: Council For Exceptional Children.

Birch, J. W. (1988). *Mainstreaming: Educable Mentally Retarded Children in Regular Classes.* Reston: Council For Exceptional Children.

Curwin, R., and Mendler, A. (1988). *Discipline With Dignity.* Alexandria: Association for Supervision and Curriculum Development.

Hidalgo, N. M.; McDowell, C. L.; and Siddle, E. V., eds. (1990). *Facing Racism in Education.* Cambridge: Harvard Educational Review.

Jordan, J. B. (1989). *Teacher, Please Don't Close the Door: The Exceptional Child in the Mainstream.* Reston: Council For Exceptional Children.

Marland, S. (1972). *Education of the Gifted and Talented.* Washington: U.S. Government Printing Office.

Scruggs, T., and Mastropieri, M. (in press). "Effective Mainstreaming Strategies for Mildly Handicapped Students." *Elementary School Journal.*

Warfield, G., ed. (1989). *Mainstream Currents.* Reston: Council For Exceptional Children.

Chapter
4

Alternative Skills and Techniques

Teaching Children to Teach Themselves

A child's mind is not a sponge. It is more a wellspring.

Alfred De Vito

INTRODUCTION: WHY?

It is generally accepted that the one who learns the most in a classroom is the teacher. This accomplishment is usually measured in perspiration units—the greater the teaching effort, the greater the perspiration and the greater the results. In any given classroom, the teacher is the individual who works the hardest, the longest, and expends the greatest amount of energy. With those things pertaining to the educational processes, the teacher is the key to what goes on in and out of the classroom. The teacher directs the traffic of educating the students, dictates what is happening, when it happens, how it happens, and with what intensity. The teacher is in charge. The full responsibility for successful learning is the teacher's. The teacher:

Elects, sometimes alone, sometimes with group sanction, goals and objectives of the lessons;

Selects and identifies the processes and techniques for achieving these goals;

Reviews the content material to either refresh or reinforce his or her own knowledge of the topics to be covered;

Anticipates difficult student-learning areas and prepares for these with ancillary materials and approaches;

Teaches the lesson, reaching inside for that extra measure of enthusiasm and vitality to insure a dynamic lesson, preparing to project excitement as the appropriate stature is assumed;

Listens to ascertain that everything is said in the clearest possible manner, observing the audience as it reacts both verbally and nonverbally to the presentation;

Remembers to change voice, posture, location in the room, to stress major points of the lesson;

Injects humor, challenging questions, and thought-provoking confrontations throughout the lesson;

Praises the responses of children;

Remembers to use the appropriate audiovisual materials as needed;

Summarizes and moves forward, readying for "What's next?"

At the end of the day the teacher may be exhilarated or deflated, not quite sure of how successful the efforts were. The nagging question, "Did they learn anything?" always hangs heavy. The teacher learns the most in a classroom because he or she is mentally, physically, and socially involved; accepts the responsibilities for learning; and has the strong desire to succeed at a high level of performance, pride, and dignity.

What have the class members been doing during teacher-dominated learning? For students, the greatest portion of the school day is spent sitting and listening. Listening to whom? Occasionally, throughout the day, a pedagogical chord is struck, and students' penciled actions can be observed, or a wry smile may cross a student's face. The teacher wonders if educational gold has been struck, or if some discomforting digestive problem has been resolved. He or she never knows. Empirical studies have ascertained that at any given moment, approximately $33\frac{1}{3}$ percent of the class is listening to the teacher. This comes through to teachers as they answer the chorus of, "Would you please repeat the question?" Teachers work diligently to increase the percentage of listeners by positioning themselves in the most advantageous place in the room. Circulation patterns and key orientation areas within the classroom are prime to eliciting attention. Sometimes this means teaching from the middle of the room, the back of the room, or facing them head on, one-on-one from the front of the room. Another attention-getting ploy is asking questions of the audience with rapidity. This may be instituted in response to observed lanquishing body languages emanating from the class members. Rapid-fire questioning techniques can be strategically directed to those class members deepest in the Land of Nod. It can also be directed to listeners in the darkest corners of the room, notifying them that education is still in progress. Another device to increase the percentage of listeners is to vary your voice. Lowering your voice, so low that members of the class must listen carefully, works. This technique, interspersed with occasional Caruso-like shrills, adds variety and usually merits attention. When teachers do all the work (and learn the most), children become passive learners. Training children to teach themselves should make them the rightful benefactors of learning.

Learning should be the responsibility of the learner. The path to learning should be illuminated, enriched, and guided. Alternate paths to the same goals should be made available by the teacher. The teacher sets the climate, the tone, the environment, the conditions, but learners must walk the path, growing more independent of the teacher as they assume more responsibility for their own education. A child should be encouraged to practice self-discipline through self-examination and reflection. The child should seek out his own source of weakness, then develop a plan of action for effective self-improvement. Self-concept improvement is a wholly desirable achievement for any individual. Developed responsibility for one's own progress moves one from a passive learner to a creative, innovative, independent learner.

TASK CARDS

An excellent way to begin involving your children individually or in groups in a variety of creative endeavors is through the use of task cards (sometimes they are called idea cards, suggestion cards, or activity cards). Many teachers like to select a theme, such as pollution, and then prepare from 15 to 20 task cards dealing with this topic. Task cards usually follow the basic form described below.

1. The front side
   a. The task card's title is in clear view and presents the topic of investigation. For example:
      —Air Pollution
   b. Glue a picture or illustration on this side to spark interest.
2. The reverse side
   a. A statement, sometimes in the form of a question, indicates the task to be solved. For example:
      —Collect evidence from your community relating to the smoky polluters.
   b. You may give suggestions on how to complete the assignment. For example:
      —Compare factory pollution to school pollution.
      —Design your own smoke chart.
      —Use a camera to show the polluters.
      —Make drawings of smoky polluters.

—Prepare a letter to the president of a company that is polluting to find out what steps his company is taking to prevent current or future pollution problems.

—Collect evidence by using petroleum jelly-coated cardboard disks located near the pollution source.

c. A collection of additional related activities titled "More" can also be included. For example:

—Are smoky polluters polluting our environment in other ways? See if you can find out.

—Prepare a pollution poem or rap and present it to the class.

Many teachers prepare a task-card area in their room for student use. The task cards are changed periodically. It is helpful to number each task card and to place the set of cards in a labeled file folder. Students should be encouraged to write some of their own task cards.

The next several pages include more task-card ideas. Please look at them and use them with your students. Task cards are not bounded by age, grade level, interest, and so on. They work well with all ages of children (and adults, too).

MORE TASK CARD IDEAS

More Themes for Task Cards

1. Go through a magazine and tear out all the pictures of things whose names begin with the letter c. Paste them all together on a piece of construction paper.

2. Collect animal pictures. Then choose an animal you are interested in and find out more about it.

3. While you are at recess, collect some things that interest you. When you come in from recess, paste them on a tagboard.

4. Find a picture of something you enjoy. Make up a commercial for it. Now try to sell this product (or thing) to your friends.

5. Count something you have always wondered about. For example, how many chairs and tables do we have in our room?

6. Take a picture of what you dislike at school and decide how you might change it. When you have decided, tape-record your suggestions.

7. Go through a magazine and tear out five pictures you like. Make up a story about them. When you are sure of your story, tape-record it.

8. Trace this shape by walking:

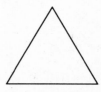

Figure 4.1 Sample task cards

CAN NOISE POLLUTION
BE FOUND IN YOUR SCHOOL?

TASKS

Tape record noises in and around your school.

Play your tape to other children. Can they identify the noise source?

Can you suggest ways to reduce noise pollution in your school? Home? Community?

Take (or draw) pictures of noise pollution problem areas.

MORE

Locate noise pollution problem areas in your community. Design a procedure for correcting them.

Measure the noise pollution with a tape recorder volume indicator or decibel meter.

Can loud noises hurt your hearing? Interview an ear doctor and then a jackhammer operator or jet engine mechanic.

What would you do if your school were located on the approach to a busy city airport? Design and implement a program of action.

Investigate the laws that have been instituted to reduce noise pollution. Try the Noise Control Act of 1972. Are there local city laws on noise pollution?

Did you know in New York City honking your auto horn except in cases of "imminent danger" costs $50.00 a toot? Is this a good law?

Trace this shape by jumping:

Trace this shape by hopping:

9. Using old magazines, cut out five long "o" words and five short "o" words and paste them on paper as decoration.

10. Find a recipe for butter, yogurt, buttermilk, ice cream, or any other milk product that is usually sold in stores. Then make it. When it's done, taste it and decide what you did right and what (if anything) you did wrong.

11. Set up an experiment to find out what conditions affect carbon dioxide (CO_2) production in a mixture of sugar, yeast, and water. Do not use more than one-fourth pound of sugar or one-fourth of a package of yeast for any one trial.

12. How much allowance do you get each week? Do you have a job? Write down how much money you get each week and estimate how much you spend and what you spend it on. Then keep a record for a week of everything you've earned and spent. Does the record agree with what you estimated?
MORE: Now plan what you'll earn and what you'll spend for another week and try to follow that plan. Such a plan is called a budget. What can you budget besides money?

13. Borrow a basic cookie recipe from your mother and then bake the cookies. Did you follow the directions exactly? What would the cookies look like if the oven were hotter? Or cooler? Would you have to adjust the time? What would happen if you put in too much baking powder? Or too little flour?
MORE: What spices would make the cookies more exciting? Cinnamon? Nutmeg? Ginger? Would you add brown sugar? Coconut? Nuts? (How much?) Experiment and create your own cookie recipe.

14. Look up some linear equations in your algebra book. Graph the equations. Make a Christmas tree by putting dots on paper and then connecting them. Could you write equations for all of the lines connecting the dots? Try it.

15. Using magazines and newspapers, make a display of a variety of geometric figures as they occur in architecture, nature, science, advertising, and other fields.

16. Pretend you are an immigrant in a foreign country. List the problems you will probably encounter.

17. SCIENCE MISSION POSSIBLE (SMP) NO. 1
Your mission, should you decide to accept, is on the card before you. It will be your job to locate the following items placed in inconspicuous areas of the room and accurately measure their length in both the Imperial and metric systems. If for any reason you are unable to do so, you may contact an associate, but not under any other circumstances. When you have completed this assignment, meet with your superior before continuing. Take precautions, because within 15 seconds this card will not self-destruct.
    The items are:

   your teacher's umbrella
   a Kleenex box
   a filing cabinet
   a bobby pin
   the chalk tray
   a magazine
   three science books in a straight line
   a one-dollar bill
   a paper clip
   the demonstration table

If you feel you have successfully completed this assignment, write what you think is the general difference between length and width. (Materials needed: meter stick and yardstick.)

18. SMP NO. 2

The heat is on now . . . the word is out. It is our job to work as a team and cool it. Check your thermometers. What do they read? Not sure? Then do this. Using your special SMP Celsius thermometer, find the temperature of the following:

the air in the room
the water from the faucet
boiling water
ice water
10 ml of alcohol

Now find the average temperature of the faucet water, boiling water, and ice water. Can you operationally define temperature? Materials needed:

10 ml graduated cylinder
water
safety glasses
100 ml beaker
ice
alcohol
candle

19. SMP NO. 3

The United States government has very rigid restrictions on gold standards. There is reason to suspect that there has been foul play. It is your job to locate the problem and expose the people involved. It is necessary for you to have a good understanding of what is meant by a standard of measurement. In order to prove your understanding, set up your own system for measuring length and weight. In other words, make your own units, but they must fulfill the requirements for a good standard of measurement. (Materials needed: These are up to you.)

20. Open a can of alphabet soup and spell as many words as you can with the letters you find in it. Write your words on a piece of paper.

21. On a piece of paper, write as many words as you can find in the word astronomy.

22. Look at a map of the United States and draw or trace the outline of one state. Turn your paper, looking at the shape until you "see" another object in it. Draw the new object.

23. Invent three animals by combining body parts of different animals that are familiar to you. Name them and draw a picture of each one. For example:

hippopotamus + elephant = hippophant

24. For 20 different letters of the alphabet, find an object in your house or outside of it whose name begins with each letter and make a list of them.

25. Animals cannot talk, yet we can tell how they feel by the way they act. How do these animals act:

   a horse, when it is scared;
   a dog, when it is hungry;
   a kitten, when it is hurt;
   a bear, when it is mad?

26. You are in charge of pizza for our next party, and we want something exciting! Create a new variety of pizza and try it out; then we will make it at school. (Hint: Must all of the ingredients bake the same amount of time?) What would you put on a Christmas pizza? A Mexican pizza? Is an ice cream pizza possible?

27. Design your own bug catcher. Show the class how it works by setting it up outside the classroom. Use any materials you like as long as it catches live bugs. (Dead bugs are no fun to watch.)
   MORE: Can you design a trap that catches only small bugs? Only large bugs? How about catching only flying bugs? (Hint: How can you attract the bugs?)

28. Find color photos of a variety of specimens of butterflies and moths. Try especially hard to find monarch, viceroy, kallima, and caligo eurilochus. Do some of the wing colors and patterns seem useful? Find some examples of camouflage in other animals. (Hint: Imagine a polar bear hunting a snowshoe rabbit in a blizzard!)
   MORE: If you could design your own butterfly, how would you design the wings for protection? Where would it live? What if it lived at the north pole? At the equator?

29. Collect at least ten different kinds of flowers (or pictures of flowers with all of the petals visible). If the flower has just a few petals, count them. If it has a lot of petals, count the sepals. (What's a sepal?)

30. Write a letter to someone you admire or wish you knew, like a movie star, athlete, author, political figure, or scientist. Locate the address and send the letter.

PUZZLER ACTIVITIES

Puzzler Activities (PA) are designed to help children learn to think on their own. PAs are problems to be solved, brief confrontations with real or fictitious situations furnished by the teacher in the form of printed handouts. Challenged to solve the problems, the students map out strategies, raise appropriate questions, and consider differing explanations. Children who engage PAs verbalize more fully about problems.

PAs are usually offered as provocative situations inviting investigative participation. Each child can contribute to these activities because little or no prerequisite knowledge is needed. This condition avoids any prerequisite content intimidation. PAs are selected for their creative engagements and expansions. PAs do not have any single right answer; some have no answer at all. PAs with no apparent answers can still be used—you can ask, "What questions, if you had the answers, would help refine the explanation?" You may furnish additional facts to maneuver the discussion to a conclusion or by asking, "What more do we need to know?" This expands the current status of the problem resolution and it continues on.

The student's response should always be accomplished by a suitable rationale for the response. You as the moderator, or better yet, a child as a moderator, can challenge or accept each response as thinking is promoted through the problem.

PAs can be a valuable adjunct to any classroom teaching situation. They can readily augment reading, social studies, science, and mathematics instruction. Try writing your own PAs. Look for source materials around the house, the school, or in the newspapers. Compile, for future use, a portfolio of interesting and puzzling activities. Train children to write and orchestrate their own PAs.

PA 1   WHAT IS WRONG WITH THE CLASSROOM CHALKBOARDS?

Most chalkboards are difficult to use. They are too high for small children and too low for tall teachers. They are inflexible and offer a variety of reasons why it is difficult to fill all the available space contained within them. Most chalkboards are dull, messy, and boring to observe. A large number of teachers dislike the feel of chalk dust on their hands. All class members seem to dislike the screeching noise that occasionally is made by squeaking chalk. And the job of cleaning chalkboards is not necessarily a "fun" activity.

Some questions to think about:

a. What alternatives are there to the use of chalkboards?
b. If no alternatives exist and chalkboards are used, how can they be improved?
c. What ideas or inventions would greatly improve chalkboard use?

What solutions to the chalkboard problem can you suggest? Write down each concern and suggested solutions.

Sample:	Concern:	Chalk dust is a problem. Some people are allergic to it. Some people feel uncomfortable with chalk dust on their hands, and chalk dust is messy as it falls on many objects in the room.
	Solution:	Use a different surface material for the chalkboard and write with a watercolor ink marker.
	Concern:	

Solution:

_____

What additional information would you like to have?

Sample: Cost of new, suggested alternatives to chalkboards.

Sample: Availability of any new suggested materials.

_____

_____

_____

Now consider these additional concerns:

   a. Are the teachers truly unhappy with the present chalkboards?
   b. Have the chalkboard changes removed allergies related to chalk dust?
   c. Will chalkboard erasers become obsolete?
   d. Will people lose jobs at factories that make chalkboards and chalk-
      board erasers?

PA 2   WHAT'S ALL THE NOISE ABOUT?

Virtually all of the children given hearing tests at the Dekro Middle School in
Indiana, New Jersey, are found to have some hearing loss. Many of the children are also emotionally upset. It is not uncommon for the children to get
into fights with one another. The teachers are unhappy with their working
conditions and are very vocal about it. Similar events in two other schools in
the area have led to their closing.
   Some questions to think about:

   a. Is this a school for children with special problems?
   b. Are these problems the result of something that happens at the
      school?
   c. Is there tension between the faculty and the students? Between the
      faculty and the administration?

Write down what you think the problems might be:

_____

_____

_____

_____

_____

_____

What additional information would you like to have?

_____

_____

_____

_____

_____

_____

Now consider these additional facts:

a. Dekro Middle School is located near the Indiana International Airport.
b. Decibel readings range from 95 to 100 in the school yard and 80 to 96 in the classrooms.

Does any of this new information change your first conclusions? If so, now what do you think the problem is? Can you suggest possible solutions to the problem?

PA 3 WHY SHOULD WE WORRY?

The world is concerned about the possible elimination of half of the species on earth by the middle of the next century. Approximately 1000 species a year are disappearing from the face of the earth, never to be observed again. Most of these are plants and insects that inhabit rain forests and wetlands. At this rate, within 100 years half of the species may be extinct. Since life began on this earth, about 99 percent of all species have disappeared, but in the cycle of things, they have been replaced by other species. The current loss is much more disastrous, because no new species are emerging to replace those that are lost.

Some questions to think about:

a. What effect does this have on human beings?
b. What effect does this have on the remaining species? For example, one mammal species becomes extinct every year. Most of these are varieties of bats.
c. Most of the remaining wild lands affected by species extinction are located in the developing nations.

What suggestions could you make that might help alleviate the problem?

_____

_____

_____

_____

_____

What additional information would you like to have?

_____

_____

_____

Now consider these additional facts:

a. There have been periods when, for example, dinosaurs died off, but never before has there been a period of such mass destruction of various species.
b. The efforts by present-day conservationists are not enough to stop the loss of these numbers of species.
c. Our information of past major extinctions that occurred millions of years ago is limited and provides us with no visible patterns to understand them.

INVITATIONS TO INVESTIGATE

Presenting children with a problem for investigation can be difficult, because teachers are confronted with children who have a wide variety of skills and abilities even though they are assigned to the same grade level. One way to overcome this problem is through the use of an "invitation to investigate." It may be defined as a problem-solving approach wherein the students analyze and synthesize.

Let's look at several illustrations of invitations to investigate.

Where Did the Water Go?

Using two test tubes, rubber stoppers, and glass tubes as shown in Figure 4.2 (page 133), prepare the following demonstration.

Fill the test tubes so that they have identical warm-water levels. Add rock salt to tube B and push the rubber stopper in or out to adjust the water level until the water level of tube B is identical to that of tube A. Ask the children to predict what will happen. Usually three predictions will be offered:

1. The water level will rise as a result of the melting rock salt.
2. The water level will drop as a result of the melting rock salt.
3. The water level will not change because the rock salt will not melt.

The Minipreparation of Audiotutorial Tapes (Mini-PATT)

A procedure that allows teachers to produce instructional tapes suitable for their own classes in a short period of time (one to three hours for a 30-minute tape) is now available using the Mini-PATT approach.

To prepare instructional tapes using the Mini-PATT system, just follow the directions.

1. Materials needed:

   a. One cassette tape recorder with microphone (an internal microphone is best)

   b. C-60 cassette tapes of good quality (less background noise)

   c. A partner, preferably a teacher or a child

2. Procedure:

   a. Decide what concept you would like to teach using the audiotutorial method. For example:
   the letter o, graphing, short vowel sounds, shapes, colors.

   b. State your instructional objectives for the concept you've selected. For example:

   The child will be able to construct a two-dimensional graph from the data presented using acceptable graphing techniques.

   The child will be able to observe an object using four of his five senses.

   c. Obtain all of the materials and supplies that you will need to implement your instructional objectives. For example:
   an object for observing or a game you've constructed.

   d. Prepare an evaluation for this concept, based on your stated objectives, to be used later to find out if your audiotutorial lesson was successful. Do not show this evaluation to your partner!

   e. Using the materials needed, teach your partner the concept and record your instructions on tape. Your partner should respond by gestures or movements of the head, not verbally. Your lesson should last about 10 to 15 minutes.

   f. After completing your audiotutorial tape, listen to the results. Record your comments regarding your product for future revision. Both positive and negative aspects should be included.

The Mini-PATT approach is an effective procedure for developing audiotutorial tapes for classroom use. Many of the Mini-PATT tapes can be incorporated into interest centers, learning activity packages, and minicourses. Will you try the Mini-PATT system in your classroom?

Source: Adapted from Jimmy R. Jenkins and Gerald H. Krockover, "The Mini-PATT Approach to Individualizing Instruction," *Science Activities*, vol. 10, no. 3 (November 1973), pp. 38–39. By permission.

Figure 4.2 Invitation to investigate example

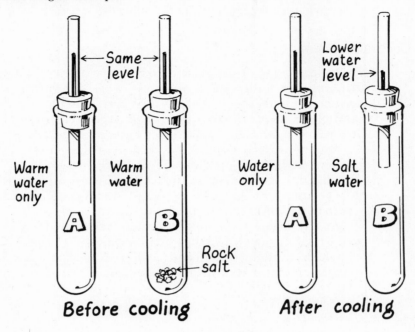

Before cooling   After cooling

Based on our experience, most children will choose the first prediction. But, after approximately one hour, the children will observe that the water level will have gone down in the tube!

Where did the water go? Children may now formulate hypotheses as to what has happened. Did the water level go down because a gas was produced? Or did the water evaporate? Did the salt absorb the water? Did the water absorb the salt? See if your children can design experiments to find out where the water went.

Further investigations might include trying table salt or sugar instead of rock salt. Are the same results obtained?

Are the volumes of any two liquids additive? Try equal amounts of methanol and water (use a 100 ml graduated cylinder). You may need to experiment with a variety of quantities.

Try other liquids such as rubbing alcohol (isopropyl alcohol) and water or motor oil and mineral oil.*

Cool It!

Inflate two balloons to the same size. Place one in the refrigerator and leave one at room temperature. Where did the air in the refrigerated balloon go?

---

*Adapted from Gerald H. Krockover, "Invitation to Investigate," *Science Activities*, vol. 8, no. 5 (January 1973), pp. 38–39. By permission.

Place a balloon in a warm oven or pan of steaming water. What do you observe happening? Where did the air in the warm balloon come from?

The Cartesian Diver

Fill a clear soda or catsup bottle to the very top with water. Set it aside. Fill a drinking glass with water to within $\frac{1}{4}$–$\frac{1}{2}$ inch of the top. Fill an eyedropper with just enough water so it will barely float upright in the drinking glass. Then place the dropper in your filled bottle of water. Place a cork in the bottleneck and press down slowly (see Figure 4.3). Excess water may squirt out, so be careful.

You will observe that the dropper dives to the bottom. When you release the pressure on the cork, the dropper rises to the top.

This activity can serve as an excellent invitation to investigate. What causes the eyedropper to dive? Air pressure? Water pressure? Explain the dropper's return to the top of the bottle when pressure is released.

An extension of this invitation to investigate involves the use of a small, wooden safety match. Cut off a small segment (7 or 8 mm). This segment should include the head and a small portion of the wood behind the head. (You may need to experiment to determine the proper length.) Place this small match bit in the

Figure 4.3 The Cartesian Diver

Test of water level in dropper

No pressure

Pressure applied with cork

water bottle. Press firmly on the cork. The match segment reacts to the pressure in the same way as the dropper.

Are the explanations for the behavior of the match and the dropper the same? Are the same components involved?

DEMONSTRATIONS TO EXPERIMENTATIONS

A classroom demonstration is a controlled performance, usually given by the teacher, to present some preselected phenomena. The outcome, barring unexpected results, is generally known. Valid arguments in favor of a well-planned and well-executed demonstration include: expediency of time, broad coverage of content, instruction in safety, broadcasting of procedures, and, in general, setting the stage for future instruction. Demonstrations are also valuable when the materials for the experiment are too costly for all students or too dangerous for students to handle. Caution, however, must be exercised to avoid overuse of demonstrations in lieu of a more student-centered approach.

The egg in the bottle, an air-pressure activity, is an example of a routine science demonstration. To present it, you need a shelled hard-boiled egg, a glass milk bottle, a sheet of newspaper, a match, and water. The newspaper is rolled into a wad so that it can be ignited and dropped to the bottom of the milk bottle. The burning paper will eventually go out. The heated air inside the glass container will expand, become lighter, and escape, making the air pressure inside the bottle less than the pressure outside the bottle. Moisten the hard-boiled egg. Quickly seal the mouth of the bottle by positioning the wet egg, blunt end first, in the mouth. This will initiate the egg's motion. If the egg is not wet, the rim of the bottle should be moistened before positioning the egg. Water serves as a lubricant and the egg should slip down inside the bottle—sometimes slowly and sometimes with a resounding thud.

The success of this demonstration depends on finding an egg the approximate size of the milk-bottle opening. The cost of eggs as well as the difficulty in obtaining 10–15 glass milk bottles (the kind that grandma used works best) with the right-size mouths make this activity better for a teacher demonstration than a student activity.

The demonstration is a good introduction to a study of air pressure. The very act of getting the egg intact inside the bottle is a bit of a mind boggler. Few people think it can be done. Accomplishing a seemingly impossible task is interpreted as a discrepancy to a viewer: it is contrary to expectation. These discrepancies are sometimes called discrepant events. Getting the egg out of the bottle intact further enhances the discrepancy. This can be accomplished by carefully adding sufficient water to the bottle to thoroughly rinse out all the burned and unburned debris. Also, the water acts as a lubricant for the egg's exit. After all the water and debris are removed, turn the bottle upside down and position the egg so it rests in the neck of the bottle. Place the bottle directly over your head. Using your thumb and first finger, form a circle against the mouth of the bottle. Place your mouth against your circled fingers and blow into the bottle as hard as you can. Be careful! Stay lively! The egg can exit slowly, or it can come out rapidly and land on you. In either event, the egg in the bottle is a dramatic demonstration that can kick off your unit on air pressure.

Demonstrations have their place. When necessary, use them. Remember, however, that the payoff for children is in their personal mastery of the skills of experimentation. Every demonstration makes you, not the students, more adept. While a demonstration may occasionally be necessary, it is not sufficient for student learning.

True scientific experimentation in the elementary school is difficult. It rarely happens, but that does not mean it couldn't. Nor does it mean it shouldn't. It just rarely happens. Experimentation calls for knowledge about the problem under consideration, as well as perseverance and fastidiousness, all housed in an open and creative mind. This is a lot to expect of elementary and middle-school pupils. The best we can do is to involve them in a variety of science activities, correlated with the grade level and background of the children, that approximate experimentation. All children need initial and sustained exposure to the experimental process (in part or in toto). To acquire a familiarity with the concept of experimentation is a complex undertaking. Its acquisition for most children will span several, or all, of the elementary school years, provided that continued instruction in the process is given.

An experiment usually seeks an answer to a question through an investigation of some observable phenomena. Experimentation involves:

delineating the problem;

constructing the hypotheses;

identifying the pertinent variables;

organizing a design compatible with the formulated hypotheses;

controlling the variables;

collecting the data;

interpreting the data;

summarizing the conclusions in light of the problem.

This is somewhat removed from either a teacher demonstration or a simple teacher-student involvement in a specific activity.

Children's abilities to experiment may be improved through the use of either teacher-structured activities or unstructured explorations. In either case, a problem needs to be identified. Children usually need assistance in identifying and stating problems. You, as the instructor, can help them phrase problems so they are manageable, understood by all, and experimentally explorable.

The planting of seeds in a tumbler garden activity is a good example of an unstructured approach. (See Figure 4.4).

Have all the students plant tumbler gardens that are equal in the following ways: size of containers; size, variety, number, and position of the seeds within

Figure 4.4 Seeds in a tumbler garden

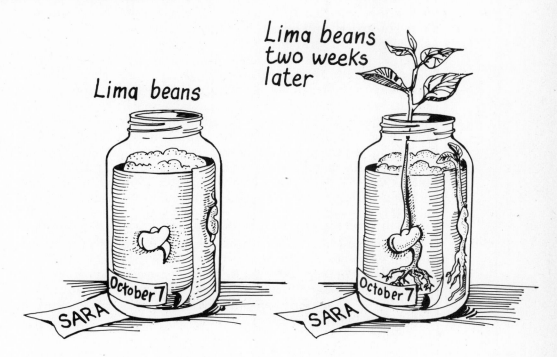

the containers; size of the paper toweling; folding of paper toweling; positioning of paper toweling within the containers; quantity of wadding; and amounts of water.

In the process of establishing equality among the tumbler gardens, you could have the children determine the volume of the containers, observe the seeds, describe the seeds externally and internally, make inferences about the seeds, predict some behavior of the seeds, classify the seeds, determine the mass and the hardness of the seeds, measure and record the amount of water furnished the seeds, and so on. All of this is valid sciencing and accumulates knowledge of seeds, but it is not an experiment. An experiment takes place in the pursuit of an answer to a question:

Does light make a difference in the growth of the seeds?

Does temperature make a difference in the growth of the seeds?

Does the amount of water added affect the growth of the seeds?

In establishing the question you wish to pursue through experimentation, avoid *why* questions. While they spark interest, they usually encompass too much. "Why are plants green?" is an excellent question, but a formidable one for elementary-school children. Who, what, when, where, and does questions are usually more manageable than why questions.

Once the question has been posed, pertinent variables (which, when modified, will produce some change in the system) must be identified. Identifying them is a critical point in determining the success of the experiment. Too often in elementary experiments, the variables are not controlled. In the tumbler-garden activity, suppose the seeds were planted with a multitude of variables operating. Not only would the activity fail to answer the question originally asked, but it would conclude little and undoubtedly raise more questions. If this is your purpose—and on occasion it may be—fine! If, at some point in the developmental sequence of the experiment, your intent is to limit the activity, to answer a specific question, you must control all variables except the one you are investigating—the manipulated variable (independent variable). Variables that respond to this manipulation are called responding variables (dependent variables). Once you have controlled the variables, the experiment—collecting and interpreting data, and so on—more readily falls into place within the scheme of the total experimental process.

Read X, Why, and Thee to find out why a why question sometimes fails.

If one could turn on a yet-to-be-invented Instantometer that could flash a student's thought in response to why, the responses would be varied. The responses might range from, "It went out because it was damp" to "It went out because it blew out," "It went out because it simply burned out," and "I don't have the foggiest notion of why it went out." The last response would probably be the most common one.

X, Why, and Thee

The day lay heavily that Friday afternoon. The noonday lunches, resting comfortably like small barbells in the stomachs of 30 sixth-grade students, were reflected in the eyes of the students. Undaunted, the elementary science teacher commenced teaching science.

"Okay, watch me carefully," cautioned the instructor. Out of a mysterious container came a smoky substance identified by the instructor as dry ice. "Is everyone watching?" queried the instructor. Injecting some mid-day humor, he added, "Notice that during the entire demonstration no finger ever leaves the hand." This was followed by the striking of a match. It was placed in close proximity to a piece of dry ice. It went out immediately.

"Can anyone tell me why this happened?" asked the instructor. He repeated, "Why do you think this happened?" Almost everyone in the classroom saw what had transpired. The match went out. The "why" was something else.

The teacher sensed the partial vacuum buildup. It moved out from the back of the classroom like a tidal wave. Buttressing himself against the cresting wave, he slowly sank, gurgling, "Why? Why? Why?"

Source: Adapted from Alfred DeVito, "X, Why, and Thee," *Science and Children,* vol. 8 (November 1970), pp. 24–25. By permission from the National Science Teachers Association. Copyright 1970.

We do not believe any of the responses would have satisfied the instructor. The instructor probably was pointing to one scientific explanation for why the match went out.

How many times have you asked the students in your class why? How many times have you read in the eyes of your students the sign, "Closed for renovations"? How does one move students from that "closed for renovations" look to an "open for innovations" look?

The instructor in this case made use of a good discrepant event. Inquiry was inherent to the demonstration. What might have gone wrong? Did the why come too soon? Perhaps the jump from observation (the eye) to explanation (the why) was too great for the students.

A problem-solving approach wherein the instructor leads the students to the answer to a why question through analysis and synthesis is preferable to performing a demonstration and simply asking why. The students should be trained to analyze the components of the activity. They should be able to ask themselves the following questions: What is involved in the activity? What characteristics do the objects involved in the activity have? How do these objects interact with one another? Observing the result of the demonstrations, what might one hypothesize about these objects? How can one set up an experiment to check these proposed hypotheses? How does this information aid in answering the question, why?

This approach assumes the students have had some training in working toward the solution of problems. If they have not had this training, a discrepant event presented in isolation may draw a blank from the audience. If it does, be prepared with supportive, sequential demonstrations that lead students to knowledge that may allow them to understand the why of the discrepant event. Consider these demonstrations:

1. Expose a piece of dry ice to room temperature.
   Observation: Under ordinary conditions, the dry ice changes directly from a solid to a gas without passing through a noticeable liquid state.
   Question: What happened to the dry ice? Where did it go?
2. Taking the necessary precautions, put dry ice in a metal pitcher. Let the dry ice evaporate. Pour the contents of the pitcher into a paper bag filled with air. Attach it to one side of an equal-arm balance (a balanced yardstick or dowel will do), and balance it with an equal size bag also filled with air.
   Observation: The paper bag to which the generated gas has been added moves downward.
   Question: What does this reveal about the generated gas?
3. Again evaporate some dry ice in a metal pitcher. Construct a cardboard trough. Incline the trough toward one or a series of burning candles. Pour the contents of the pitcher into the trough.
   Observation: The generated gas flows downward and extinguishes the candle.
   Question: What does this reveal about the generated gas? Is it lighter or heavier than air?

4. Wrap a thin wire around a lighted candle and lower the candle into a metal pitcher filled with air. Repeat this, lowering the burning candle into a metal pitcher in which dry ice has been evaporated. Compare the two activities.

Observation: In the pitcher filled with air, the candle continues to burn. In the pitcher filled with generated gas, the candle quickly goes out.

Question: Will this generated gas support combustion?

The questions in demonstrations 1–4 build a sequence that leads to the explanation of why the burning match went out when placed in proximity to the dry ice.

Why questions can be difficult. The biggest fear of many prospective teachers seems to be that students will ask them questions like these:

"Why is the sky blue?"

"Why can't animals talk?"

"Why do snakes shed their skins?"

Students need time to reflect on the why of things. Students need prerequisite knowledge to make an instantaneous response. If this is lacking, students need a strategy and time to employ the strategy to arrive at a response to a why question. If students lack a strategy, concrete, sequential demonstrations or activities should be provided that lead them to a solution of why problems. Remember to uncover the pieces and permit the students the opportunity to weld ideas together. Try it. WHY NOT?

POINTS TO PONDER

Select a creative activity and present it as a teacher demonstration. Next, modify the activity and approach it as a creative experiment.

STICKERS, STAMPS, AND SHORTCUTS TO SUCCESS

Stickers are bright, colorful, and energizing. They have tons of kid appeal and they are usually given for excellent papers, good behavior, and holiday surprises. They say to a student, "You are okay! You succeeded!" Why not use these positive, colorful, and creative reinforcers to liven up your lessons and make every student in your room successful?

Stickers can be used as decorations on individualized learning games or they can be used to signal the correct answers. Small stickers or colored dots are very economical. You do not always have to use the extra-large, bubble-up, eye-moving, scented ones. Every time the stickers match in a learning game, you win! If there is not a match, you can try again until you succeed. In this case every student is a winner, every day.

Inked stamps can also provide an inexpensive way to code correct answers or provide positive reinforcement. A variety of different colored stamp pads and a drop of peppermint, strawberry, or cherry flavoring can give students a colorful and scented reward. You can even have a "stamp it" center where students can give their own papers a positive stamp.

Creative teachers spend a good deal of time making activities to interest students and to make learning fun. There are many practical shortcuts. For example, keep learning games small, no larger than a file folder, making storage and retrieval easy. Include directions on every game. Directions can be printed on labels and attached easily to games, or they can be typed and saved on a computer. You will remember the directions clearly when you first develop a game, but next year when you pull the materials from storage it will take time to recall the directions. Printed directions will also inspire the students to use games without your assistance.

Want to find materials easily and have them ready to use? Here are some organizational tips. Color-coded materials are not only attractive but beneficial. If all of your math activities are in yellow folders or in yellow plastic containers, you can put your fingers on them quickly. Arrange all game pieces and directions for a game in a Ziploc bag, and staple the bag to the inside of the folder. This keeps all the playing pieces in one spot. Cards for games can be coded by number or letter so if something gets lost, it can be easily returned to the proper folder. Label the tab of each folder. Even if you have the name of the game on the front of the folder, the tab is what you see in your file drawer.

Laminate, laminate, laminate! What more can be said? This is one shortcut you do not want to miss. Does it take time? Yes. Does it cost money? Yes. Is it worth it? Yes.

If you make learning games for your classroom, it takes time. Most of the time is your free time, after school and on weekends. Your time is very valuable. The materials you use are expensive and you will want to be able to use the games year after year. Lamination is essential. It makes games look professional and it makes them durable. If you do forget to label anything before it is laminated, you can always use a permanent marker. A game used only one day without lamination will collect its share of fingerprints, peanut butter, and smudges.

To cut your production time in half, assemble a supply box. Include a metal-edged ruler, graph paper, and an X-acto knife for cutting quick, straight lines. (*Note: Use caution when using an X-acto blade.*) Put pictures over graph paper, cut with the knife blade, and presto, 90-degree angles are a snap. Add a glue stick and a roll of double-sided tape. Glue sticks are fast, neat, and they dry instantly; avoid glue that has a water base because it will crinkle paper. Double-sided tape is also a valuable adhesive, and can be used for heavier weights of paper. A good paper punch, stapler, and scissors are essential. Incorporate sets of thin and thick permanent markers and an assortment of stickers, dots, and labels. Freezer Ziploc bags, quart and gallon sizes, are great for storing game pieces and will last longer than thinner bags. Keep a supply of colored file folders and index cards handy. A sharp paper cutter is worth its weight in gold. Various sizes of rubber letters and numbers can be used for titles and sequencing activities. Clear contact paper is useful for covering items that cannot go through the laminator.

Be prepared. You never know when you will be inspired to make a game at midnight.

Once you start making learning games and see how excited and eager students are to use them, you will be on the lookout for all kinds of free and inexpensive materials. Keep partly-used or sample workbooks. Coloring books are wonderful for simple patterns. Magazines and catalogs contain pictures for art work. Potato-chip cans, shoe boxes, film containers, ready-made icing cans, and detergent lids will all be seen in a new light. Creative recycling will become part of your life.

SKILLETTES

Sometimes students need skills and concepts presented to them in a variety of ways. Skillettes are mini-lessons or learning activities that are designed to teach basic skills in a game format. They provide interest and reinforcement so students can learn. They take the boredom out of seat work.

When designing skillettes you will want to create three-to-five different activities or games for each skill. For example, if you were creating a skillette for the vowel a, you would want one game for a long a, one game for short a, and one game for both long and short a. Questions should have one correct answer so self-checking can be incorporated into each skillette. Skillettes can be developed for individuals, partners, or teams of students.

It helps if you have students do skillettes in a sequential order. Number the activities and design a pathway so students can check off each activity as they finish (Figure 4.5). Numbering makes it easier for students to find the next activity and to return the materials to the appropriate place. Remember, variety is the spice of life. Be creative and design all types of games.

The following set of learning activities can be incorporated into skillettes. They can also be used in book kits and modules.

Wrap ups (Figure 4.6)

Wrap ups provide extra practice for simple drill activities. They can be made using various size pieces of poster board. This is an excellent way to use scraps. The idea is to match the question with the answer. Self-checking is provided on the back. Wrap ups are designed for one student at a time.

To make a wrap up, start with a piece of poster board or heavy tagboard.

1. Cut a piece of poster board about 3 inches by 8 inches. You should be able to hold the poster board comfortably in your hand.
2. Write or glue questions down the left-hand side and answers down the right-hand side of the poster board.
3. Cut notches next to each question and answer.
4. Punch a hole at the top of the card and attach a long piece of string, yarn, or shoelace.
5. Starting on the left side, wrap the string from the first question

Figure 4.5 Pathway

Figure 4.6 Wrap ups

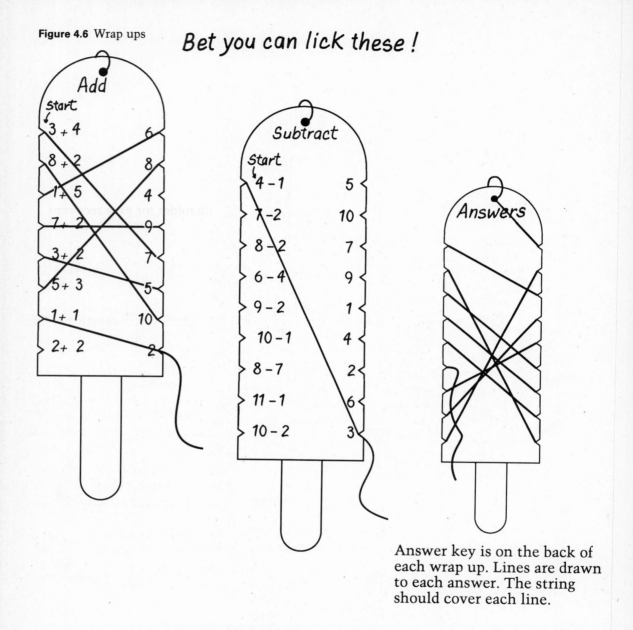

Bet you can lick these!

Answer key is on the back of each wrap up. Lines are drawn to each answer. The string should cover each line.

around the front of the card to the correct answer on the right-hand side.

6. Move the string around the back of the card until you reach the second question. Repeat.
7. Keep wrapping until all questions are answered.
8. With a pencil, lightly sketch in the answer lines on the back of the poster board.
9. Test the card again.

10. Darken the answer lines by using a straight-edged ruler and a thin permanent marker.
11. Title the front of the card.
12. Include a simple set of directions and an arrow so students will know where to start. You may want to mark the first answer on the front of the card to get students moving the string in the right direction.
13. Remove the string and laminate the card or cover it with clear contact paper.
14. Punch through the hole to remove the lamination film and cut the film from the notches.
15. Tie yarn or string onto the card.
16. These cards can be stored in a labeled file folder for easy recovery.

Extending Wrapups

—Design wrap ups about social studies, geography, or history information such as dates and events, countries and continents, cities, capitals, and states.

All age levels of students enjoy wrap ups. It is a fun way to practice basic skills, especially math facts. You can add pictures or stamps for interest.

Flip-and-Match Books (Figure 4.7)

Are you looking for a simple way to present new material, reinforce vocabulary, or engage students in a hands-on learning activity? Flip-and-match books may be just what you need. Students match the correct answers that are housed in a flip book and check to see if they are correct. Flip books are easy to store and all the parts stay together.

1. Design a matching game to teach a skill. Vocabulary words, math problems, historical events, and shapes make good flip-and-match books.
2. Cut 3-inch by 5-inch index cards in half vertically.
3. Write questions on one half of the cards, and the answers on the other half.
4. Code the questions and answers by placing matching stickers on the back of each card.
5. Cut a front and back cover for the set of flip-and-match cards. A 6-inch by 4-inch cover will give you plenty of room. Design and title the cover.
6. Place directions on the inside of the cover.
7. Laminate the cards.
8. Bind the note cards and covers with a spiral binder or book rings. Leave a half-inch gap between the sets of cards in the binder. Four book rings, two for each set, help to keep the cards straight and easy to flip. There are games that use small plastic rings. It may be worthwhile to check out your local toy store.

Figure 4.7 Flip and match books

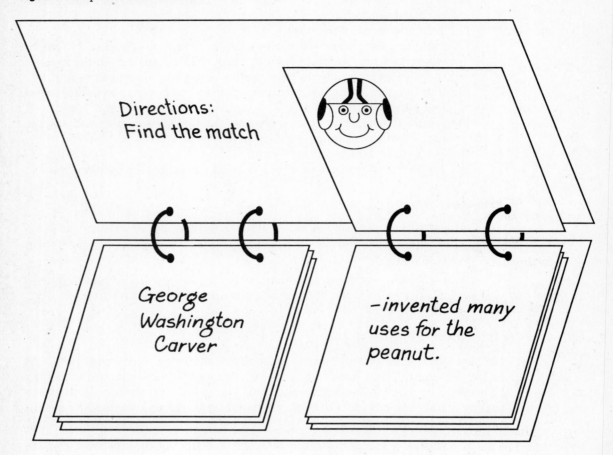

 Matching stickers, numbers, or symbols can be placed on the back of matching cards for easy self-checking.

Extending Flip-and-Match Books

Make a flip-and-match book for you and your school.

Make a history or geography flip-and-match book using three stacks instead of two stacks. These could be labeled time (year), person or place, and event.

Flip-and-match books can contain more than two sets of cards. Extended books work well for creating the beginning, middle, and end of a story. Students can also design flip-and-match books to study basic math facts, historical events, or leaf identification. Ideas and illustrations from workbooks can be incorporated.

Window Folders (Figure 4.8)

You will enjoy window folders as much as your students do. Do you think it is important to have your students know basic facts? Do you have old workbooks stacked on your shelves? Do you want to recycle scrap paper in your classroom? Do you want to spend less time at the copy machine? If you answered yes, read these simple directions.

1. Take a page from a workbook, a sheet on money, vocabulary words, math facts, or punctuation, and glue it completely to the back, inside page of a file folder.
2. Cut a hole under each question using an X-acto knife.
3. Flip the file folder cover behind the question page and write the answers to the questions in each hole.
4. Write directions on the inside of the file folder and label the tab.
5. Label and cut one extra hole at the bottom of the card so students can write the page number on their papers.
6. Laminate the file folder.
7. Cut through the lamination film with an X-acto knife. (*Note: Use caution when using an X-acto knife.*)

The student uses the card by placing a piece of scrap paper behind the window folder. The answer to each question is written in the open area beneath the question. When the student completes the drill sheet, the window folder is closed. The scrap paper is placed outside the window folder so the answers show through the holes. Students simply check and correct. Encourage your students to mark each correct answer, then to go back and find which problems they missed. The window sheets can be given to the teacher for approval. Since the students mark the correct answers, it will be easy to locate where students are having difficulty.

To conserve on file folders, cut them in half and make two games from each file folder. To save time, type the directions for the game on computer labels and attach them to the window folders. It also helps if you make a pattern out of tagboard after you have perfected the first window folder. This will make drawing the holes a snap. Transparency sheets and markers can also be used to save paper.

If you are afraid your students may look at the answers, remember this is just a drill activity. It is a time for students to learn, to make mistakes, and to eliminate misconceptions. We all make mistakes; hopefully we learn from them.

Figure 4.8 Window folders

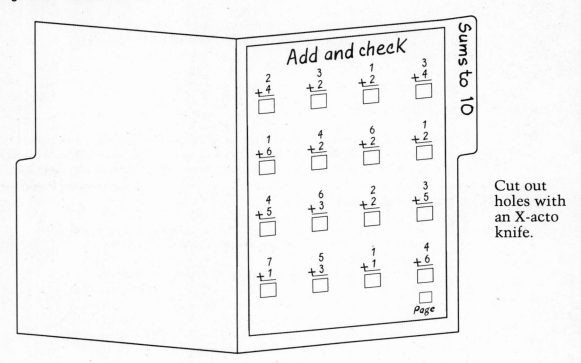

Cut out holes with an X-acto knife.

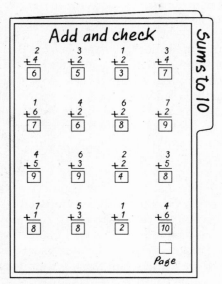

Bend the front cover behind the question page. Write the answers on the front cover for self-checking.

Students will slide pieces of scrap paper between the folder flaps. When they remove the paper, the answers will appear for easy self-checking.

Extending Window Folders

—Make window folders for other mathematical operations such as subtraction, multiplication, and division.

Instant-Winner Punch Cards (Figure 4.9)

Instant-winner punch cards are used to reinforce basic skills or concepts such as math facts, reducing fractions, mental math, formulas, simple vocabulary, homonyms, synonyms, and/or antonyms. You make instant-winner punch cards by placing all the questions on the front side of a card and all the answers on the back side. One student or a pair of students can use the card. You look at the question and answer it silently or orally. Then you poke a pencil, golf tee, or straw through the hole and flip the card over to check your answer. If you are working with a partner, he/she will tell you if you are correct. To add interest, instant-winner punch cards can be made from various shapes of tagboard.

1. Cut out a shape from a file folder or tagboard.
2. Write the title and simple directions in the center of the card.
3. Punch a hole near the edge of the shape for each question. Try to space the holes evenly.

Figure 4.9 Instant winner punch cards

Poke a straw or a pencil through the hole and check the answer on the back.

Answers are on the reverse side for easy self-checking

4. Write or glue a question next to each hole.
5. Write or glue the answer for each question on the back of the card next to its respective hole.
6. Laminate the tagboard. If you use heavier poster board, use clear contact paper.
7. Place your instant-winner punch cards in a Ziploc freezer bag with the golf tee, straw, or pencil.
8. Put the Ziploc bag inside a labeled file folder.

Instant-winner punch cards are perfect for drill. They provide immediate reinforcement and are fun! Students can even design their own drill games.

Extending Instant-Winner Punch Cards

—Design instant-winner punch science cards matching chemical formulas to the chemical; for example, HCl-hydrochloric acid, H_2O-water.

—Design instant-winner punch cards for English words and their Latin roots; for example, perimeter-peri (around).

—Design instant-winner punch cards for volume formulas for a cube, cone, and sphere.

Mystery Middles (Figures 4.10A and 4.10B)

Looking for a new way to teach contractions, multiplication tables, vocabulary words, different languages, or formulas? This may be the way to crack the monotony and add a little excitement to the day. Mystery middles are effective with elementary and middle-school students and can be developed for any subject area. The question is on the outside. After the student has thought of the answer, he/she opens the mystery doors to find the answer. Students can use mystery middles individually or with a partner. To make a mystery middle, you will need tagboard or construction paper, markers, scissors, and a package of brads.

1. First design a mystery middle. The front shape may be an egg, ball, ear of corn, tulip, haystack, leaf, or geometric shape. Use your creativity. This shape will be cut in half.
2. Make a pattern for the back shape. It can be a chick, a geometric shape, a flower, a frog, or any shape that corresponds with the front shape.
3. Write the question or problem on the two front pieces.
4. Write the answer on the back piece.
5. Laminate all pieces individually.
6. Poke a small hole through all three shapes near the base so the two front pieces open and close in front of the back piece.
7. Align the pieces and put a brad through the hole.
8. Mystery middles can be placed in a Ziploc bag and stored in a labeled file folder.

Figure 4.10A Mystery middles (Example 1)

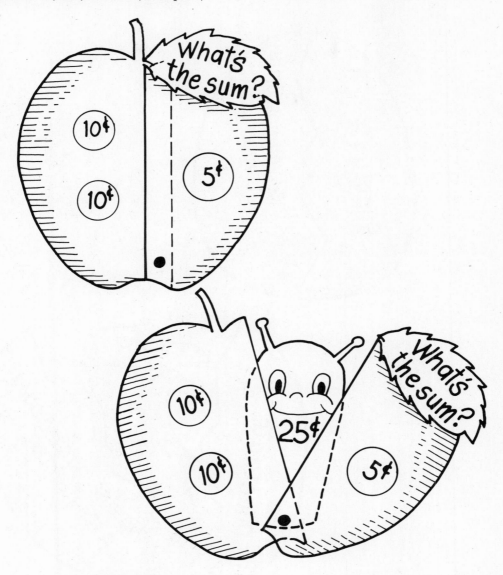

9. You can place the directions on the file folder or in the Ziploc bag.
10. Remind students to put the front pieces together when they are finished.

Extending Mystery Middles

—Design a flexible mystery middle. Each mystery door can have a window cut in each panel. Behind each door insert a small circular disk

Figure 4.10B Mystery middles (Example 2)

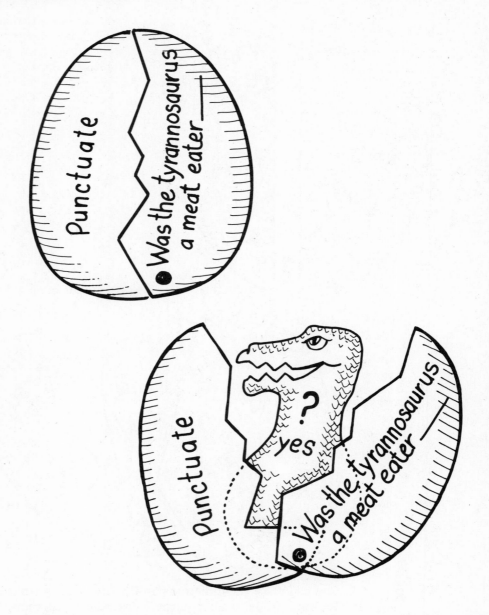

attached by a brass brad. On each disk write numbers. The disk behind each door can be spun, bringing different numbers into view representing changing values. A wheel or disk with the appropriate responses can be made for the mystery middle. Color codings could be used so the students can see if the response is correct.

Peek-A-Boo Pockets (Figure 4.11)

Peek-a-boo pockets provide an interesting way for students to manipulate materials, solve problems, match answers, and feel a sense of accomplishment. A peek-a-boo pocket takes time to make and a little knowledge of sewing, but it is well worth the time and effort. One peek-a-boo pocket can be used all year for a variety of drill activities. Once you have the peek-a-boo pocket made, concentrate on making game cards and tongue-depressor answer sticks.

To make a peek-a-boo pocket you will need the following materials:

$\frac{1}{2}$ yard clear vinyl plastic (.008 inch or .010 inch), which is available in stores for covering chairs. This will make five peek-a-boo pockets.

Polyester sewing thread (any color).

A roll of 1-inch colored plastic or cloth tape. This will make two peek-a-boo pockets.

A transparency pen.

1. Cut two pieces of clear vinyl. One piece should be 8 inches by $10\frac{1}{2}$ inches. The other piece should be $8\frac{3}{4}$ inches by $10\frac{1}{2}$ inches.
2. Cover all edges of the clear vinyl pieces with the plastic or cloth tape by wrapping $\frac{1}{2}$ inch of the tape on the back and $\frac{1}{2}$ inch on the front. If it is not exact, it will not matter.
3. Place the 8-inch piece of vinyl on top of the $8\frac{3}{4}$-inch piece and align the left sides together. Anchor with paper clips.
4. Draw a vertical line 4 inches from the left-hand side and stitch along this line.
5. Draw a horizontal line $\frac{1}{4}$ inch from the bottom. Stitch a horizontal line across the entire bottom of the pocket.
6. Starting from the stitched line at the bottom, draw horizontal lines $1\frac{1}{4}$ inches apart to the top of the vinyl on the right side of the peek-a-boo pocket. The lines should start from the middle and move to the right edge. Stitch over the lines. You will have room for eight tongue depressors.
7. Do not stitch the left side of the vinyl or the top of the left side. The poster board will fit into this space.
8. Wipe the peek-a-boo pocket with a damp cloth to remove transparency marker lines.

Now that you have the peek-a-boo pocket, you are ready to make the question cards and answer sticks. To make the question cards, you need tagboard or poster board. To make the answer sticks, tongue depressors work well. You may also need clear fingernail polish, contact paper, and a permanent marker.

1. Cut a piece of tagboard or poster board $3\frac{3}{4}$ inches by $11\frac{1}{2}$ inches. The extra length can be used to label the card and list directions.
2. Draw horizontal lines starting at the bottom of the tagboard to correspond to the stitch lines. These should be $1\frac{1}{4}$ inches apart.

Figure 4.11 Peek-a-boo pockets

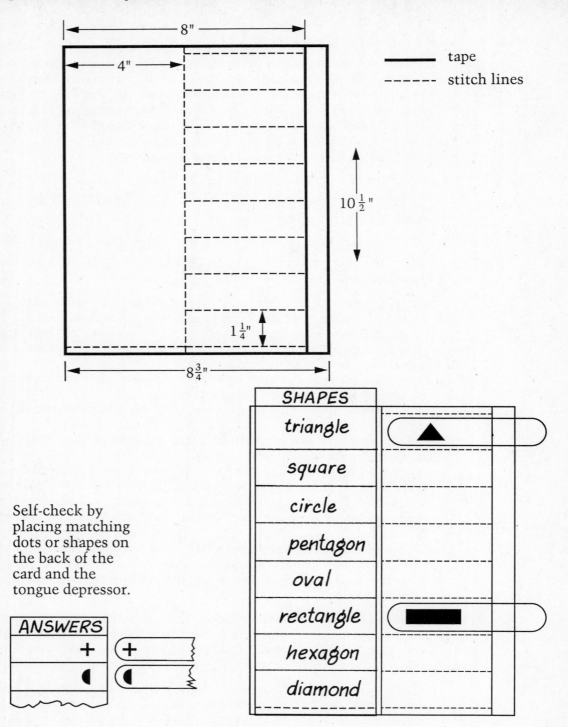

Self-check by placing matching dots or shapes on the back of the card and the tongue depressor.

154

3. Write a question or problem in each space. Questions from workbooks can be glued to the tagboard. Questions can also be typed onto computer labels and placed in each space.

4. On the back of the tagboard, place a different sticker near the right edge in each of the eight spaces starting at the bottom. The top space can be labeled "ANSWERS."

5. Laminate the card.

6. Place the answer on one side of each tongue depressor.

7. Place the tongue depressors in the peek-a-boo pockets that correspond to the questions.

8. Turn the peek-a-boo pocket over and place a sticker on the back of each tongue depressor that corresponds to the sticker on the question card.

9. Code the tongue depressor by placing a colored dot on the stick or drawing a colored line with a marker. This will help to identify a stick if it gets lost from the set.

10. Cover stickers or labels with clear contact paper or clear nail polish so they will not tear. If you use permanent markers on the tongue depressors, you do not need to coat or cover them.

11. Place tongue depressors in a labeled Ziploc bag, and store the card and tongue depressor in a labeled folder.

Extending Peek-A-Boo Pockets

Make a set of tongue-depressor answer sticks matching prefixes to root words.

Make a set of tongue-depressor answer sticks matching geometric shapes to mathematical formulas for either area or volume.

Make a set of tongue depressor-sticks matching capital cities to their respective states.

Slip and Slide (Figure 4.12A and 4.12B)

It is time to slide into some fun drills. You can do this by making slip-and-slide cards. Place the questions on one side of the card and the answers on the other. Self-checking is very easy. One way to make slip-and-slide cards is to make a tachistoscope (T-scope).

1. Take a piece of tagboard or file folder and cut it into a T-shape (8 inches by 3 inches). You can make five T-scopes and one slider out of each file folder. These will fit nicely into another file folder for easy storage. A pattern is available in Figures 4.12A and 4.12B.

2. Write the title and questions on the front side of the T-scope.

3. Write the answer directly behind each question on the T-scope.

4. Construct a slider by cutting a $6\frac{1}{2}$-inch by 2-inch rectangle. A problem window and an answer window are cut into the slider with an X-acto knife. *(Note: Use caution when using an X-acto knife.)*

Figure 4.12A Slider

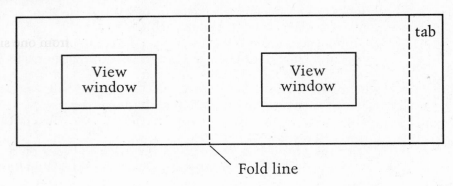

Figure 4.12B Slip and slide

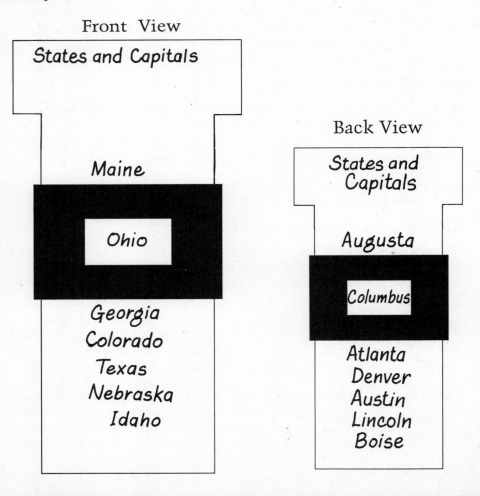

5. Directions can be placed on the folder, on each T-scope card, or on the slider.
6. Laminate all pieces.
7. To make the slider, score a vertical line 3 inches from one side. Fold. Score a second vertical line $3\frac{1}{8}$ inches from the score mark. Use double-sided tape to close the slider.
8. Insert the T-shaped card and you have an instant slip-and-slide card.
9. Store in labeled file folder.

A second type of slip-and-slide card can be made with a piece of tagboard and a tall potato-chip can with a plastic lid.

1. Cut a piece of tagboard into $2\frac{3}{4}$-inch by 11-inch strips to fit into a potato-chip can.
2. On the top of the strip, write the title of the card and simple directions.
3. Draw a series of horizontal lines every $\frac{1}{2}$ inch or $\frac{3}{4}$ inch down the slider strip.
4. Make the same horizontal lines on the back of the slider strip.
5. Write questions on the title side of the tagboard and answers on the back side. Each answer is written directly on the back of the question.
6. Laminate the slider cards.
7. Cover the potato-chip can with contact paper.
8. Cut a slit across the top of the plastic lid. The slit should be open enough to insert the slider card, but thin enough to hold it.
9. Store the cards in labeled file folders.

The student inserts the slider card and slowly pulls the card to reveal the first question. The student turns the can to see the back of the card, which shows the answer. The student continues until all questions on the slider card have been answered.

Slip-and-slide cards provide immediate reinforcement and are fun for students to use. Students can use blank cards to make their own slider cards. It is helpful to create a pattern and make a stack of copies for future use. Some copy machines can even copy the pattern on tagboard. This is a real time saver.

A third type of slip-and-slide card has two question windows and an answer window, as seen in Figure 4.12C. This format is very useful for math drill.

1. Use a 3-inch by 5-inch index card for the card holder.
2. With an X-acto knife, cut three windows $\frac{3}{4}$ inch by $\frac{1}{2}$ inch in the card. *(Note: Use caution when using an X-acto knife.)* Keep the flap on the third window because this is the answer window.
3. Tape two 5-inch by $\frac{1}{2}$-inch strips to the back of the card holder. This will keep the question/answer card in place.
4. Place an addition, subtraction, multiplication, or division sign between the first and second windows. You can make the holder multi-operational by leaving the card blank and writing the sign of operation with an overhead pen.

Figure 4.12C Slip and slide

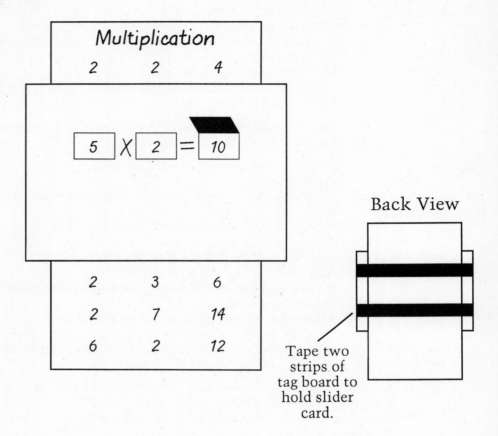

5. Cut a question/answer card about 4 inches by 7 inches out of tagboard.
6. On the question/answer card write three columns of numbers. The first and second columns will represent the numbers of the problem. The third column will contain the answers. It helps to put the question/answer card in the holder when you are writing the numbers so the numbers will be in the correct places.
7. Make several cards for each skill. Number each card in order of difficulty.
8. Laminate the cards and the holder. With an X-acto knife, slit the strips on the back of the holder. *(Note: Use caution when using an X-acto knife.)*
9. Store in a labeled folder.

A fourth type of slip-and-slide card can be made by using a creative shape of cardboard and a question/answer strip. The question/answer strip may be made of tagboard, poster board, or a paint stick.

1. Cut out a creative shape using the tagboard.
2. With the X-acto knife, cut two vertical slits through the creative shape about $\frac{1}{2}$ inch or $\frac{3}{4}$ inch apart and $\frac{1}{2}$ inch wider than the question/answer strip. *(Note: Use caution when using an X-acto knife.)* The strip can be made from poster board, tagboard, or a paint stick. A 2-inch strip works well unless you need room for words or sentences.
4. Label the top of the question/answer card.
5. Draw horizontal lines every $\frac{1}{2}$ inch or $\frac{3}{4}$ inch on the front and back side of the strip.
6. Write on each space.
7. Weave the strip through the two slots so the question is visible on the front side of the shape.
8. Turn the card and write the answer on the back of the strip. You can place the answer directly above the tagboard strip. Write the word "answer" on the strip and draw an arrow pointing toward the answer.
9. Laminate the card and the question/answer strip.
10. File in a labeled file folder.

Extending Slip-and-Slide Cards

Make a slip-and-slide card set for parts of speech; for example, verb-action word, adjective-descriptive word.

Make a slip-and-slide card set for parts of a letter; for example, salutation (greeting).

Make a slip-and-slide card deck for Latin prefixes; for example, geo-(earth). Geometry is a measure of the earth.

Make a slip-and-slide card deck for colors. What two (or three) colors give another color? For example, blue and yellow make green.

Make a slip-and-slide card deck for various map symbols.

Wheels of Knowledge (Figure 4.13)

With a turn of the wrist students can challenge themselves. A wheel-of-knowledge game can be created with one or two wheels. They can be used to encourage language development, practice phonetic drills, improve vocabulary, or sharpen math facts. They can add a nice twist to seat work.

1. To design a single wheel of knowledge, draw and cut a creative shape approximately 4 inches by 5 inches in width. Shapes can correspond to a subject area, a story, or a learning-center theme. Cut out the view window, which will be approximately 1 inch by $\frac{1}{2}$ inch.
2. Cut a 3-inch circle that will rotate behind the shape. It may be helpful to make a paper model before you use tagboard or a file folder.
3. Position the wheel so it rotates past the view window. Depending

Figure 4.13 Wheels of knowledge

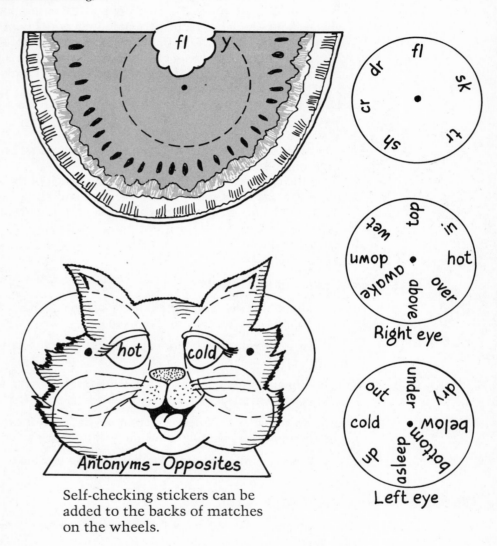

Self-checking stickers can be
added to the backs of matches
on the wheels.

on the skill, you may need the view window on the right, left, top, or
bottom.

4. Poke a hole in the center of the circle and in the shape. Attach with a
brad.
5. Add words, pictures, or problems with the wheel in place. This
will help to keep the spacing correct.
6. If you have answers to your wheel-of-knowledge game, write the
answers directly behind the view window.
7. Disassemble the parts before you laminate each piece.
8. Reassemble and place in a labeled file folder.

A wheel-of-knowledge game with two wheels offers more flexibility. One wheel contains the questions and the second wheel contains the answers. The student has to rotate both wheels to make the correct match. Different sets of wheels can be created to vary the level of difficulty. It is a good idea to color code and number each set of wheels.

1. To design a double wheel-of-knowledge game, cut out a shape that is large enough for two 3-inch wheels. Simple pictures from primary coloring books work well for the shapes, especially faces with eyes. The eyes become the view windows.
2. Cut two 3-inch wheels that will rotate behind the view windows. You may want to make a model and practice before you cut your shape and wheels from tagboard.
3. Using an X-acto knife, cut the view windows from the shape. *(Note: Use caution when using an X-acto knife.)*
4. Position the wheels so they rotate past the view windows.
5. Attach the wheels with brads.
6. Place the words, pictures, or problems on the question wheel while it is in position.
7. Write or place the answers on the second wheel. The answers should *not* be in order.
8. Code each question and answer on the back of the wheels with a sticker or symbol so students can self-check.
9. Disassemble and laminate each part.
10. Reassemble and place in a labeled folder. Additional wheels can also be stored in Ziploc bags in this folder.

Extending Wheels of Knowledge   Construct wheels of knowledge for:

fractions: common and decimal fraction equivalents;

cloud formations and their corresponding names;

rocks and mineral constituents: for example, granite-feldspar, quartz, and mica; or rocks and corresponding characteristics: for example, gneiss-banding;

leaves of trees matched with correct tree names;

exponential descriptions matched with correct numerical values; for example, 10_3 equals 1000.

Flip Folders (Figure 4.14)

There is always another way to let students experience success. Flip folders can give students positive reinforcement, tempt their curiosity, and teach them some basic skills. Sequential activities such as putting the sentences of a paragraph in order or listing historical events work very well in flip folders.

Flip folders can be constructed by using a file folder, tagboard, a picture, a glue stick, a marker, and scissors.

Figure 4.14 Flip folders

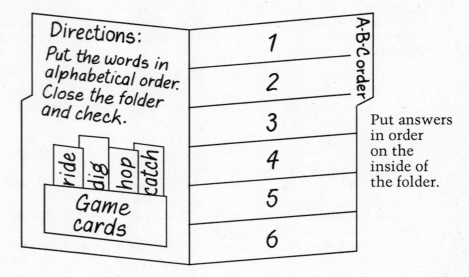

Put answers in order on the inside of the folder.

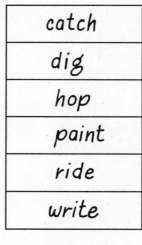

Write game cards in the correct order.

Glue entire picture on the back of the game cards.

After the picture is glued to the back of the game cards, cut the game cards apart. When the student puts the cards in the correct order, closes the folder, and flips it, the picture should be in the correct order.

1. Cut the tagboard to fit the inside of a file folder.
2. Write the questions on the front of the tagboard.
3. On the back of the tagboard, glue an interesting picture. Make sure you glue the entire picture to the tagboard so when you cut the picture apart, the edges stay together.
4. Cut the tagboard into five to eight pieces.
5. Write the answers on the inside back flap of the file folder so they correspond to the tagboard pieces.
6. Label and put directions on the folder.
7. Laminate the pieces of the puzzle and the file folder.

When you play this game, you place the questions on the correct answers with the picture side facing the file folder. After all of the pieces are in place, you close and flip the folder. If all of the questions have been answered correctly, the picture will appear in proper order.

It does help to draw the lines on the file folder so the student knows where to place each piece. Using only five to eight pieces is also important. If you use too many pieces, the answer cards will shift and lose position when you flip the folder.

Extending Flip Folders

Use flip folders to enhance the process of inferring. When only a few pieces are in the correct order, revealing only portions of the picture, have the students make inferences about the complete picture.

Design a flip folder placing a map on the reverse side. Use geographical game cards arranged in some prescribed order to determine the orientation of the map.

Place a treasure map on the reverse side. Arrange game cards that locate the treasure in an order that best describes the most desirable route to it. How do different routes compare? Which is the most expedient route to the treasure?

Concentration (Figure 4.15)

Concentration is a matching game where students turn over two cards at a time and try to make a match. It has wide appeal for all ages and can be used for all subject areas.

1. Make one set of cards with the questions and one set with the answers. The number of cards may vary with the grade level, but eight to ten pairs of cards per game is a good number. The cards should all be the same size and color.
2. Identify each question and answer pair with matching stickers on the same side as the question and answer.
3. Laminate all cards.
4. Put in a labeled folder with the directions.

Figure 4.15 Concentration

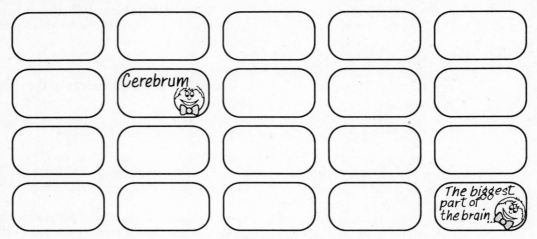

Flip two cards at a time; if they
match you win. Self-checking needs to
be on the same side as the writing.

Cerebrum

The biggest part of the brain containing centers for speech, sight, hearing, touching, tasting, and smelling.

One or two students may play the game. To start, place all cards face down on the table. The first person turns over two cards. If there is a match, the person keeps the cards and gets an extra turn. If there is not a match, the cards are returned to the face-down position. The next player then selects two cards. The game ends when there are no more cards. The player with the most cards wins.

Extending Concentration   Make concentration cards for all areas of the curriculum, such as:

> science: for example, insects, rocks, clouds, trees, leaves, simple machines, food groups, and parts of the human body. Use the picture or the title shown versus the description.

> art: for example, colors versus their descriptive names; artists versus their styles or tools versus the names of the tools of art

> mathematics: for examples, geometric shapes versus names or descriptions of the shapes

Think of your own matching pairs for social studies, spelling, English, and so on.

Puzzle Cards (Figure 4.16)

Puzzle cards can be created for any subject. You make puzzle cards by writing the question on the left side of the card and the answer on the right side. Then you creatively cut each card into two pieces making a mini-puzzle. Students match each question and answer, then check by putting the shapes together. If the puzzle pieces fit, the answer is correct.

1. Write the question on one half of the card.
2. Write the answer on the other half.
3. Cut the card in half using a different cut for each card. Cards can be cut horizontally or vertically.
4. Laminate each card.
5. Place pieces with directions in a Ziploc bag.
6. For easy access, place the game in a labeled folder.

You can design an entire set of puzzle cards for vocabulary words, math problems, social studies events, or foreign language drill. Students at all grade levels enjoy using puzzle cards. Colorful note cards or creative notepads can be used to add a little variety to puzzle cards.

You can also purchase blank puzzles. Use a permanent marker to write questions and answers on the puzzle pieces. Students fit the puzzle together, revealing the questions and answers.

Extending Puzzle Cards

> Make a three- (or four- or more) piece puzzle-card deck to enhance increased spatial relations awareness.

> Vary the interface of the pieces; for example, straight and curved lines, 45- and 90-degree angle cuts.

Figure 4.16 Puzzle cards

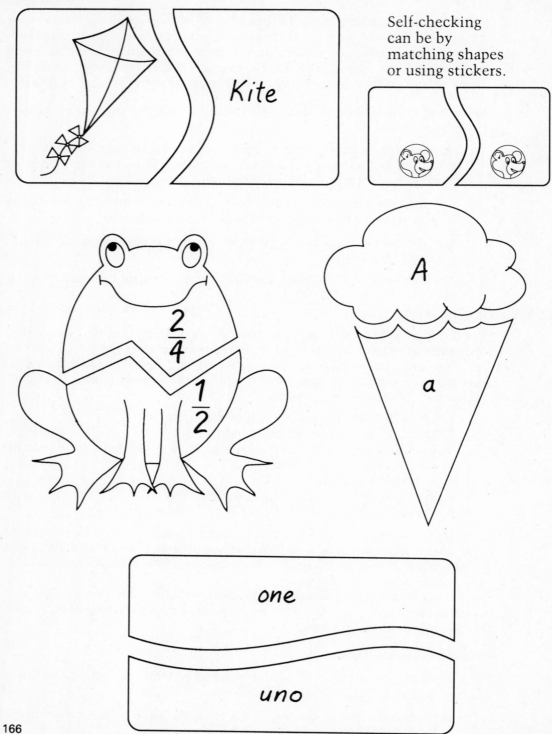

Self-checking can be by matching shapes or using stickers.

166

Sort and Check (Figure 4.17)

It is always exciting to sort objects, words, problems, sentences, and/or punctuation marks into categories, then check to see if you are correct. Sort-and-check games can be used for any subject area and at any grade level. Students can work individually or in pairs.

Sort-and-check games are easy to construct.

Figure 4.17 Sort and check

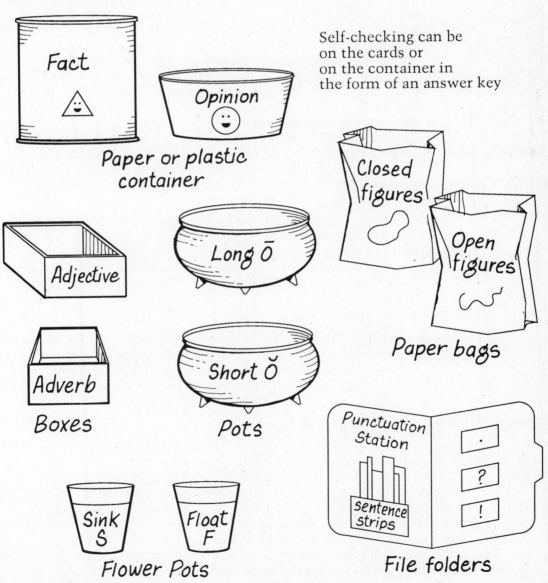

Self-checking can be
on the cards or
on the container in
the form of an answer key

1. Collect materials to be sorted. These can be words with long and short e; various types of sentences without punctuation marks; number of syllables cards; true and false questions; pictures of open and closed figures; objects that will sink or float; sentences that represent the beginning, middle, or end of a paragraph, or historical events that took place during different decades. The list is limited only by your imagination.

2. Label the containers where you are going to place the sorted materials. Add variety by using all types of containers such as oatmeal boxes, small baskets, cans, envelopes, library pockets, detergent caps, or strawberry baskets.

3. Make an answer key and place it on the back or on the bottom of each container. You can also place a special sticker on each container that will match the stickers on the cards.

4. Make a set of materials or cards that need to be sorted. Place answer stickers on the backs of these materials to correspond to the correct container.

5. Laminate cards and answer keys.

6. The cards and answer keys can be stored in labeled file folders or inside the sorting containers.

7. After the students have sorted the materials into the various containers or pockets, they can turn the cards to see if they are correct or they can look at the answer key.

The possibilities for sort and check are endless. Younger students like real objects and large containers. Older students are content with cards and envelopes. It is a great way to get students thinking and making decisions. Sort-and-check cards are nonthreatening and easy for students to use. Students can even make their own sort-and-check games.

Extending Sort and Check

—Initiate the construction of classification systems based on the separation of various characteristics or traits. Extend this from a one-stage separation to a two- or three-stage separation system based on other observed attributes, characteristics, or traits of the objects.

Poke-and-Discover Cards (Figure 4.18)

Poke-and-discover cards are simple to construct. All you need are multiple-choice questions and answers on any subject. The questions can be taken from a book, or you can design your own. Questions from workbooks can be cut apart and made into poke-and-discover cards. To use the card, a student reads the question, decides on an answer, covers the hole with a finger or inserts a straw, then turns the card to see if the correct answer was selected. Poke-and-discover cards can be used individually or with a partner.

To make poke-and-discover cards you need one question and one correct answer plus two incorrect answers for each card.

Figure 4.18 Poke and discover cards

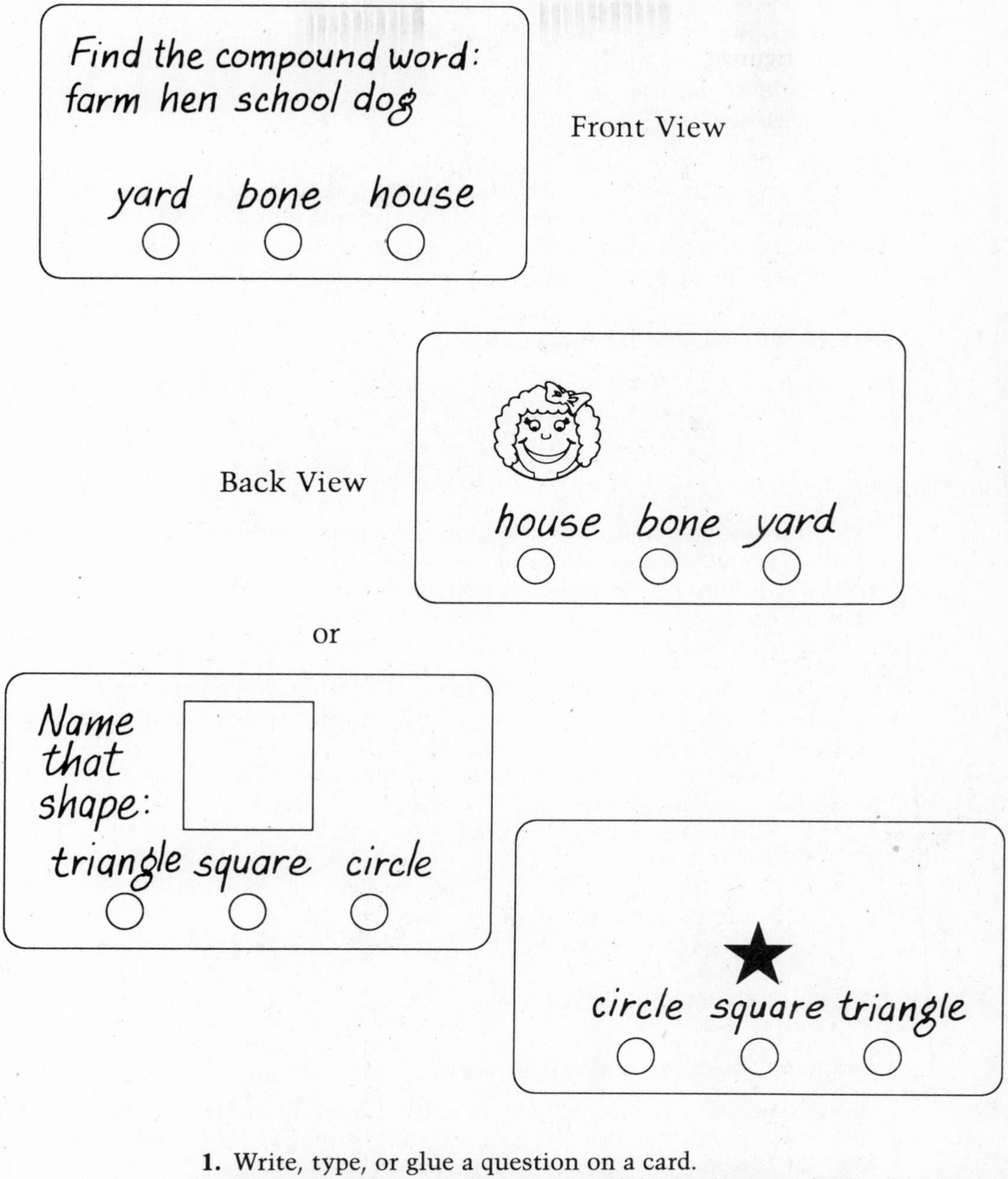

Find the compound word:
farm hen school dog

yard bone house
○   ○   ○

Front View

Back View

house bone yard
○   ○   ○

or

Name
that
shape:

triangle square circle
○   ○   ○

circle square triangle
○   ○   ○

1. Write, type, or glue a question on a card.
2. Write the answers near one edge of the card. Answers should be spaced so you can punch a hole at the side or under each one.
3. On the back of the card place a sticker, stamp, or mark near the hole of the correct answer.

4. Number the set of cards and code each card in some way so you can easily return it to the correct folder if a card gets lost.
5. Laminate the cards and punch through the lamination.
6. Place the cards with directions in a Ziploc bag or envelope.
7. Place the bag or envelope in a labeled folder for storage and easy retrieval.

Lower elementary students like to place a soda straw or golf tee through the correct hole. Upper elementary students just like to place their finger over the correct hole. You can cut poke-and-discover cards into any shape or use standard, rectangular-shaped cards. Students really enjoy making and using their own poke-and-discover cards.

Extending Poke-and-Discover Cards

Design poke-and-discover cards for compound sentences, chemical compounds, vocabulary, and so on.

Question-and-Answer Clocks (Figure 4.19)

Dial your way to a positive learning experience with question-and-answer clocks. The questions and answers are easy to match and easy to check. This is a good way to turn seat work and pencil-and-paper drills into fun activities. Students can work by themselves or with a partner. Clocks can be developed for all subject areas. Students can even make their own clocks.

1. Cut out a circle from a file folder, or use a colored paper plate.
2. Put questions on the left side of the plate and answers on the right side.
3. Make two arrows from a file folder or from scraps of poster board and attach them with a brad in the middle of the circle.
4. Match one arrow with the question and the second arrow with the answer.
5. Mark the correct matches on the back of the circle or plate with matching stickers, stamps, or marks.
6. Disassemble the parts and laminate. Some paper plates can even be laminated.
7. Reassemble the clock and put it in a labeled file folder.

Extending Question-and-Answer Clocks

Expand this by placing one or more circles or disks (in receding diameter size, with the smallest one on the top) rotating about the same center brass brad so that more information can be processed. For example, the outer disk may contain capital cities, the next smaller disk may contain states or provinces, and the third (the smallest disk) may contain the country. The reverse should have the continents displayed.

Figure 4.19 Question-and-answer clocks

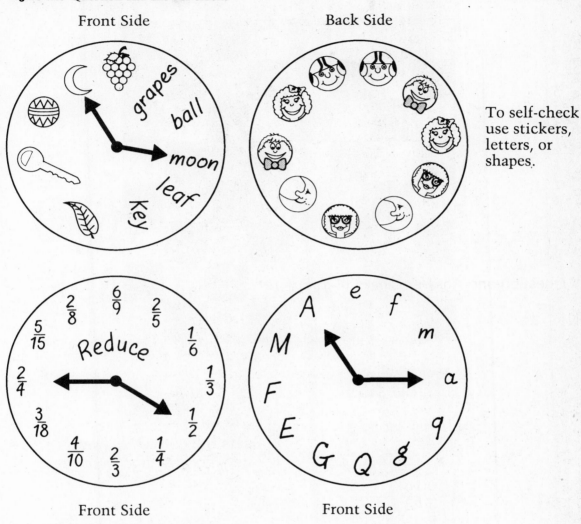

Front Side

Back Side

To self-check
use stickers,
letters, or
shapes.

Front Side

Front Side

Checker Match (Figure 4.20)

Do you have an old checkerboard sitting on a shelf? It is time to dust it off and
polish up your skills. Learning drills of all kinds can be incorporated into a
checker game. Most students enjoy playing checkers and already know the
rules. You add the content.

1. Make two sets of 12 checkers each. Each set can be cut from a different color of tagboard.
2. On each checker, place a question. It may be easiest to type it on a
   label and attach it to the checker. Number each question from one to
   twelve.

Figure 4.20 Checker match

Spelling words

Math facts

Words and definitions

If the student spells a word correctly or gets the correct answer, he/she can move a checker.

Multiple choice questions

3. Make an answer key for each set of checkers. Number the answers to correspond to the questions. Color code the answer sheet.
4. Laminate the checkers and place them with the answer key in a Ziploc bag.
5. Store game pieces in a labeled file folder.

When the students play the game, they turn the checkers upside down on the checkerboard. As each student makes a move, he/she turns over the checker, reads the question, and answers it. If the answer is correct, the student takes his/her turn. If the answer is incorrect, the student loses a turn.

If you want an easier method, just use the regular checkers and make question cards. When each person takes a turn, he/she flips one question card and gives the answer. If the answer is correct, the player can move. If the answer is incorrect, the player loses a turn. Rectangular cards are easiest to cut. You can type the questions with a computer and print them on labels. Place the labels on the cards and laminate. Number each card and provide an answer key.

This is also a fun way to practice spelling words. Place the spelling words on cards. One partner turns over a card and reads the word. The other spells the word. If the word is spelled correctly, the student can move a checker. Older students enjoy checkers. It makes school a little more exciting. Checker match can be used with any subject at any grade level.

Extending Checker Match

Design a new game. Design a three-dimensional checker-match game.

A checkerboard is a grid. It can be useful for graphing. It has real spaces and thus lends itself to mathematical spatial problems relative to distances within the area and volume if a three-dimensional arrangement is utilized. Design a game wherein correct answers to questions receive an assigned value based on adjacency to discrete squares assigned by you and your students.

Permit students to stack checkers one on top of the other wherein the values assigned to a correct response can be multiplied according to the number of checkers in a stack.

Pocket Cards (Figure 4.21)

If you have a series of questions that have answers, you are ready to make pocket cards. These cards are designed to give students immediate reinforcement of basic concepts. A student starts with a pocket that is filled with question cards. He/she looks at the first question or problem, which is written at the top of the card. The student determines the answer to the problem, then lifts the card. The answer can be printed on the lower half of the card or placed on the reverse side. When the student is finished, he/she shuffles the cards and returns them to the pocket.

Pocket cards are simple to construct.

Figure 4.21 Pocket cards

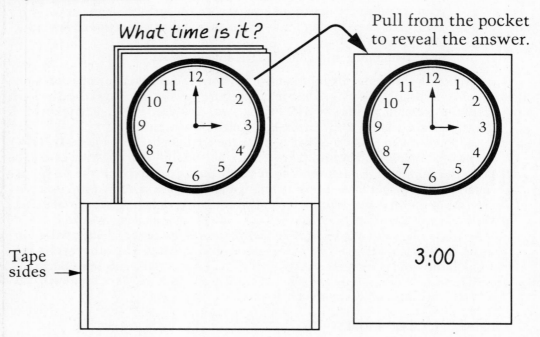

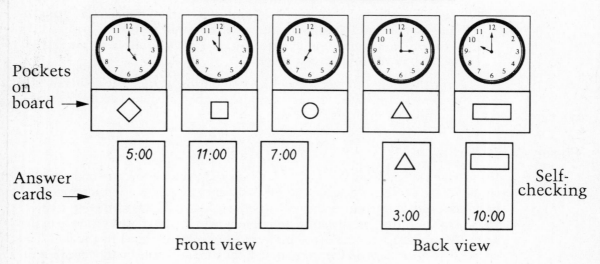

1. Take a $6\frac{1}{2}$-inch by 6-inch piece of tagboard or construction paper and fold a 2-inch pocket at the bottom of the paper. The size can vary to meet your needs. Library pockets also make wonderful pocket cards. They are sturdy and ready to use.
2. Secure the sides of the pocket with tape. Colored tape adds strength and a decorative touch.
3. Make a set of question cards to place in the pocket. Write or glue the question on the top portion of the card. The answer can be on the bottom of the card or on the back.
4. Laminate the pocket and each card. Use a razor blade or X-acto knife to cut a slit on the pocket. *(Note: Use caution when using an X-acto knife.)*
5. Store pocket cards in a labeled folder.

If you would like to make an action bulletin board, you can put the questions on the pockets and staple the pocket cards to the bulletin board. Then make a set of answer cards that can be placed in the pockets. Self-checking can be used by placing a matching dot both on the pocket and on the back of the answer card.

Extending Pocket Cards

Design a pocket-card deck for: What temperature is it? What degree is it? What kind of angle is it (acute, right)? What month is it?

Thumbprint Cards (Figure 4.22)

Thumbprint pocket cards are also wonderful to use with students. They are similar to pocket cards, but offer students multiple-choice answers.

1. Make a pocket card from a piece of tagboard 6 1/2 inches by 6 inches. Fold up a 2-inch flap. This will give you plenty of room to hold a set of index cards. The size may vary to meet your needs.
2. On the bottom of the pocket card draw three finger-shaped prints where you place the letters A, B, or C.
3. Write or glue a question and three answers on each 3-inch by 5-inch index card. The answers can be coded A, B, or C or placed in the A, B, or C position.
4. Near the bottom of the index card put a sticker or mark in the A, B, or C position of the correct answer.

The student reads the question, decides on the answer, puts a finger over the correct answer space, and lifts the card to see if he/she selected the correct answer.

You can use questions from workbooks or design your own. Thumbprint cards add a nice touch to basic drill work.

Figure 4.22 Thumbprint cards

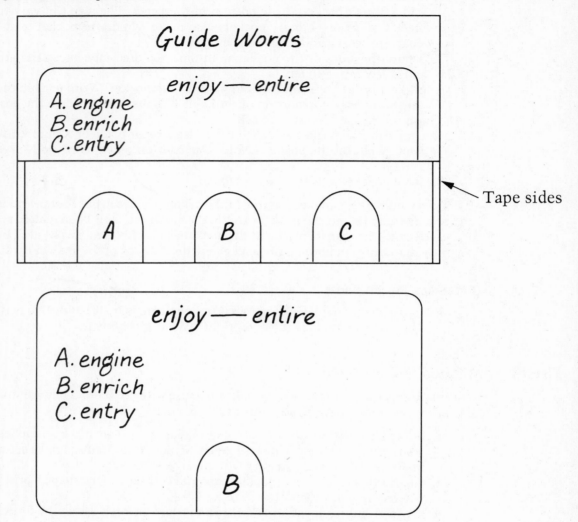

Pull the card from the pocket
to reveal the answer.

File-Folder Match (Figure 4.23)

Pocket cards can be incorporated into file folders. File-folder match games are fun to use, simple to maintain, and easy to store. Students can take them to their desks to use instead of workbook pages. They are fun to use because students manipulate and sort the materials. Since the games are self-correcting, students can see immediately if they understand the material. File-folder match games

Figure 4.23 File-folder match

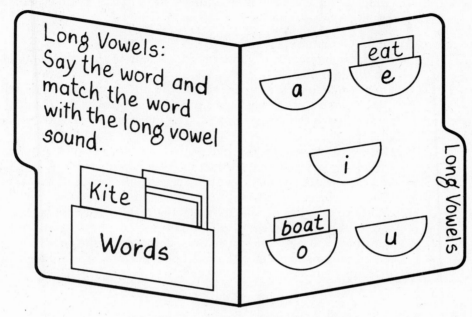

A self-checking sticker or letter
can be placed on the back of
each word card.

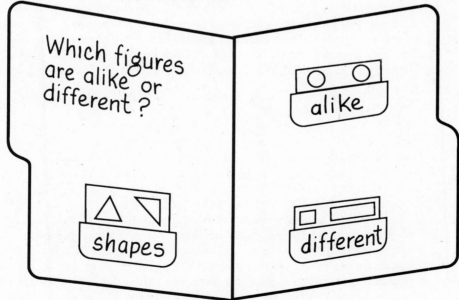

can be developed for all subjects and grade levels. Students can match parts of speech, guide words, math problems, punctuation marks, periods of history, or vocabulary. Look in workbooks to get ideas.

1. Design a matching game.
2. Place the name of the game on the outside of the folder and label the tab of the folder.
3. On the inside of the folder include the directions for the game.
4. Glue a library pocket or tape a piece of tagboard to the inside flap of a folder. Leave the top side open. The question cards will be placed in this pocket.
5. On the other side of the folder, place answer pockets. Answer pockets can be any size, but $2\frac{1}{2}$-inch by 2-inch cards work well. These are places in which students will insert the answers and check to see if they are correct.
6. Self-checking can be added by placing matching stickers on the back side of the question cards and on the front of the answer pockets.
7. Laminate the cards and the folders. Cut a slit in the top of each pocket so the cards can be slipped into the pockets while the student plays the matching game.

Rubber-Band Cards (Figure 4.24)

Rubber-band cards are matching games. Anything that has a question and a correct answer can be made into a rubber-band card. A student matches the question on the left side of the card to the answer on the right side by stretching a rubber band or a piece of elastic from the question to the answer. The answer can be checked by turning over the card. A line is drawn between the answer and the question. The rubber band should cover the line.

To make a rubber-band card, use poster board or a half of a file folder.

1. Write, type, or glue the questions on the left side of the folder and the answers on the right side.
2. Cut out a $\frac{1}{4}$-inch V-shaped notch next to each question and answer.
3. On the back side draw a light pencil line between the question and answer. Check it with the rubber band. If the line is correct, remove the rubber band and use a metal-edged ruler and a thin permanent marker to darken the line.
4. Place a title on the front of the card.
5. Type and save the directions on the computer so they can be printed and used on the other rubber-band cards. Place the directions on the front of the card.
6. Laminate the card and cut out the notches.
7. For convenience, you can store the cards and rubber bands in Ziploc bags and put the games in a labeled folder.

Figure 4.24 Rubber-band cards

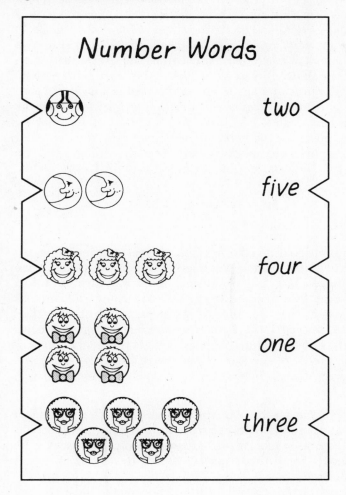

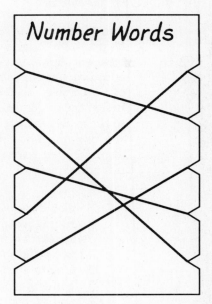

Self-checking is on the back. Rubberband lines should match answer lines.

Back view

Rubber-band cards can be made by using pictures, vocabulary words, and/or matching questions from workbooks. Rubber-band cards work well for fact and opinion questions or even guide words. The possibilities are endless.

If you use rubber bands, you need various sizes. You can also purchase elastic cord that can be cut into various lengths. Elastic cord does not fly as far as rubber bands in the classroom; you might as well keep temptation to a minimum.

You can also make double rubber-band cards. The easiest way to make a double rubber-band card is to cut a folder in half vertically so you have two $5\frac{1}{2}$-inch pieces. This makes four drill activities and allows the tagboard to be a little stronger, so the card does not bend under the stress of the rubber bands.

Place your questions, answers, directions, and labels on the front side. You will notch through both layers of file folder. Now comes the tricky part. With both flaps together, mark the answer lines on the back of the second flap instead of directly on the back of the question flap. Be sure you mark the answers in pencil first and test the card with rubber bands. If everything is in place, draw the lines with permanent marker.

When you are ready to make the second set of questions, turn the file folder inside out. The smaller cards are a nice size to handle. They are stronger and you can find rubber bands to fit. They also double the amount of drill work for the same cost of lamination.

FILE-FOLDER GAMES

File folders are perfect for game boards and other creative-learning activities (see Figure 4.25). Brightly colored file folders are attractive and durable. They open onto a student's desk to make a large playing surface. They fold together into a compact size for easy storage. They can be decorated and laminated. The tabs can be labeled so the games are easy to find. All game pieces can be attached inside the folder, making games portable. Directions can be laminated directly to the folder surface, so they do not get lost. File folders are relatively inexpensive and may be available as school supplies. (Check with the office secretary. She may even give you her used ones.) If you have never made a file-folder game, it is time to start.

1. Design a pathway using a variety of colored dots or stickers. You can also draw creative pathways with permanent markers. Add the traditional board game phrases such as lose a turn, go back two spaces, take an extra turn, move ahead three spaces, and/or free space. You can even include a shortcut.
2. Create a set of game cards that relate to the content or skill you are going to teach. If the pathway is generic, you can interchange the cards and the game boards, allowing for more flexibility.
3. Include answer keys for each set of cards. Answer keys can be easily identified by drawing around the edge of the card with a marker or by putting a colored dot around the edge of the card.
4. Write a set of directions for the game. Include the number of players, how to determine who starts the game, how to play, and how to get to the finish line. Directions can be laminated to the inside of the game folder or placed in the Ziploc bag with the playing pieces. It is best not to put the directions on the outside of the folder, because the students may need to refer to them when they are playing the game.
5. Label the tab and decorate the front of the file folder. If you have a series of file-folder games, number the tabs. Rubber numbers work

Figure 4.25 File-folder games

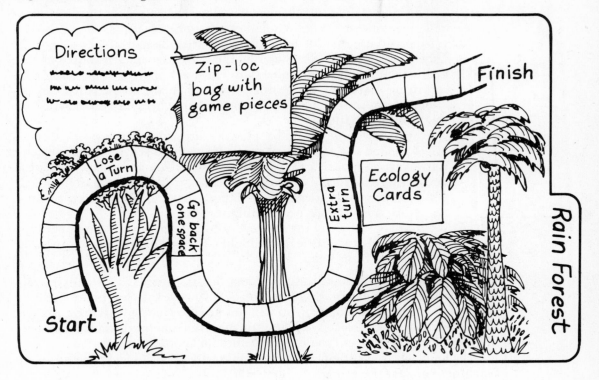

well. The numbers will be helpful for students in finding or returning the folder games.

6. Laminate the file folder, directions, and all cards that will be used in the game.

7. Collect all the playing pieces, spinners, and/or dice and put them in a quart-size Ziploc freezer bag.

8. Staple the back of the Ziploc bag to the inside of the folder near an edge. If the game is attached to the outside of the folder, it will be torn when placing the game in and out of the filing cabinet. Put a piece of clear contact paper or tape over the ends of the staples. When students play the game, they can flip the ziploc bag off the game board.

If you feel you do not have the time to create file-folder learning games, look around your classroom for old workbooks or drill sheets. File-folder games can be made with any drill sheet or workbook page. It just takes a little ingenuity, the temptation to move away from drill sheets, and the desire to make learning exciting and meaningful for students. File-folder games can also be purchased from teacher supply stores. The basic part of the folder is already constructed. You just personalize each folder for your class and add self-checking. If you want to cut your copying and grading time to a minimum, invest in some file folders.

1. You will need two copies of any workbook or drill sheet you wish to convert into a file-folder game. One copy can be used for the directions and questions, the other cut and used for answer cards.
2. It is best to use one file folder for each drill sheet.
3. Label the tab of the file folder and put the page and/or source of the drill sheet. The page numbers are extremely helpful in finding and returning materials to the file. Graphics, pictures, or titles can be clipped from the original drill sheet and attached with a glue stick to the front of the file folder.
4. On the inside of the file folder, glue the directions in a prominent spot.
5. Make a game out of the drill sheet. Poke-and-discover cards, concentration games, puzzle cards, window folders, sort-and-check activities, wrap ups, rubber-band cards, pocket cards, milk-box computer games, and light-box cards are game techniques that can be used to turn your seat work into a hands-on learning session.
6. Incorporate self-checking into every file folder game. Remember this is drill work. Students learn from this. Expect them to make mistakes and to learn from them.

Yes, it takes time to make the file folders, but it is worth it. Normally, teachers spend hours each day grading workbooks. If you use the time making games the first year a book is adopted, you will not need to grade a workbook page in that content area for at least five years. You may find that this is much more productive. The next year you could make games for another subject area.

Teachers who have tried file-folder games and activities feel positive about teaching. They use their time more constructively and they are more efficient in meeting the individual needs of their students.

How will the students respond? Students in your class will begin to be enthusiastic about school and seat work. Learning is more fun when you can make choices and be more responsible. Students will spend more time on task because they will enjoy learning. Students will have the opportunity to work with others, helping each other with directions and mastering the material.

Parents will have fewer daily papers to correct in the evening with their children, but they will have happy children who are excited about school. Creative and productive writing assignments, reading, and creative projects will become a part of your educational program. Parents will find these activities more rewarding and meaningful. Tests and evaluation checklists will keep parents informed of their child's progress.

LIGHT BOX AND FILE-FOLDER ELECTRIC BOARDS

As you begin to personalize instruction in all aspects of the curriculum, you will need tools to assist you in designing student-centered learning experiences. The light box may be just the activity to involve the student in a fun and challenging way. A light box is used in conjunction with file-folder electric boards that you can make to specifically meet the needs and interests of your students. When the student touches one probe to the correct answer, "sparks will fly," or at least a light will turn on telling the student he/she is correct.

If you plan to make a light box, you will need to go to an electronics store to purchase the following supplies:

> AA batteries (four)
>
> battery holder for batteries
>
> lamp assembly that holds a flashlight bulb
>
> lamp (light bulb)
>
> set of probes
>
> electrical tape or a soldering iron and solder

Once you have your parts, it only takes about 15 minutes to assemble them. A diagram has been provided in Figure 4.26. You can strip and twist the wires and tape them with electrical tape. Soldering works best for keeping connections together for a long time. If you do not have a soldering iron, ask the shop teacher, the janitor, a neighbor with a garage full of tools, or a local TV repair person. "Seek and you shall find." This person may help you make the entire light box. The light box can be housed in a Band-Aid can, an oatmeal box, a frosting can, or a stuffed animal. Just remember that you will need to have access to the batteries. They wear out! File down the tips of the probes until they are dull. Sharp points will damage your file-folder electric boards.

Now that you have the light box, you will need to construct a file-folder electric board. (Figures 4.27A and 4.27B.) Assemble the following materials before you get started:

> file folder (colored if possible)
>
> masking tape
>
> aluminum foil (heavy duty works well) or aluminum pie pans or TV-dinner pans
>
> markers
>
> pictures (optional)
>
> vinyl numbers or letters (optional)
>
> lamination tissue
>
> paper punch
>
> X-acto knife
>
> pencil
>
> scissors
>
> double-sided tape

Figure 4.26 Light box

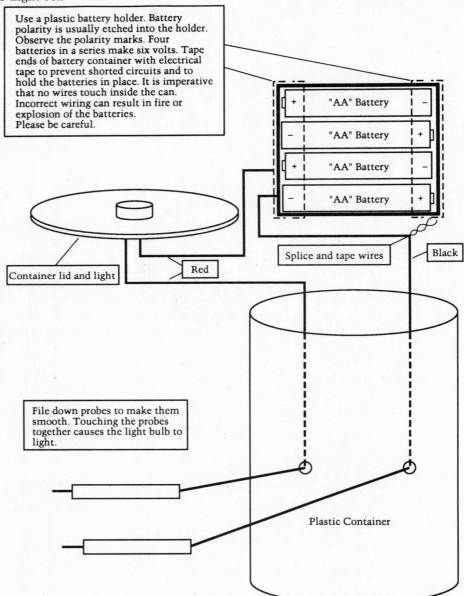

Use a plastic battery holder. Battery polarity is usually etched into the holder. Observe the polarity marks. Four batteries in a series make six volts. Tape ends of battery container with electrical tape to prevent shorted circuits and to hold the batteries in place. It is imperative that no wires touch inside the can. Incorrect wiring can result in fire or explosion of the batteries.
Please be careful.

"AA" Battery

"AA" Battery

"AA" Battery

"AA" Battery

Splice and tape wires

Black

Container lid and light

Red

File down probes to make them smooth. Touching the probes together causes the light bulb to light.

Plastic Container

1. On the front side of the file folder, print or glue a series of questions and answers. Place the questions near one edge of the folder and the answers near another, leaving room for a paper-punch hole. You can use workbook pages, math problems, logic puzzles, shapes, or diagrams. You just need something with a question and an answer. You can also use stickers and designs to add an artistic touch.

Figure 4.27A Electric board

Outside view of folder

Homonyms

● you   hare ●

● hair   pair ●

● hi   bare ●

● bear   high ●

● wait   ewe ●

● pear   weight ●

2. Label the tab of the file folder and place a number on the tab if you are making a series of folders.

3. Open the file folder and, on the inside of the front cover, make pencil marks between the question and the correct answer.

4. Laminate the file folder before you tape the aluminum strips to it. If you need to "rewire" your folder you can pull off the strips without tearing the folder.

5. Punch holes near the edge of the folder for each question and answer.

6. Cut a ½-inch strip of aluminum foil or the foil pie pan the length of the first pencil line. This needs to be thinner than the masking tape. If you use foil, double or triple the weight of the foil over the hole. Better yet, cut a small square from the aluminum pie pan and place it between the hole and the foil strip. This will prevent the students from wearing out the folder by placing holes in the foil with the probes.

7. Place small pieces of tape at the ends of the aluminum foil to anchor the strips to the folder.

8. Cut a long piece of tape and place it over the foil strips. Make sure to

Figure 4.27B Electric board

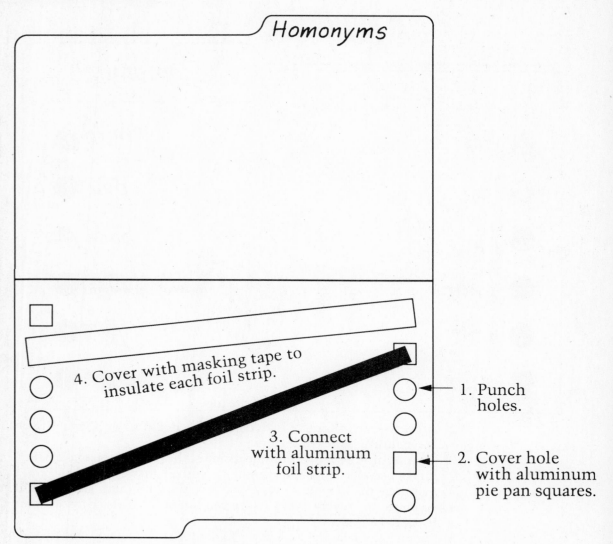

cover the foil completely; this acts as the insulation. Trim with your X-acto knife. *(Note: Use caution when using an X-acto knife.)*

9. Turn over the file folder and use the probes from the light box to test the question and answer. If you have a good connection, the light will shine.

10. Go to the next pencil line and continue the process until each question is linked to its answer. Remember to check each strip before you progress to the next question. Repairs are much easier if you catch them early.

11. Close the folder with double-sided tape.

Students love file-folder electric boards and light boxes. Upper elementary and middle-school students can even make their own. It is a wonderful way to blend a science lesson on electricity with any other subject. If students give a report, have them make a file-folder electric board to quiz their classmates. They can include vocabulary words, basic facts, or map skills. The school secretary may even have some used file folders that can be recycled for this educational activity.

Bet you can't make just one!

Extending the Electric Board

—Design and construct a three-dimensional electric board. This can be accomplished by joining four electric boards together or using a small cardboard box. The aluminum foil can be connected from one face to any other face (or to the same face). This allows for more diverse responses and greater complexity.

Milk-Carton Computer

You will need a clean half-gallon or gallon milk carton, a cardboard strip, and some blank cards to construct a milk-carton computer as shown in Figure 4.28.

1. Carefully open the top of the milk carton to gain access to the inside.
2. Cut a rectangular "input" opening about 3 inches below the top and an "output" opening about 3 inches above the bottom. Make the openings large enough for the cards to go in and out easily.
3. Cut a tagboard strip (file folders are wonderful) to the width of the input and output openings on the milk carton.
4. Tape the strip to the outside of the top slot. Thread the tagboard strip through the milk box and out the bottom slot. Curve the strip slightly on the inside. Send a card through the slot to see if it slides out or if it gets stuck on the inside. If it gets stuck, adjust the strip until the card slides through the computer with ease. When you reach this point, bend the strip over the outside edge of the bottom slot, trim, and tape it in place.
5. Close the milk carton and cover it with contact paper. Cut out the slots with an X-acto knife. *(Note: Use caution when using an X-acto knife.)* Make sure you cover the milk carton so that you can get into it if you need to make repairs. Place a set of directions on the milk-carton computer.
6. Write a question on one side of each card and the answer on the other side (upside down). See the example in Figure 4.28. You might want to try sets of cards on shapes, colors, formulas, rock identification, math facts, vocabulary words, weather symbols, constellations, and so forth. Label or number each set of cards so that if a card gets lost, it can easily be returned to the proper set.
7. Have students place the cards (question side up) in the input opening of the computer. The cards will come out the output opening, answer side up. Pretty neat!

Figure 4.28 Milk-carton computer

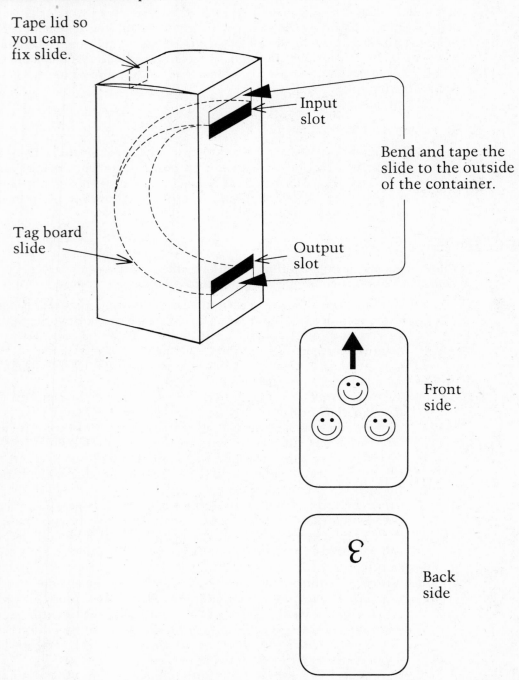

Tape lid so you can fix slide.

Input slot

Bend and tape the slide to the outside of the container.

Tag board slide

Output slot

Front side

Back side

8. Laminate the set of cards and place the cards in a Ziploc bag.
9. Store sets of cards in labeled file folders.
10. Challenge your students to make their own individual milk-carton computers and input/output cards.

Foam Computer

Foam computers are easy for students to use and provide immediate reinforcement. A student inserts a set of question cards into the foam computer. The student reads the question, then presses the foam in front of the selected answer to see if the answer is correct. The front card is then removed and placed at the back of the set of cards. See Figure 4.29.

Materials needed:

12- by 6- by 4-inch cube of foam

file folders or poster board

adhesive dots

ruler

electric knife or bread knife

pictures

marking pen

1. Draw a line vertically down the center of the 6-inch piece of foam so you have two 3-inch sections. Cut a slit with an electric knife or a bread knife about $1\frac{1}{2}$ inches deep.
2. Starting at the left side, mark one 4-inch section and four 2-inch sections. Cut each section to the depth of $1\frac{1}{2}$ inches.
3. Make a set of cards to fit the computer. File folders or poster board can be used. Each card can be divided into a question section (the 4-inch area) and the answer sections (the four 2-inch areas). Write the question and answers on the top half of the card. On the bottom of the section(s) with the correct answer(s) place a sticker(s) or dot(s). You can have more than one correct answer.
4. You can use both sides of the card.
5. After you are finished, insert the cards into the long slot. Push on the foam to check for the correct answer(s).
6. Laminate each card.
7. Place each set of cards in a labeled file folder.

Cards can be sectioned and laminated, but left blank. Students can then write on the cards with washable markers to make their own cards. Students can even make smaller foam computers for their personal use.

Do-Box Centers

These are shoeboxes that contain activities. You or your students can gather materials for a particular theme and place them in a shoe box. The shoe box

Figure 4.29 Foam computer

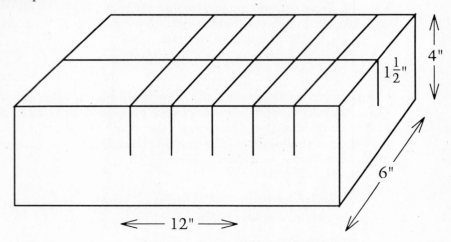

Cut foam block with a knife.

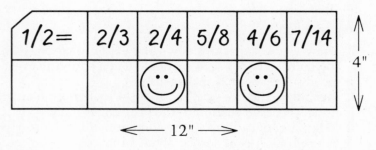

Computer card for
foam computer

To double each card put questions
and answers on both sides.

can be divided into compartments and activity cards can be placed in each compartment. Students can then pull out the box and select an activity card to conduct a particular activity. Some do-box themes might include The War of 1812, Christopher Columbus, Apollo, or Global Warming. Try constructing do boxes. Your students will love them.

Action Bulletin Boards

Finally, let's consider the aid that every teacher uses (and abuses)—the bulletin board. Many school bulletin boards are merely that—boards for bulletins, made by teachers mainly to please other adults. We like to refer to bulletin boards designed for children as "action" bulletin boards. They have the following characteristics:

They often present children with a problem in the form of a question.

They involve the children by using task cards or by having the children contribute to the bulletin board.

They are continually changed as children perceive that they need changing.

They are often tied to an interest center.

Are your bulletin boards action bulletin boards? We've provided an example of real action bulletin boards in Figure 4.30 (page 192). Compare it to existing bulletin boards!

COOPERATIVE LEARNING

Cooperative learning is a set of instructional strategies used by a heterogeneously selected group of students to study assigned material in a cooperative way where all members of the group are responsible for the maximum learning of others. Cooperative learning as outlined by Johnson and Johnson (1988) includes positive interdependence of group members, individual accountability, and shared leadership and responsibility. The teacher is responsible for teaching social skills, observing each group, and giving feedback in relationship to the group process. Each group analyzes its effectiveness.

Students are grouped according to specific guidelines. High-, medium-, and low-ability students are placed in the same group as well as task-oriented and nontask-oriented students. Racial background, economic status, and physical attributes are also considered in the grouping process. Major emphasis is placed on helping others learn and on working cooperatively. Specialized training is necessary before implementing this form of cooperative learning.*

Jigsaw teaching is a form of cooperative learning that engages students in the learning process. It incorporates various skills such as research, problem solving, decision making, organization, and public speaking. It allows students to work independently as well as in groups. Students examine small pieces of information until they become experts. Then in small groups or in one large group, the students pool their ideas or share their information. A large project can be conquered in a short period of time. Each student is responsible for collecting data, working problems, finding information, or assembling materials to complete a portion of a project. Students are actively involved in the learning process and feel a strong sense of accomplishment.

---

*For more information, contact David Johnson, Roger Johnson, or Pat Roy at the Cooperative Learning Center, 202 Pattee Hall, University of Minnesota, Minneapolis, Minnesota 55455.

Figure 4.30 Action bulletin board

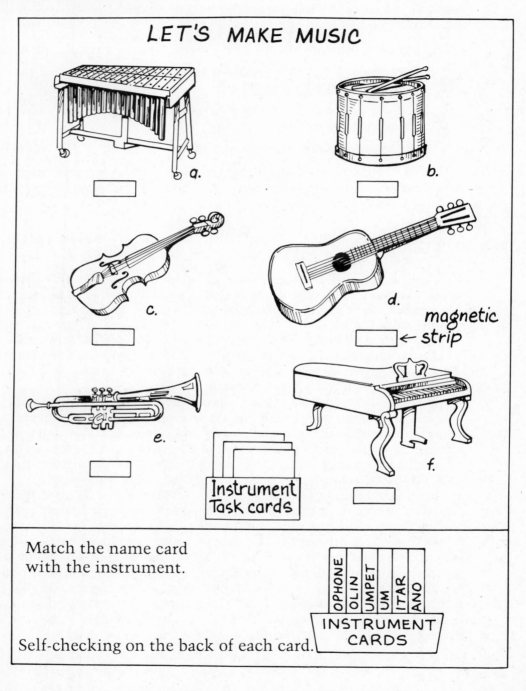

Jigsaw teaching can be used in any subject area, or for any topic that can be divided into parts. It is a strategy that can introduce new topics, develop concepts, reinforce skills, encourage problem solving, or summarize lessons. The teacher becomes the facilitator. The students put the pieces together. With the help of all, the total picture emerges. The following jigsaw activities can be easily adapted for use in elementary or middle-school classes.

Clues for All—Language Arts and Critical Thinking

Mysteries   Students can be given character roles in a mystery. Each student arrives at the scene of the crime in costume, with props, and in character. As they enter the setting (an old house in your community), the mystery unfolds. Each student takes part in the mystery and reveals clues to the solution. At the end of the enactment, the mystery is solved.

Character Sketches   After reading a story, each group of students could be responsible for writing a character sketch to reveal the personality traits, physical attributes, and hidden motives of a selected character to the class.

Anthologies   Each student could interview residents of a community to research local legends, rope-skipping rhymes, or historical events that could be compiled into a class anthology. This could also be done with poems, short stories, cartoons, or myths.

Newscasts   Students apply for jobs as newscasters, such as anchor, special interest, sports, entertainment, or meteorologist. Each news team presents a 10-minute weekly newscast. Every day a different news team would be responsible for the news. They could compete for ratings and be paid accordingly through a classroom mini-economy. This is a great way to learn current events and to gain experience in public speaking.

Parts of Speech   Allow small teams of students to present parts of speech to the class. The students would be responsible for teaching the lesson, providing drill and practice sheets, devising a test, and assisting fellow students in learning the material. It really works, especially with upper elementary or middle-school students who think they already know everything.

Story Analysis   Different teams of students could be responsible for reporting on one element of a story such as plot, character, setting, or theme. This encourages students to focus on one aspect, and as a team the students do an excellent job of story analysis.

Young Authors Convention   Each student researches an author of choice and reads one of the author's novels. At the Young Author's Convention each author arrives in costume and must remain in character. The authors meet, have tea, introduce themselves, relay some personal information, and tell the group about their most recent novels or books.

Ask the Experts—Science or Social Studies

Current Articles   Select articles from subject-specific magazines or newspapers that relate to current science topics or political events. Long articles can be divided into sections, with each student becoming an expert on his/her part. Students write questions about information they do not know. A science seminar or press conference can be held where students ask each other questions to discover the "rest of the story." Two articles with opposing viewpoints can also be used to keep the conversation lively.

Teamwork—Mathematics: Problem Solving

Problem-Solving Teams   Divide students into teams of four or five students each. Each team should have a leader. Pass out a set of 10 to 15 problem-solving cards. The leader writes the number of each card down the side of the paper and then makes an answer chart. Within the specific time limit, 20 to 30 minutes, the team works as many of the cards as possible. The leader is responsible for passing out the cards to team members and recording the answers. Two different team members should solve each problem. If the solutions match, the problem would be considered correct. If the solutions do not match, the leader would give the card to another person on the team to solve. At the end of the 20 to 30 minutes, the team with the most correct answers wins. After using this activity, students will beg for problem-solving days.

New Material   Teams of students can be given a new chapter or a set of new math problems and asked to help each other discover what they know and what they do not know. At the end of the time period, each group can discuss with the teacher what areas need to be emphasized and what areas can be eliminated or reviewed quickly. This saves a tremendous amount of time and makes the students more responsible for the instruction.

United We Stand—Social Studies and Research Skills

United States   Each week students can research information about one or two states. Research topics may include, for example, natural resources, employment, historical events, monuments, writers, musicians, national parks, topography, and artists. Students select the questions they want to research. On a designated day, the students form into a seminar group to share information. A secretary, usually the teacher or a student, collects the information and makes a summary sheet of the findings. Reference books should be available for the students.

American Indians   Have groups of students research different aspects of the life-style of a group of American Indians such as the Woodland or Plains Indians. Groups of students would find information related to food, clothing, housing, and tools. As a culminating activity, students could combine their research findings to illustrate a mural. As students study each type of American Indian tribe, they can make a different mural and then compare the murals.

Time Lines   Students can research a selected topic, such as inventors, scientists, artists, political events, family history, and wars, and construct a time line to show the events. Time lines can be overlapped to show the relationship between historical and scientific events. Students can also be given an event, such as the Russian missile crisis, to research. After they find information about the event, they can explain the event to the class and place it on a class time line. A computer program, such as *TimeLiner* by Tom Snyder Productions, can be used to produce computer-generated time lines.

Culture Wheels   Each student can select a country to investigate. He or she uses photographs or draws pictures to illustrate the life-style, customs, clothing, religion, housing, economy, family life, and government of a country. Students learn about the different cultures by viewing a display of the culture wheels and listening to individual presentations given by other students.

Folders   A series of folders can be organized that contain informational readings, articles, stories, or pamphlets to enrich a selected topic. It helps to number each folder. Students can select folders to gain background information on a variety of topics. After students have had time to read several folders, the class can meet to exchange information.

Artifact Boxes   The Artifact Box Exchange Network (University of Connecticut, 231 Glenbrook Drive, Storrs Hall, Room 28, U-7, Storrs, CT 06268) provides an excellent opportunity for students to research, investigate, and solve a puzzle. Students collect 25 artifacts from the community, such as maps, memorabilia, brochures, soil samples, manufactured items, rocks, and newspaper clippings, and write clues about each item. The artifacts are put in a box and sent to a group of students somewhere in the United States who are also participating in the Artifact Box Exchange. Your class then receives an artifact box from a mystery community. The students examine each clue by using maps, atlases, and other reference materials to determine the source of the artifact box. Each artifact serves as a clue. Clue by clue, the students piece together the puzzle and discover the town where the artifact box was assembled. Your students then communicate with the students who developed the box. What a fantastic way to use reference materials and to learn about other communities in the United States.

CONTROVERSIAL ISSUES

Creative teachers do not skirt the ethical issues. They realize that education can help children recognize and identify dangerous situations and can help prepare students to deal with them. Rather than simply presenting one side of an issue or just its emotional aspects, creative teachers begin with an issue and have the children present as many sides of it as possible. Creative teachers do not choose sides; they allow children to make decisions so that when they are confronted with real life, they will make wise judgments.

One effective way to study controversial issues is to create controversy folders. Select articles from local newspapers, state publications, and national magazines that relate to a controversial issue you want your class to study. Find articles that discuss differing points of view. Assemble the articles in a folder, putting the pro articles on one side and the con articles on the other. Mark each article accordingly. Key points can be underlined. Students can read the articles and make their own decisions. Students can write position papers or defend a point of view through class debates. Some examples follow.

Issue 1: Smoking

Close-up

1. The average life expectancy of a 25-year-old male nonsmoker is six-and-one-half years greater than that of a man who smokes one or more packs a day.
2. The death rate from lung cancer is ten times greater for cigarette smokers than it is for nonsmokers.
3. Cigarette smoking is a habit among a minority of adults and even a smaller minority of teenagers.

POINTS TO PONDER

Will you smoke? Why or why not? Does smoking make you more popular? Does smoking make you more sophisticated? How expensive is smoking? Do nonsmokers have the right to stop smokers from smoking in public places?

Additional information for Issue 1 can be obtained from the National Tobacco Institute, Raleigh, NC 27614; and the American Cancer Society, 219 East 42nd St., New York, NY 10017.

Issue 2: Drugs

Close-up

1. Drug use is increasing among younger children (although it varies widely from one school to another).
2. No single cause or set of conditions clearly leads to drug dependency; it occurs in all social and economic classes.

3. Most states have laws requiring instruction in drug education, but most instruction occurs too late in a child's life.
4. Narcotic drugs include some of the most valuable medicines known as well as some of the most abused.
5. A drug is a medicine that helps to make sick people well, but it can also make well people sick.
6. Never take drugs that belong to someone else. They can make you sicker.
7. Some things look like drugs, but they are actually poison. They are marked with either the sign of the skull and crossbones (old method) or the snake—(SIOP) (new method).
8. Drugs are for sick people.

POINTS TO PONDER

Cite alternative ways of getting "high" that are not self-destructive. State wise uses of drugs and problems in the use of over-the-counter drugs.

Additional information for Issue 2 is available from the Drug Enforcement Administration, Department of Justice, Washington, DC 20537; The Drug Abuse Council, Inc., 1828 L St., NW, Washington, DC 20036; and National Institute on Alcohol Abuse and Alcoholism, 5600 Fishers Lane, Rockville, MD 20852.

Issue 3: Death

Close-up

1. Death is one part of the cycle of living things.
2. Death is not the same thing as going to sleep.
3. Funerals are mechanisms used by society to cope with death.

POINTS TO PONDER

What happens when a loved one dies? Have you ever had a pet die? How do burial customs in different countries compare?

Additional information for Issue 3 is available from The Last Dance, 3rd edition, 1991. Lyne DeSpelder and Albert Strickland, Mayfield Publishing Co., 285 Hamilton Ave., Palo Alto, CA 94301; and Death Studies Journal, Hemisphere Publishing Corp., 79 Madison Ave., Suite 1110, New York, NY 10016.

Issue 4: Sexuality

Close-up

1. An understanding of basic reproduction is vital for the continuation of our species.

2. A misunderstanding of sexuality leads to major problems in the intermediate grades, including sexually transmitted diseases, pregnancy, birth-control problems, and negative feelings about sexuality.

POINTS TO PONDER

Why are there variations in growth of secondary sex characteristics in children (breast development, underarm hair, menstrual cycle)?

What are some misconceptions about reproduction, nocturnal emissions, and masturbation?

What physical and emotional problems are associated with sexual development in children?

What problems are associated with increased recognition and interest in the opposite sex? Do the changing roles in dating and family life result in confusion for adolescents? If so, what problems are encountered?

Additional information for Issue 4 is available from National Guidelines for Sexuality Education, SIECUS, 130 W. 42nd St., Suite 2500, New York, NY 10036; and *Sexuality Education: Theory and Practice*, 2nd edition, 1991, Clint Bruess and Jerrold Greenberg, Macmillan Publishing Co., New York, NY 10016.

External/Internal Rewards

Briefly described, external rewards are external kudos that are awarded to individuals (or schools) for a job well done. Monies, prizes, awards, badges, and plaques are given to students (or schools) for outstanding attendance records, high test scores, high grades, super attitudes, and so on. These are overt acts designed to provide incentives for obtaining the fruits of acquired learning. It is felt that these rewards will motivate learning.

Internal rewards emanate from within the individual. The child is taught to be responsible for his or her own progress. The child is taught that one improves oneself through continual self-examination, searching for one's own strengths and weaknesses for the purpose of self-improvement.

Internal rewards are the development of one's own self-concept wherein one learns to control one's own behavior and destiny. Each is responsible to himself. This involves a need for self-discipline, self-denial, and the self-realization that attitude is integral to one's performance and that success comes from continual application to study and work. Inherent in this process is the need to persevere with patience, to be undaunted by failures, and to profit from the opinions and mistakes of others. The product of internal growth is the development of one's self-concept leading to a creative, innovative, independent thinker who knows herself and the society within which she must operate—and can maintain a satisfactory balance between the two.

POINTS TO PONDER

Which approach is best? Would your choice be good for everyone? Are there other choices? What system of rewards would you recommend? Describe them.

Clarifying Values

All of the issues previously mentioned, and you can think of others, relate to values and their clarification. Children have certain experiences as they grow and learn, from which general guides to behavior will evolve. These guides tend to give direction to life and may be called values. Our values show what we tend to do with our time and energy.

Choosing values involves seven requirements in three categories.

Choosing a Value

1. It must be the result of free choice.
2. It must be chosen from among alternatives.
3. It must be chosen after thoughtful consideration of the consequences of each alternative.

Prizing a Value

4. We must be happy with the choice.
5. We must publicly affirm our choice.

Acting with Our Value

6. We must do something with the choice throughout life—read about it, form new friendships, or spend money on the choice we value.
7. We must use the value in several different situations and at several different times.

Through these steps, we define the values that guide us.

Values-clarification activities that creative teachers use fall into several categories, including:

1. Rank Ordering: Present a situation and three alternatives. Have each of them ranked from 1 to 3 by each child. Then discuss the rankings in an open and nonjudgmental fashion. Here is an example:

    If you had $15 million to spend, how would you rank the following as ways to spend it?

    Clean up polluted rivers and streams.
    Develop a new form of energy for fuel.
    Send an astronaut to Mars.

2. Values Continuum: Copy the illustration below on the blackboard (Figure 4.31). Note the continuum line drawn between the polarized positions on the smoking issue. Suggest that each student mark on the continuum line where he or she stands on the issue. Then discuss choices. Select another issue that can be polarized and repeat the procedure.

Figure 4.31 Values continuum

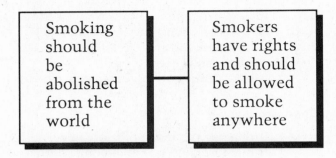

3. I'm Proud: Have each student tell you what he or she is proud of. Suggest a variety of situations such as:

What did you do in English class today that you are proud of?
What have you done recently for a friend that you are proud of?
Which experiment that you completed are you proud of?

4. I'm Successful: Have each child prepare a success chart on which each tells how he or she helped somebody, learned something new, gained respect from people, did something his or her family was proud of.
5. My Strengths: Have children tell each other what their strengths are, and then have each child prepare a list of his or her strengths.
6. I Think for Myself: Have children list times when other people decide for them, times when they are allowed to think for themselves, times when they are *not* allowed to think for themselves, and times when they *must* think for themselves. Then ask them, "When are you allowed to think for yourself in school?"

Write down some feelings or needs of others to think about when thinking for yourself.

POINTS TO PONDER

What accomplishments have you made in your teaching career that you are proud of?
What are your teaching strengths?
Select an issue of concern to you and place it on the value line. Ask your classmates to do likewise.

GAMES

Are you ready for Groovy Zoo, Quizmo, Animal Friends, Beat the Path, Word Pursuit, Who Am I?, Pollution Solution, The Survival Game, Animal Dominoes, Draw Me, Trapped, Glacierama, and Bogy? These are but a sampling of more than a hundred games that students and teachers have developed themselves. Games can be used to reinforce skills that have already been introduced, such as graphing and classifying. But games can also be used as motivational devices for the instruction of a skill, or even for evaluation purposes. Children enjoy solving problems and being involved in thinking activities by playing games. Games can also be used to reinforce the skills of socialization and interaction with peers through sharing, taking turns, and verbal interaction. Games can serve as one mechanism for the humanization and relaxation of the classroom atmosphere. Although some games are original, many educational games are patterned after popular commercial games. Many require paper and pencil only; others require a game board and game cards. We will present several examples; you will be able to think of many more. Some of the ideas and rules are explained on the next few pages, change them to fit your needs and the needs of your students. After you've got the idea, develop a game to reinforce the skill of measuring metrically or of reinforcing math facts.

Here are some examples:

1. Groovy Zoo (a classification game, invented by three third-graders!). You will need a file folder to make a playing board with a start, a finish, and a pathway of spaces, each space naming a typical animal characteristic; four or five model clay animals, such as a fish, a rabbit, a turtle, and a snake, to be used as counters by the players; and a numbered spinner.

   Each player takes one of the clay animals as a counter and places it on the playing board at the starting point. Each player spins a turn in the regular playing order. The number a player spins is the number of spaces he or she may advance if the clay animal has the characteristic named on the unit the player will land on; if the animal doesn't have that characteristic, then the player must stay where he or she is and wait for another turn. The first player to reach the finish wins.

2. Quizmo (a comparative observation game). You will need to make a set of animal-description cards. Each card will carry a good description of a certain animal, but will not name that animal. You will also need a different set of player cards. Player cards are pieces of manila board divided into 16 squares. Each square carries the name of an animal that is described in the set of description cards.

   One person is the "caller" for the game. The caller draws a description card from the deck and reads it; the player covers the name of the animal described. The first person to correctly cover four names in a horizontal, vertical, or diagonal row wins.

3. Who Am I? (a descriptive observation game). This game uses the playing board and spinner used in Groovy Zoo. But for each characteristic named on the front of the board, you will have to list the animals that have that characteristic on a separate sheet. No more than four should play this game at one time.

   The players decide on a playing order, then they spin in turn. Each player moves the number of spaces indicated by the spinner. When the player lands on a space, he or she must read the characteristic named there and then name an animal that has it. If the player cannot, he or she must go back to where he or she began the turn. Answers can be checked by referring to the answer sheet. The first one to reach the finish wins.

4. The Animal Game (an observing and ordering game). You will need a game board, a deck of 72 cards, and two or more players. Your game board should have the pictures of about 100 different animals on it. (You may also want to number the pictures and make a keyed list of the animals' names.) Each card in the deck should name one animal characteristic. Limit the total number of characteristics you use to about 30, and use them each twice or three times on different cards.

   Each player is dealt nine cards. The remainder of the deck is placed, face down, by the board, and the top card is placed face up beside the deck. Each player, in turn, takes the upturned card or the top card of the deck and adds it to his/her hand; then he/she may match a card with one of the different animals, or may discard that or another card onto the face-up card. When a player accumulates three cards that describe one of the animals on the board, the player may place those cards over the animal's picture (but only in turn!). The first player to "go out"—to get rid of all of his or her cards—wins.

5. Draw Me (an observing and inferring game). All that's needed for this game is a bit of imagination, an object or a picture, paper, and pencils. Pass out the pencils and paper to all of the players. Then, holding the object or picture so that no one can see it, describe it without naming any of its parts. Your description should be limited to how the object looks—its size, shape, color, texture, and so forth. The object of the game is to see who—if anyone—can correctly draw the object you are describing. Sound too easy? That's only because you haven't tried it!

6. Animal Dominoes (an observing and matching game). You'll need to make a set of at least twenty-eight animal-domino cards. Each card should be divided into equal halves, with each half carrying a picture of a mammal, bird, fish, amphibian, reptile, or insect (this is their relative value, in descending order). The domino cards should carry every possible combination of pictures—double mammals, mammal and bird, mammal and reptile, bird and insect, and so on.

   Seven of the cards should be dealt, face down, to each of the two to four players. The player with the highest double-mammal cards begins the game by placing the double face up at the center of the table. The player to his or her left must play a match or draw another card from the "bone pile" (the leftover cards). If the player still cannot play a match, he or she loses the turn. The players continue to match or draw until one player has matched all of his or her cards; that player wins.

BOOK KITS

Book kits are designed to supplement or replace basal reading textbooks. Each kit includes not only the appropriate book, but also the necessary accessories to go with it, which may include:

—computer diskettes

—videotapes

—cassette tapes

—filmstrips

—flannel-board shapes

Any book will work as long as you include the necessary ancillary materials. Each book kit should include the following components, contained in individual envelopes or file folders, when deemed appropriate:

reading assignments and discussion questions printed on 4-by-6-inch index cards. These questions can be discussed with a friend, teacher, or in small groups.

spelling words taken from the book

sequencing activities

games

art activities

creative investigations

puzzles

task cards

skillettes

activities using the spelling words that are designed to increase competence in pronunciation and in understanding of meanings

vocabulary words that are introduced in the book

vocabulary activities that are structured to provide help with word meanings

an evaluation question that is thought provoking and requires a creative answer

a culminating task-card activity

a supplemental list of books related to the book-kit theme

All materials for the book kit can be stored in a box or in a large folder. Include a pathway sheet to help direct students through the activities. Give students choices. As students progress through the book kit, they can check off the activities they have completed. At the end of each book kit, include an evaluation sheet so that students can tell you what they like and dislike about the book kit. This information is important, because it will help you make the kit more appealing to students and it will help you know what to include in other book kits.

To decorate the outside of the folder or box, photocopy the cover of the book being used. Add a touch of marker, and you have an attractive and informative cover. Also photocopy information about the author and the list of additional books written by the same author. Include this information on the outside of the folder or box.

Book kits can be used to reinforce and develop the same skills found in basal readers. And book kits allow the child to increase reading competency while having freedom of selection.

It takes approximately one to two weeks for a child to complete a book kit, working about one to one-and-one-half hours per school day. The greatest cost is in buying the books; however, many books are already in the school library.

As an example, let us use an intermediate-level paperback book, such as Scott O'Dell's *Island of the Blue Dolphins* (Boston: Houghton Mifflin, 1960).

Into a container such as a large file folder, a dress box, or cardboard box, you will need to place:

1. The book (You will need to read it first!) and all media materials related to this paperback book. Try locating records, films, filmstrips, and tapes for starters.
2. A pathway to guide the students through the book kit.

   —Number each activity.
   —Students can also choose from lists of optional activities as noted on the pathway.
   —Pathways are a way of recording progress.

3. A list of discussion questions relating to the book, placed on index cards.

   Why do you think Ramo thought of the red ship as a red whale?
   What are toyon bushes?

4. A list of spelling words from the book, such as:

   cricket, carcass, horizon, utensils, anchor, punish

5. A list of spelling activities to go with the words.

   A crossword puzzle using at least ten of the new words.
   Unscramble the message in this code. Some clues are provided:
   VJG (The) FQNRJKP RWTUWGB DA (by) VJG YCTTKQTU KP
   (in) ECPQGU OCPCIGCQ VQ HNGG NTQO VJKU FCPIGT

6. A list of vocabulary words from the book, with sentences showing the context in which they're used.

> toyon bush. "The toyon bush shielded Karana."
> kelp. "The kelp beds were clearly seen from the shore."

7. Vocabulary activities using the new words.

> Select one of your vocabulary words and find several pictures to illustrate its meaning.
> Take your vocabulary words and place them in several categories. Try colors, nouns, or verbs, and other topics of your own choosing.

8. Thought-provoking evaluation questions.

> What do you think was the most exciting episode in this book and why do you feel this way?
> Name three different emotions Karana felt while on the island. Give three incidents that would show each of these emotions.
> Explain your feelings about this book.

9. Several culminating task-card activities.

> Prepare a picture book of the animals mentioned in this book. Write a short paragraph about each of them.
> This particular Indian tribe was superstitious. Find several superstitions and illustrate them. How did your favorite superstition get started?
> Find four or five poems about the sea and share them with a friend.
> Prepare your own map of the *Island of the Blue Dolphins.* Include the landmarks mentioned in the book. Be sure to include a map key.
> Find out about other islands. What is an island anyway? Look up Hawaii and Easter Island or countries like Japan and Britain.

10. A supplemental book list for those children who wish to read additional books related to the subject.

> Try finding dolphin books, island books and/or such books as *Tinkerbelle, Kon Tiki, Swiss Family Robinson;* and magazines such as *National Geographic, Ranger Rick,* or *National Wildlife.* The list can be limitless.

11. An evaluation sheet that relates to the book kit.

> Have the students evaluate each activity and the book.
> Ask them what they would change or add to the book kit.

Why don't you try to prepare several book kits and introduce them to the children? Find out if they like them and want more.

MODULES

An alternative creative-teaching technique is that of modular instruction. Before we examine several actual instructional modules, let's consider the components of a module and its advantages and disadvantages. Modules are also sometimes called learning-activity packages, unit packages, teaching-learning units, mini-courses, mods, individualized learning experiences, and so forth. Keep in mind that only the name changes, the idea is the same. We will use the general term module to refer to any type of learning package that is designed to involve children on an individual basis. Any curricular subject can be used as well as any theme approach. We have utilized modules at all levels—preschool through adult—and have found them to be effective learning tools.

What Is a Module?

A module is an instructional unit that can stand on its own, and is based on a single concept or area. A module is designed to assist the student in attaining a specified objective or instructional goal. All materials and activities needed to attain this goal are included in the module. Teachers wishing to individualize their instruction should design a preassessment evaluation to use with their instructional modules. As a result, only those students requiring a specific goal are required to become involved in a specific module. In the same manner, a postassessment evaluation allows the student and teacher to determine whether or not the module assisted the student in becoming competent in a specific goal or objective.

Components of a Module

A module usually contains the following components:

The title, plus any necessary background information;

the instructional objectives (usually no more than two to four since we are dealing with packets of instruction);

a preassessment evaluation to determine if the learner needs the module for competency;

a list of all materials needed for the student to perform the modular activities;

the instructional procedures, which include any necessary readings, laboratory activities, or investigations;

a pathway to record the student's progress;

a generalizing experience (making the specific module applicable to other topics and areas);

a postassessment evaluation. We prefer to use a generalizing experience as a postassessment evaluation; however, you may wish to prepare a separate postassessment evaluation.

Advantages and Disadvantages of Modules

The advantages and disadvantages of modular instruction are continually debated. Here are the advantages (strengths) and corresponding disadvantages (weaknesses) of modular instruction:

Advantage: Provisions can be made for the assessment of each individual child.

Disadvantage: Sometimes individualization takes place at the expense of the entire class.

Advantage: Modules reduce the amount of time the teacher lectures to the whole class and increase the personal contact between teacher and students.

Disadvantage: The teacher sometimes finds himself or herself spending too much time answering procedural questions.

Advantage: Modules allow the teacher to spend less time covering material the student already knows.

Disadvantage: Sometimes group review can be beneficial for all students.

Advantage: The modular approach is self-instructional, with the child proceeding at his or her own rate or pace.

Disadvantage: Not all children can discover or work at their own pace, and some may find the experience unsatisfactory.

Advantage: Modules require fewer materials and less equipment, since not all students are doing the same thing at the same time.

Disadvantage: There may be 25 different things going on at the same time in the classroom.

Advantage: Modules allow increased individual involvement in one's own instruction.

Disadvantage: Group interaction is reduced due to individual pacing.

Advantage: Since modules are small segments of learning experiences, they can be easily updated.

Disadvantage: Modules take too much teacher involvement and time after school to create.

Are modules worth the effort? We suggest you try some with your students and then be the judge. You may wish to duplicate the examples presented here or try writing some of your own. We cannot decide if modules are for you; only you can make that decision.

As we prepare our own instructional modules, we find it helps to ask ourselves five questions. When you prepare your own modules, try asking yourself:

1. What does the student need to know about this idea, concept, or skill? (Or, what are my specific instructional objectives?)
2. Does the student already know the information? (What form should the preassessment evaluation take?)
3. What materials will I need to provide for the student to achieve the objectives?
4. How will I manage the program, and what will the student be doing? (What is the instructional procedure?)
5. How will the student and I know that he or she has arrived? (What would be a good generalizing or postassessment experience?)

Module 1   Classifying Colors and Shapes

Level: Primary grades, or K–3

Objectives: At the end of this module the student should be able to:

identify each of the following shapes: circle, triangle, and square;

identify each of the following colors: red, blue, green, yellow, orange, purple, black, and brown;

identify two-concept objects: red circle, blue square, yellow triangle.

Preassessment Evaluation: First, the child is shown color cards and is asked to identify what color they are. Then the child is shown cardboard shapes and is asked to identify them. Finally, the child is shown colored shapes (such as a red triangle) and is asked to identify them by color and shape.

If the child does not successfully complete each preassessment task (does not score 90 percent), then he or she should do the module.

Materials needed: Three shoe boxes, wood or plastic building blocks of various colors; a magnet; wires shaped as circles, triangles, and squares; and cardboard squares, triangles, and circles that are yellow and green, as well as the original cardboard pieces from which they were cut.

Instructional procedure: Prepare three activity boxes that can be given to a child for instructional purposes, their contents as indicated below:

1. A construction box, with all of the colored building pieces. Ask the child to build a yellow building or a red building.
2. A magnet box, with a magnet and the wire shapes of circles, squares, and triangles. Ask the child to pick up a square, circle, or triangle.
3. A puzzle box, with the yellow and green cutouts of squares, triangles, and circles. Ask the child to put a green circle in the circular hole, or a yellow triangle in the triangular hole.

Generalizing experience: Give the child a piece of paper with the outlines of a circle, square, and triangle on it. Also provide the child with a box of crayons with the eight basic colors. Then ask him or her to find the circle and color it red.

Continue this procedure using a variety of the possible combinations until the skill has been satisfactorily reinforced.

Module 2   Controlling and Manipulating Variables in Capillarity

Level: Intermediate grades, or 4–6

Objectives: At the end of this module the student should be able to:

identify and name five variables that are important in influencing either the rate at which the water moves or the maximum height to which it rises;

construct an investigation in which he or she holds all but one variable constant;

identify the dependent and the independent variables in the investigation.

Preassessment evaluation: Give the student a shallow plastic dish or cup containing water about three centimeters deep. Give him or her three- by ten-centimeter strips of two different colored materials, such as paper towel or cotton. Ask the student to show that the liquids move at different rates in different materials by constructing an investigation that will allow you to observe this phenomenon. Have the student name the independent and dependent variables. The student will not need to proceed if:

he or she can construct an investigation in which he or she holds all but one of the variables constant;

he or she can name the independent and dependent variables in his or her investigation;

he or she can name five variables that influence the rate at which the water moves or the maximum height to which it rises.

Materials Needed: Three or four different types of material, four or five plastic dishes or cups, clock with a second hand, liquid, meter stick.

Instructional Procedure: Using a strip of blotting paper and a shallow dish with water, the student observes water moving easily up the blotting paper. After this action has been observed, the student should prepare a list of inferences that suggest what variables are important in influencing either the rate at which the water moves or the maximum height to which it will rise. Then he or she should design an investigation in which all but one of the variables are held constant while only the independent variables are manipulated. The interpretation of students' observations will be a sure test of their inferences. Typical observations that students will make are:

The height of the water is almost the same on any two strips of blotting paper used.

The water moves up the strip.

The water moves up the two strips at about the same rate.

The student should then try to determine why the height of water was the same for the two strips. Students will need to consider the variables in these questions:

Were both strips the same size and shape?

Were both strips put the same distance into the water?

Were both strips in the water for the same length of time?

Were both strips made of the same material?

Did both containers hold the same liquid?

Was the temperature of the water in both containers the same?

Would it make a difference if both strips of paper were held by a different person?

Does color of material influence the rate at which the liquid rises?

The student should see the need for keeping all but one of these variables constant in the investigation.

Next, the student should suggest questions to consider for the next portion of this investigation. Sample questions might include the following:

Would the waterline be the same if the two strips of paper differed in width?

How does the rate at which the water rises depend on the width of the blotting paper?

Would the waterline be the same if the two strips of paper were dipped in the water to different depths?

Does the rate at which the water rises depend on the type of material that the strips are made of?

Would the waterline be the same if the two strips of paper were left in the water for different amounts of time?

Does the height of the waterline depend on the temperature of the water?

Would the height of the waterline be the same if two colors of the same type of paper were used?

The student should design an investigation to test some of the questions he or she has proposed. He or she should keep in mind that all variables but one must be kept constant. The student should be able to identify which variable is the dependent variable and which is the independent variable.

Generalizing Experience: The student should be given two plastic containers and two identical strips of material different from those used before. Put water in one container, and put cooking oil to the same depth in the other. Ask the student to investigate the question: Do different liquids move at different rates in the same material? Ask the student to prepare a list of variables he or she has identified. Then ask the student to select one variable from this list and conduct an investigation to try and answer the questions raised by the isolated variable. The student should be able to name the dependent and independent variables in his or her investigation.

If the student does not successfully complete the module, he or she should try again, using a different liquid and strips of a new material.

Module 3   Controlling and Manipulating Variables in Evaporation

Level: Middle school, or 7–9

Objectives: At the end of this module the student should be able to:

> identify and name five variables that are important in influencing the rate at which water evaporates;

> construct an investigation in which he or she holds all but one variable constant;

> identify the dependent variables in the investigation.

Preassessment Evaluation: Give the student a balance with two sponge cubes of identical size to hang on each side of the balance. Ask the student to prepare a list of factors that would affect the evaporation rate. Have the student prepare an investigation that will allow her or him to check any two of these factors. Have the student name the independent and dependent variables in the investigation. The student will not need to proceed if:

> he or she can construct an investigation in which he or she holds all but one of the variables constant;

> he or she can name the independent and dependent variables in the investigation;

> he or she can name five variables that are important in influencing the rate at which water evaporates.

Materials needed: A single-beam balance, sponge cubes, plastic sandwich bags, light bulb with reflector, hot and cold water.

Instructional procedure: The student should attempt to think of factors that would influence the evaporation rate of water from the sponge cubes. He or she should attempt to rank these factors in order of importance, as he or she sees it. He or she should then attempt to design an investigation in which all but one of the variables are held constant. The student should manipulate one of the variables while holding the other ones constant. A list of typical variations that could influence evaporation and be tested in an investigation follows:

Shine a light source on one sponge.

Use hot water on one sponge and cold water on another.

Put a closed plastic bag around one sponge.

Shine a light on both sponges, but protect one with a thin, transparent sheet.

Use different-sized or different-shaped sponges of the same mass.

Fan air past one sponge.

Cut one sponge with ragged edges.

The student should attempt to identify which factor is most important in the evaporation process. A good way to identify this factor is to time how long it takes the balance to become unbalanced when each modification is considered. The student should also attempt to relate the experiments to nature—that is, determine the effect of the sun, wind, and surface area upon evaporation.

Generalizing Experience: The student should be given a container of water and asked to list those factors he or she would consider as explanation for increased water evaporation. He or she should then design an investigation to determine the evaporation rates for this method. The student should be able to name the dependent and independent variables for the investigation.

If the student does not successfully complete the module, he or she should return to the instructional procedure and, using a different liquid, conduct another investigation.

THEORY INTO ACTION

We have presented three examples of modules, developed and used for kindergarten through the middle grades and junior high. These modules are not perfect. They will need to be continually revised to keep pace with student comments and teacher observations.

Modules emphasize skills and concepts, not the memorization and regurgitation of facts, facts, and more facts. The emphasis in the primary grades is on basic learning skills such as observing, inferring, measuring, and predicting. The emphasis in the intermediate grades is on integrated learning skills such as formulating models, interpreting data, and controlling and manipulating variables. Skills are as valuable as content. You can always look up an answer pertaining to content. Try looking up a skill!

During the middle, junior-high, and high-school years, emphasis should be placed on the further development of the skills previously mentioned. In addition, emphasis should be placed on a greater sophistication in the use of hands-on materials for investigations.

How do you begin to develop modules for your students?

To begin module implementation, you might start by preparing a core of modules for your classroom at a minimal level of student performance. Each child entering should receive an evaluation related to your instructional goals so that a profile of each student can be prepared revealing his or her strengths and weaknesses. In this way, you, as the teacher, will know where this individual is in relation to the performance outcomes set by you, or you and the student. Once this evaluation has been accomplished, a list of resources should be developed. There are many resources available from national professional organizations, such as the National Council of Teachers of Mathematics or the International Reading Association, which can serve as good starting points. In time, a portfolio of activities of both a core and supplemental nature will evolve, allowing you to provide a sequence of instruction for each student, taking him or her from where he or she is to where he or she should be. Undoubtedly, on the first time around, these modules will be difficult to develop. It will take time, and a reduction in an individual teacher's work load may be needed to accomplish real development. Teachers who take the time to personalize their instruction and prepare modules of instruction, however, have their directions and goals in mind for their instructional program. Unless we take the time to do this, we will remain on that never-ending treadmill of vague instruction. The role of the teacher must shift from one of a custodian of education to that of an architect and a creator of the instructional program in schools.

We have reviewed many skills and techniques, including (just to refresh your memory):

task cards;

the minipreparation of audiotutorial tapes;

invitations to investigate;

skillettes;

book kits;

light boxes;

milk-carton computers;

foam computers;

cooperative learning;

games;

puzzler activities;

modules.

Many teachers ask us if mechanisms are available to incorporate all of these alternative creative-teaching endeavors into one concerted teaching effort. The answer is a resounding YES! On to interest centers!!

THEME INTEREST CENTERS: A GREAT PLACE TO START

Since interest centers are flexible and build on the vast array of learning activities, they attract children. With the trend to the integrated-theme curriculum, open-concept learning, and individualized instruction, interest centers are right on target. Interest centers can usually be divided into three categories: content, skill, and theme. Let's examine each type.

Probably the most traditional and easiest type to assemble is a content interest center. It is based on a particular area of content, such as magnets, plants, or electricity. Thus, in a magnets interest center, all activities (task cards, modules, games) would be tied to the content area of magnets.

The second type is the skill interest center. Its sole purpose is the development and reinforcement of a particular skill, such as classifying or graphing. All activities (task cards, modules, games) would be tied to the skill area of graphing or classifying.

The third type (the most forward-looking and true to life) is the theme interest center. This center is based on broad themes (solutions, change, future, relationships, frontiers, adaptation, communication, creativity, cities, freedom, farming, technology, progress, environment). Within the theme interest center, we find content and skills drawn from a variety of subject areas and integrated. Since they are so comprehensive, theme interest centers require imagination and creativity of a teacher.

An interest center may be placed in any strategic location in your room, area, or school. An increasing number of teachers are organizing their instruction based on a great variety of interest-center approaches. As one teacher remarked to us: "Interest centers allow me to be with my students. I can communicate with them on a personal basis and I can encourage group discussions. I wish I had learned how to make an interest center in college."

Making an Interest Center

The first step in making an interest center is developing the related teacher- and student-created materials. These materials include teacher guides, student textbooks, reference books, activity sheets, task cards, modular activities, films, tapes, games, computer software, and action boxes.

All of these materials should be arranged in a sequence based on your instructional goal(s) for the center. Many teachers use a preassessment evaluation to determine which students need which portions of the center. Remember to include evaluation materials related to the interest center's purpose (content quizzes, tests, competency measures, and also attitudinal measures).

Display the materials in an attractive, eye-appealing manner. Plastic bas-

Figure 4.32 The interest center

kets or packing boxes should be obtained for storing interest center materials when they are not in use.

We have shown a sample theme interest center in greater detail on the next two pages. This example is not intended to be comprehensive. It is a summary of the types of ideas that can be incorporated into one center. Take a look at it and you'll be on the road to a "filling" interest center. Yours probably will be good enough to eat!

Theme Interest Center on Cooking

Task cards: Find your favorite recipe and prepare it to serve to the class.

Media: Find films, slides, transparencies, tapes, pictures, and other materials related to the theme of cooking. Prepare activities to go with them.

Audiotutorial tapes: To teach children to follow directions, prepare several tapes dealing with recipes and have children follow them. Try popcorn, muffins, Rice Krispies cookies.

Book kits: Good starters for a book kit are Vicky Cobb's *Science Experi-*

ments You Can Eat (New York: J.B. Lippincott, 1972) and *More Science Experiments You Can Eat* (New York: J.B. Lippincott, 1979). Go to the library; you'll find many more ideas for book kits.

Skillettes: Prepare skillettes relating to such skills as classifying, following directions, computing with fractions, or using measuring containers.

Light boxes: Prepare light-box cards related to the spelling of certain foods or matching food names with their pictures.

Games: Invent several food games patterned after existing games. Develop:

"Concentration" by matching food pictures;

"What's My Line" by asking, "What's my cooking-related occupation? Is it butcher, baker, butler, or cookbook writer?"

What about the Food Chain Game, or Who Eats Whom?

More ideas include:

Field trips to the grocery store, factory, restaurant, bakery, home kitchen

Foods, lands, customs, and people

Your own class recipe book

Food mobiles and centerpieces

New food inventions

Food cost investigations

Spoon, fork, knife: Where did they come from and why do we use them?

Investigate diets and your health.

What foods will make you healthy?

Do an individual calorie journal.

Invitations to investigate: There are all sorts of possibilities here. Try something like the following:

—Why does dough rise?

—What can you learn about mold? What does it have to do with food?

Puzzler activities: See PA 4 below.

PA 4   WHAT'S COOKING?

You live in a totally electric house with modern appliances in the kitchen. Because of a severe electrical storm last night, you will be without electricity for the next three days. You had planned to have five guests for dinner during this period. In spite of the electrical blackout, you decide to go ahead with your plans. You have a propane camp stove, an ice chest, a box of matches, and water. What will you prepare for dinner? Why?

Since the electric can opener, blender, microwave, and electric stove won't work, will you have to change your meal plans? What other appliances will be affected by the loss of electrical service for three days?

What provisions will you make for washing dishes after the meal?

RESEARCH SAYS . . .

Activities As Instructional Tools

According to a research report published by the Institute for Research on Teaching at Michigan State University (Brophy and Alleman 1991), "Everything in the curriculum, not only the activities but also the content, is viewed as a means for helping students to acquire important dispositions and capabilities, not just to acquire cultural literacy construed in a narrow, 'name recognition' sense."

They further assume that the content should be organized into networks structured around important ideas and that these ideas should be taught for understanding (not just memorization) and for application to life outside of school. A goals-driven curriculum designed to teach important ideas for understanding and application will provide a basis for a broad range of activities that call for students to think critically and creatively in the process of conducting inquiry, solving problems, or making decisions.

Parade of Facts Not a Content Base for Good Activities   As a basis for identifying worthwhile activities, the typical parade of facts curriculum that emphasizes breadth of coverage over depth of development of ideas has severely limited potential. Rather than providing important ideas taught for understanding and application, it restricts teachers to reading, recitation, and seat work. The activities are mostly low level, calling for retrieval of definitions or facts (matching, fill in the blanks) or isolated practice of part-skills. Such curricula cannot be improved by replacing work sheets with better activities, Brophy and Alleman caution. The knowledge component must be replaced or supplemented in ways that emphasize important generalizations that can provide a content basis for better activities.

Activities To Accomplish Goals   A second set of assumptions concerns the nature and role of activities. Brophy and Alleman assume that activities are not self-justifying ends in themselves, but are means for helping students to accomplish curricular goals. Activities fulfill this function by providing structured opportunities for students to interact with curricular content, preferably in ways that engage students in processing it actively, developing personal ownership and appreciation of it, and applying it to their lives outside of school.

Any particular activity might be designed to provide opportunities for students to apply their existing knowledge to questions or problems relating to new content, to synthesize and communicate what has been learned, to think critically about the content, or to make personal decisions or take personal actions that relate to it.

Sets of activities should include opportunities for students to do something with the content—in the context of problem solving, decision making, or other higher order applications. This is more likely to occur when major long-term goals, rather than short-term, content-mastery objectives, are used as the primary criteria for selecting activities. (Brophy and Alleman, 1991)

The researchers conclude by stating,

The final assumption is that the success of an activity in producing thoughtful student engagement with important ideas will depend not only on the nature of the activity itself but also on the nature of the teacher structuring and the teacher-student discourse that occurs before, during, and after the time period in which the students respond to the activity's demands. Activities are likely to have their maximum impact when the teacher (a) introduces them in ways that clarify their purposes and engage students in seeking to accomplish those purposes; (b) scaffolds, monitors, and provides appropriate feedback concerning the students' work on the activity; and (c) leads the students through appropriate postactivity reflection on and sharing of the insights that have been developed. (Brophy and Alleman, 1991)

Included in this assumption is the notion that teachers will lead students through activities in ways that engage them not just cognitively but also affectively (implying sufficient interest in and feelings about the content as well as motivation to accomplish the activity's purposes).

Even though students fear ambiguity and risk and may initially resist worthwhile but demanding activities, some encouraging evidence exists to suggest that when teachers plan good activities and implement them in ways that emphasize their value as worthwhile learning experiences, students will not merely cooperate but come to perceive the class as both more valuable and more interesting than other classes.

PAUSE FOR A SUMMARY

Creative-teaching alternative skills and techniques include task cards, puzzler activities, audiotutorial tapes, invitations to investigate, skillettes, book kits, action boxes, games, modules, and interest centers.

Task cards (sometimes called idea cards, suggestion cards, or activity cards) are an excellent way to involve children in individualized instruction.

Puzzler activities are brief confrontations with real or fictitious situations supplied by the teacher. They challenge the student to map out strategies, raise appropriate questions, and consider different explanations or solutions.

The minipreparation of audiotutorial tapes (Mini-PATT) allows teachers to produce instructional tapes suitable for their own classes in a short period of time.

Invitations to investigate are problem-solving situations that allow students to analyze and synthesize an experimental observation.

Skillettes are short, discrete lessons designed to introduce or reinforce a single skill.

Book kits are designed to supplement or replace basal reading textbooks. Each kit includes not only the appropriate book, but also all of the necessary accessories.

Action boxes provide simple ways for children to quiz themselves.

Games can be used to reinforce skills, to motivate students, or to evaluate progress. Games serve to relax the classroom atmosphere.

A module is an instructional unit that can stand on its own and is based on a single concept or area.

Interest centers usually can be divided into three categories: content interest centers, skill interest centers, and theme interest centers. Theme interest centers are the goal of teaching children to learn *how* to learn.

Cooperative learning provides an effective mechanism to foster positive learning experiences for children.

REFERENCES

Bloom, B. S., ed. (1956). *Taxonomy of Educational Objectives: Handbook I: Cognitive Domain.* New York: McKay.

Brophy, J. (1990). *The De Facto National Curriculum in Elementary Social Studies* (Elementary Subjects Center Series No. 17). East Lansing: Michigan State University, Institute for Research on Teaching, Center for the Learning and Teaching of Elementary Subjects.

Brophy, J., and Alleman, J. (1991). "Activities as Instructional Tools." *Communication Quarterly*, vol. 13, no. 2, pp. 1, 4. East Lansing, MI: Institute for Research on Teaching.

Brophy, J., and Alleman, J. (1990). *Activities as Instructional Tools: A Framework for Analysis and Evaluation* (Occasional Paper No. 132). East Lansing: Michigan State University, Institute for Research on Teaching.

Johnson, D., and Johnson, R. (1988). *Circles of Learning.* Alexandria, VA: Association of Supervision and Curriculum Development.

Chapter
5

Creative Evaluations
Evaluations and Trust!

The slowest learners in our schools are not the pupils, they're the educators who run them.

Lester Velie

Do all of you remember the story of Peter Rabbit? Here's a new version.

The Tale of Peter and the Rabbit

"Class, look at this picture and tell me what you see." said the teacher. Hands went up, but the teacher called on Peter, whose hand had not been one of them. "Peter, what is it?"

"It looks like a rat."

The class laughed. Someone said, "Peter is so stupid. He doesn't know a rat from a rabbit."

The teacher said, "Peter, what's the matter with your eyes? Can't you see that it has long ears?"

"Yes," said Peter weakly.

"It is a rabbit, isn't it?"

"Yes," he said.

"Today's story is about a rabbit," said the teacher, pointing to the picture and then the word. "It's a story about a hungry white rabbit. What do you suppose a rabbit eats when he's hungry?"

"Lettuce," said Mary.

"Carrots," said Suzy.

"Meat," said Peter.

The class laughed. Someone said, "Peter is so stupid. He doesn't know what rabbits eat."

"Peter, you know very well that rabbits don't eat meat," said the teacher.

"That depends on how hungry you are," said Peter. "When I'm hungry I'll eat anything my mother gives me, even if I don't like it."

"Don't argue, Peter," said the teacher. "Now class, how does a rabbit's fur feel when you pet him?"

"Soft," said Suzy.

"Silky," said Mary.

"I don't know," said Peter.

"Why?" asked the teacher.

"'Cause I wouldn't pet one. He might bite me and make me sick like what happened to my little brother the time one got on his bed when he was sleeping."

The class laughed. Someone said, "Peter is fibbing. He knows his mother doesn't allow rabbits in bed."

After the class had read the story and had recess, the teacher said to the supervisor, "I hate to sound prejudiced, but I'm not sure that this busing from one neighborhood to the other is good for the children."

The supervisor shook his head sadly and said to the teacher, "Your lesson lacked one very important ingredient."

"What was that?" asked the teacher.

"A rabbit," said the supervisor.

Source: Eugene Grant, "The Tale of Peter and the Rabbit," *Phi Delta Kappan,* vol. 49, no. 3 (November 1967), back cover. Copyright 1967. Phi Delta Kappa, Inc. By permission.

TEACHING, TESTING, AND THE THREE DOMAINS OF LEARNING

If we expect to teach the whole child, then we should expect to teach in all three learning domains (cognitive—content; affective—attitudes; and psychomotor—physical motion). Unfortunately, most instruction in schools deals with only the lowest levels of cognitive instruction (the Terrible Three) at the expense of the higher cognitive levels and with complete neglect of the affective and psychomotor domains.

The role of the teacher is to teach in all three domains of learning.

The Cognitive Domain (Content)

Cognitive learning is accumulating content knowledge and may be classified into six levels: knowledge, comprehension, application, analysis, synthesis, and evaluation (Bloom 1956). Whenever possible, cognitive learning should focus on the four higher levels of learning rather than just on knowledge or comprehension. To assist you in recognizing the different cognitive levels, try classifying these questions using the levels shown on the Cognitive Chart of Action Verbs (Figure 5.1).

Level   *Question*

_____ **1.** Name each of the weather map symbols.

_____ **2.** Which of the characteristics below are important in describing a rock's texture?

_____ **3.** Obtain a blank map of Australia from your teacher. Study both the average precipitation map and elevation map shown below. On the basis of these two maps, where do you think the river systems originate in Australia?

_____ **4.** Select the profile of the stream with the greatest potential energy.

_____ **5.** The features on the map are sand dunes. What is the direction of the prevailing winds in this area?

_____ **6.** Energy exists in many different forms. State three of them.

_____ **7.** The scale diagram below represents the orbits of Mars and Mercury. The minimum distance between Mars and Mercury is 106 million miles. What is the radius of the Mars orbit?

_____ **8.** Leap year occurs every fourth year, and then February has 29 days instead of 28. What is the purpose of leap year?

_____ **9.** Time zones have been established for the earth. What are the advantages and disadvantages of having time zones?

_____ **10.** Why are historians interested in the origin of the moon's surface?

After you have classified each question according to cognitive level, check your answers with those below. If your answers are different from ours, try to infer why.

ANSWERS TO COGNITIVE LEVELS

1. Level I (Knowledge)—*name* indicates knowledge
2. Level IV (Analysis)—making inferences about which characteristics are important
3. Level V (Synthesis)—deducing and inferring
4. Level II (Comprehension)—understanding relationships

(Answers continued on page 224)

Figure 5.1

COGNITIVE CHART OF ACTION VERBS

I. Knowledge—recalling the terminology, specific facts, principles, generalizations, and theories unique to a subject area.

1. Identifies
2. Names
3. Chooses
4. Lists
5. Selects
6. Distinguishes

II. Comprehension—translating knowledge into one's own thoughts and words, thus enabling one to understand relationships.

1. Computes
2. Measures
3. Matches
4. Demonstrates
5. Selects
6. Balances

III. Application—using previously acquired knowledge and understanding to solve problems in new or unique situations.

1. Compares
2. Groups
3. Arranges
4. Calibrates
5. Dissects
6. Operates

IV. Analysis—reducing ideas to their component parts.

1. Selects hypotheses
2. Estimates
3. Interrelates
4. Limits
5. Infers
6. Reflects

V. Synthesis—putting parts together to make new patterns and to encourage divergent thinking.

1. Proves
2. Extrapolates
3. Interpolates
4. Predicts
5. Infers
6. Deduces

VI. Evaluation—the most complex of all cognitive learning, it requires the combining of the previous five levels.

1. Controls variables
2. Rejects
3. Verifies
4. Questions
5. Interprets
6. Doubts

From Robert B. Sund and Anthony J. Pickard, *Behavioral Objectives and Evaluational Measures: Science and Mathematics,* pp. 41–42. Copyright 1972. Columbus, OH: Charles E. Merrill Publishing Company. Reprinted by permission.

5. Level III (Application)—solving problems in a different situation
6. Level I (Knowledge)—stating or naming from memory
7. Level V (Synthesis)—putting parts together to make new patterns
8. Level III (Application)—using previous knowledge in new or unique situations
9. Level VI (Evaluation)—making interpretations based on the five lower levels of learning
10. Level VI (Evaluation)—making interpretations

How well did you do? Try writing your own list of questions that illustrate your ability to recognize all six levels of the cognitive domain. Now let's move on to the affective domain.

The Affective Domain (Attitude)

The most important of the three domains of learning is the affective domain (attitude). As we have said before, the affective outcomes of school learning should be of primary importance to the teacher. Once a child's attitude has formed, it is very difficult to change. A child's self-concept (the way a child feels about himself) is paramount to good learning experiences. A child spends from 10 to 16 years in school, a total of more than 20,000 hours devoted to school and related activities. Students enjoy few hours in which they are not judged by teachers, peers, family, and others. At no other time in their lives will students be judged by so many so often. Unfortunately, rather than considering the affective aspects when designing instruction, most textbooks, teachers, and schools focus on the lowest level of how to learn for later life—factual (cognitive) material as opposed to affective learning.

Many studies have shown a relationship between cognitive success and positive or negative attitudes toward school. If children have a series of positive school learning experiences, they are likely to develop a generally positive attitude about school and learning. If, however, the learning experiences are generally negative and their achievement is regarded as inadequate by themselves, the teachers, and the parents, students are likely to develop a negative attitude toward school and learning. Unfortunately, once a negative attitude has been instilled in a student in elementary school, it is almost impossible to change in later life. Academic self-concept is clearly defined by the end of the primary grades, and the teacher must bear a major responsibility for assisting the student in acquiring a positive or negative opinion about school and learning.

Four major attitudes that are a part of literacy and that can be evaluated are (a) curiosity, (b) inventiveness, (c) critical thinking, and (d) persistence. Definitions and examples of various kinds of behaviors associated with the four areas are (Science Curriculum Improvement Study, 1973):

(a) *Curiosity.* Children who pay particular attention to an object or event and spontaneously wish to learn more about it are being curious. They may give evidence of curiosity by using several senses to explore the world around them;

asking questions about objects and events;

actively investigating cause and effect;

showing interest in the outcomes of experiments, stories, and problems.

(b) *Inventiveness*. Children who generate new ideas are being inventive. These children exhibit original thinking in their interpretations. They may give evidence of inventiveness through verbal statements or actions by

using manipulatives and materials in unusual and constructive ways;

suggesting new ideas, experiments, or approaches to problem solving;

describing novel conclusions from their observations and experiences.

(c) *Critical thinking*. Children who can provide sound reasons for their suggestions, conclusions, and predictions are thinking critically. They may exhibit critical thinking, largely through verbal statements, by

using evidence to justify their conclusions;

predicting the outcome of untried activities;

justifying their predictions in terms of past experience;

changing their ideas in response to evidence of logical reasons;

pointing out contradictions in reports by their classmates;

investigating the effects of selected variables, new ideas, or different problem-solving strategies;

interpreting observations.

(d) *Persistence*. Children who maintain an active interest in a problem or event for a longer period than their classmates are being persistent. They are not easily distracted from their activity. They may give evidence of persistence by

continuing to investigate materials after their novelty has worn off;

repeating an activity in spite of apparent failure;

completing an activity even though their classmates have finished earlier;

initiating and completing a project.

POINTS TO PONDER

Try identifying an affective behavior and classifying it. Classify each of the ten statements below. Check your answers with the ones provided, and then write ten examples of your own.

Classify each statement:

a. Curiosity
b. Inventiveness
c. Critical Thinking
d. Persistence
e. Not an Affective Behavior

_____   **1.** The student asks why mass is recorded as weight.

_____   **2.** The student ignores past experience when making a conclusion concerning whether or not life exists on Mars.

_____   **3.** The student repeats a mathematics problem after apparent failure.

_____   **4.** The student correctly states an addition fact.

_____   **5.** The student suggests using a pendulum to make a sand picture.

_____   **6.** A student checks out a thermometer to conduct a change-of-state experiment with ice at home.

_____   **7.** A student suggests an experiment to record the respiration rate of a goldfish.

_____   **8.** The student tests the reaction rate of two different kinds of metals with acid in addition to the required metal.

_____   **9.** After receiving a grade of C on his/her activity, the student repeats the activity and submits additional results.

_____   **10.** After listening to an answer from a classmate during a discussion about evolution, a student presents evidence in opposition to the first answer.

Here are the answers. How well did you do?

1. c	4. e	7. b	10. c
2. c	5. b	8. a	
3. d	6. a	9. d	

The Psychomotor Domain (Physical Motion)

The psychomotor domain is concerned with the development of muscular skill and coordination. This domain includes such skills as using tools (hammer, screw driver, wrench), reading rapidly, drawing geometric shapes, playing a musical instrument, typing on a computer keyboard, using a microscope, and playing sports. While intellectual skills enter into each of these psychomotor skills, the primary focus is on the development of the psychomotor skill involved. Most successful teachers divide their emphasis among the three domains as follows:

K–3 Teachers
20 Percent Cognitive Instruction
40 Percent Affective Instruction
40 Percent Psychomotor Instruction

4–6 Teachers
    40 Percent Cognitive Instruction
    30 Percent Affective Instruction
    30 Percent Psychomotor Instruction

7–12 Teachers
    50 Percent Cognitive Instruction
    25 Percent Affective Instruction
    25 Percent Psychomotor Instruction

College Teachers
    60 Percent Cognitive Instruction
    20 Percent Affective Instruction
    20 Percent Psychomotor Instruction

POINTS TO PONDER

How do you plan to divide your instructional time among the three domains? Justify your decision.

EVALUATION AND COMPETENCY TESTING IN THE COGNITIVE DOMAIN

As we turn toward the evaluation of children, we find that creative teachers evaluate children using all three domains: cognitive, affective, and psychomotor. Creative teachers provide an environment that encourages ALL children to succeed. They realize that evaluation is a continual process and of an individualized nature. They understand that the so-called unsuccessful students (as viewed in schools) can be successful because these students have many desirable attributes:

They are very inventive in the use of nonstandard oral language.

They are able to progress and to be successful when dealing with things that interest them.

They show considerable insight into human behavior.

They are not as easily frustrated as many straight-A students.

They are apt to frustrate the school system with some highly imaginative approaches.

They approach and deal with various situations in unusual or unconventional, but appropriate, ways.

They are curious about all things.

As illustrated in our module examples in Chapter 4, creative teachers preassess children according to a set of performance objectives. This procedure is also called criterion-referenced testing. Then activities are designed, based on the results of the preassessment, to help the child succeed. Success can be measured by postassessment. Many teachers provide children with profiles of skills so that everyone—the child, the teachers, the parents, and the administrator—can be informed of a child's progress (see the sample profile, Figure 5.2, page 229). More and more schools are adopting the profile and conference report as a positive alternative to grading. If you, however, must administer grades, a skills profile can provide the necessary information. If the children and you agree that they must achieve a postassessment score of 90 percent of the possible points for an A, your grading scale has been established.

We should point out, however, that since success is our goal, children enrolled in classes taught by creative teachers will probably earn more As than ever.

Test items used by creative teachers in science are not low-level cognitive-knowledge questions such as:

Draw the Beaufort wind symbol for the wind coming from the northwest at 37 miles per hour.

Change 35°F to its corresponding Celsius temperature.

Instead their questions, written at a higher level and involving thinking, are like the following:

Using the materials provided, construct a four-stage classification scheme.

Given the following data, construct a graph and make two predictions from it, one of which is an extrapolation and one of which is an interpolation.

Write several assessment items of your own. Remember that they should involve thinking and allow for a variety of answers. In addition, skill questions related to the content discipline should also be included.

EVALUATION IN THE AFFECTIVE DOMAIN

When you feel good about yourself, your accomplishments, and your friendships, life is wonderful and school is an exciting place to be. Creative teachers want each child to have a positive self-image. They want to know about the emotional needs of each child. They spend time talking to students about their families and friends, about the special times in their lives, and about school.

Another way teachers find out about the affective needs of students is through attitude surveys. Attitude surveys encourage students to examine their feelings about themselves, how they relate to others, and how they work at school. There are no right or wrong answers or grades. Attitude surveys are just a way for students to discover more about themselves and for teachers to learn more about their students. Ask your students what makes them feel good about themselves and why. Ask them about how they study. Ask them about their friendships. Ask them questions about riding on the bus or walking to school.

Figure 5.2 Sample profile

SAMPLE PROFILE OF A STUDENT'S SKILLS IN SCIENCE

Name _____

Section _____

Preassessment date _____

Postassessment date _____

Module number	Science process	Number of points possible	Preassessment score	Postassessment score	Change plus or minus
1	Observing	6			
2	Inferring	8			
3	Measuring	14			
4	Using Numbers	10			
5	Classifying	10			
6	Space/time	8			
7	Communicating	12			
8	Interpreting data	8			
9	Controlling variables	10			
10	Experimenting	10			
11	Defining operationally	6			
12	Instructional objectives	8			
	Totals	110			

Find out how they feel about the lunchroom and the playground. A bad experience can affect the entire day. If you understand their concerns, you can help your students search for solutions.

The attitude survey in Figure 5.3 can be used with upper elementary students or modified for lower elementary or middle-school students. Leave room for open-ended questions at the end of the survey to gain more information about topics of your choice.

Figure 5.3

ATTITUDE SURVEY

1 = Super

2 = Good Job

3 = Needs Improvement

	September			January			May		
	1	2	3	1	2	3	1	2	3
How I feel about myself:									
1. Follow directions									
2. Put forth my best effort									
3. Use my creativity									
4. Pace myself to get lessons and projects done on time									
5. Learn something new every day									
6. Have a positive attitude about myself and others									
7. Am enthusiastic									
8. Show interest in new ideas									
9. Am willing to try again									
10. Feel accepted by others									
How I relate to others:									
1. Listen to others politely									
2. Keep my hands and feet to myself									
3. Respect the material and property of others									
4. Share my talents with others									
5. Reinforce others by giving positive comments									
6. Work and play cooperatively with others									
7. Am courteous with others									

	September			January			May		
	1	2	3	1	2	3	1	2	3
8. Have friends at school									
9. Have friends riding the bus or walking to school									
10. Play with others on the playground									
How I work at school:									
1. Finish homework and other school projects on time									
2. Ask questions to gain more understanding									
3. Stay on task									
4. Participate in class discussion									
5. Listen attentively to the teacher and my classmates									
6. Work independently when needed									
7. Enjoy solving problems									
8. Revise work when necessary									
9. Am eager to come to school									
10. Evaluate my school performance									

I feel good about:

September _____

January _____

May _____

Things I would like to improve:

September _____

January _____

May _____

Goals I plan to accomplish:

September _____

_____

January _____

_____

May _____

_____

It is beneficial to have the students complete the same survey several times during the year so they can see if their attitudes have changed. The teacher can also complete the survey for each student. To add a personal touch, schedule a conference with the student to compare and discuss the survey charts. This is also a wonderful time to have the students write a few affective goals that can be assessed during the next conference. Attitude charts can also be shared with parents during parent-teacher conferences.

A child's self-concept and attitude can be positively reinforced through the use of Happy Notes (Figure 5.4). These can be purchased commercially, computer generated, or designed by students. Make it a habit to send at least three

Figure 5.4 Happy note

positive notes each day. You can write the notes at the end of the day so you can reflect on the positive aspects of the students for that day, or you may write them first thing in the morning to start your day on a positive note. It will certainly brighten your day and alert parents to the fact that you are looking for the good in their children. To help you keep track, make a record in your grade book of who gets a positive note and the date. If you notice that a student has not received any positive messages for a while, it is time to send some.

To make a set of positive note cards, just divide an $8\frac{1}{2}$- by 11-inch sheet of paper into four pieces and have the students design a positive note that includes a picture and a positive statement. These can be copied, cut, and used all year. The students love to receive positive notes, especially if they have done the art work.

Affective evaluation can also take place while students are engaged in open-ended thinking activities. As an example:

> I took a trip with my family to the zoo. It was big and noisy and crowded. It was fun, too, until I got separated from my parents. I looked around and they were gone.

What would you do?

Write an ending for the story.

How would you know if your decision was right or wrong?

For older students:

> This is your first year at the middle school. You have decided to participate in a variety of school activities. You are on the basketball team and the school's academic team. Basketball practice is after school, and the academic team meets during activity period. You have just found out that your academic team has won the regional competition and will participate in the state competition on the same day as the basketball tourney.

You have to make a decision. You are a valuable member of both teams. What will you do? How will you know if your decision was right or wrong?

The values continuum or line is also excellent for affective evaluation.

On the chalkboard, draw a line with a large circle on each end:

Figure 5.5 Value continuum

Then choose a two-sided issue; the greater the polarity, the better. Present the issue to the students and explain the two opposing views. Write a one-word summary of one view in each circle. Next, present two other views that lie in between the extremes. Mark these on the continuum line. Have each child decide his or her position on the issue and mark it on the line. Finally, have the children discuss their views on the issue.

As an alternative to the chalkboard sketch, you can chalk the circles on the floor and tape a line between them. Follow the procedure above, but have the children move to the place on the tape continuum that represents their views on the issue. Try these opposing points of view for starters:

take lunch versus buy lunch

conserve energy versus use energy

drug testing in schools versus no drug testing in schools

zoos versus free animals

calculators in schools versus no calculators in schools

Reaction situations like the next one also work well for evaluative purposes. Remember, there can be more than one correct response.

The teacher assigns a science project to each class member. Your father does most of the project, but you turn it in and say you did the whole project yourself. The teacher asks you for an explanation because you couldn't have done it yourself.

What is your reaction?

Is it positive or negative?

What other response could you have made?

Is this reaction positive or negative?

Now write some of your own reaction situations.

EVALUATION IN THE PSYCHOMOTOR DOMAIN

The psychomotor domain is concerned with the development of muscular skills and coordination. Children involved in creative hands-on activities are actively doing things. Invariably things need to be measured, cut, and joined together, fashioned into some construct enhancing a lesson or some theme project. In the process, children may be scissoring, gluing, hammering, sawing, and even possibly drilling and soldering. These are but a few of the psychomotor skills necessary for a successful hands-on program. Activities should be designed to provide children experiences in the appropriate skill for the age level and for the task at hand.

One psychomotor evaluation example that utilizes the skill of measuring and is concerned with how students change throughout the school year and into the future is:

> *Have each child record the following information in the fall, winter, and spring: height, weight, hair color, sex, and one measurement of your choosing. Which information changed? Why? Which information stayed the same? Why? Next, have the students collect this information about themselves from three years ago. Then have them predict how this information will be different three years and six years from now.*

In conclusion, evaluation is a serious segment of the educational process. We can use evaluation as a learning experience or as a bludgeon. Much evaluation presupposes that what is being taught is desired by the learner. When, as educators, we commit ourselves to teaching what is relevant, and when we present this learning as deeply rooted in experience and in an open dialogue, based on mutual trust and respect between student and teacher, then good education is taking place.

POINTS TO PONDER

Design a psychomotor checklist to record the development of the students in your class. Select skills that are appropriate for your students. Two examples follow (Figures 5.6 and 5.7). How might you adapt them for your students?

COMPETENCY TESTING

Most people would agree that after more than 12 years of schooling at a yearly cost exceeding $2500 for each child, a high-school graduate should be able to read and write. We are, however, continually amazed by newspaper headlines that tell us about high-school graduates suing school systems because they are illiterate. Colleges are being forced to provide more remedial reading and writing courses. Publishers are having college textbooks rewritten at the ninth- or tenth-grade reading level.

Minimum-competency testing has appeared on the scene. More than three-quarters of the states have passed laws or regulations requiring minimum-competency testing. Two-thirds of these states require that tests be given, and nearly one-half require a passing score as a condition for high-school graduation. Furthermore, competency testing is sifting down to lower and lower grade levels. In some states, elementary-school children must pass approved tests before they can be promoted. Many states require minimum-competency tests before children can be promoted to grade seven.

Although some states test all the basic skills, most competency testing is being done in reading and mathematics. Creative teachers recognize that certain skills are needed for lifelong learning and they assist *each* student in acquiring these skills. While we refer to skills such as observation, inference, measurement, formulating hypotheses, and communicating as basic skills,

Figure 5.6 Primary psychomotor checklist

PSYCHOMOTOR CHECKLIST
Primary

The following psychomotor skills are important in the physical development of your child. Progress is indicated by:

   +   mastered skill
   −   working toward the mastery of that skill

	Preassessment	*Postassessment*	
1. Uses tools correctly and with ease:	September	January	May
a. pencil	___	___	___
b. scissors	___	___	___
c. paste/glue	___	___	___
d. crayons	___	___	___
e. ruler	___	___	___
f. computer mouse	___	___	___
g. computer keyboard	___	___	___
2. Demonstrates coordination in:			
a. walking	___	___	___
b. skipping	___	___	___
c. jumping	___	___	___
d. running	___	___	___
e. catching balls	___	___	___
f. walking on a balance beam	___	___	___
g. hopping on one foot	___	___	___
h. climbing playground equipment	___	___	___
3. Uses fine motor skills to:			
a. tie a bow	___	___	___
b. fasten butons	___	___	___
c. string beads	___	___	___
d. arrange blocks	___	___	___
4. Claps or moves to rhythm patterns	___	___	___
5. Pantomimes simple stories	___	___	___
6. Imitates movements	___	___	___
7. Focuses attention on work for an appropriate amount of time	___	___	___

Figure 5.7 Intermediate psychomotor checklist

PSYCHOMOTOR CHECKLIST

Intermediate Elementary—Middle School

The psychomotor domain is concerned with the development of muscular skill and coordination. Below is a list of psychomotor skills that are necessary for intermediate or middle school students. Progress in each area is indicated by:

+ outstanding skills
/ satisfactory skills
— skills that are being developed

	Preassessment	Postassessment	
	September	January	May
1. Uses correct posture in:			
a. sitting	____	____	____
b. standing	____	____	____
2. Demonstrates coordination in:			
a. walking	____	____	____
b. running	____	____	____
c. catching	____	____	____
3. Exhibits appropriate levels of energy	____	____	____
4. Participates actively in physical education/recess	____	____	____
5. Focuses attention on educational tasks/assignments	____	____	____
6. Demonstrates sense of balance	____	____	____
7. Holds pencil in correct manner	____	____	____
8. Organizes work space	____	____	____
9. Uses the following tools correctly and with ease:			
a. scissors	____	____	____
b. ruler	____	____	____
c. protractor	____	____	____
d. compass	____	____	____
10. Uses computer keyboard appropriately	____	____	____
11. Draws geometric shapes accurately	____	____	____

they are, in reality, the minimum-competency skills needed for lifelong learning. Teaching these skills will assist students in meeting the minimum competencies in reading and mathematics required by most states.

POINTS TO PONDER

What competencies should a teacher test for? How do you avoid having minimum competencies become maximum competencies? Should minimum-competency test scores be used to evaluate teachers? Why or why not?

How can pre- and postassessments along with a student profile meet the needs perceived by minimum-competency testing?

Cite the pros and cons of a minimum-competency testing program in elementary school, secondary school, and college.

PORTFOLIO ASSESSMENT

A portfolio is defined as a case or folder that holds one's work samples. In education, portfolios are used by teachers to collect samples of a child's schoolwork. Portfolios are used at all grade levels as a part of the assessment process. Portfolios have been a part of art assessment for many years and they are now becoming accepted for all areas of the curriculum. More than 20 states now utilize portfolio assessments as part of the complete assessment package.

Advocates of portfolio assessment recommend that a set of criteria for portfolio sets of students' products needs to be developed. Furthermore, two portfolios should be developed for each student. One portfolio should contain daily work samples. Special evaluation samples should then be selected from the daily portfolio to be placed in the second or formal portfolio.

The effective use of portfolios as an assessment tool can: (1) provide students with a means to reflect on their own curricular activities, (2) supply teachers with a range of sources from which to plan instruction, and (3) provide students and teachers with opportunities to discuss progress as well as instructional needs. Portfolio assessment allows students to share information about their progress with other students, parents, teachers, and administrators. It allows the teacher to assess the learning that seems to have taken place by individual students and the entire class, and to determine the quality of the instructional strategies used by the teacher.

Portfolio assessment allows students in language arts, for example, to provide work samples that require students to:

1. construct their own meanings;
2. integrate new ideas drawn from specific tasks;
3. integrate reading, writing, speaking, and listening in a more natural environment.

In mathematics, a sample assessment item for a student's portfolio might be:

A relative of yours has just moved to the United States. She rides the subway each day to work. She is not familiar with U.S. money. She needs

75 cents in exact change to ride the subway, and only nickels, dimes, and quarters may be used.

Using the paper provided, draw or write an explanation for your relative that will help her to know what coins to use for the subway ride. Place the paper in your daily portfolio.

In science, a sample assessment might be:

Materials have been provided for you to build an electrical circuit. After you have built the circuit, test the conductivity of the materials provided and record the results in a data table that you construct.

Place a drawing of your circuit and your data table in your portfolio.

In social studies, a sample assessment might be:

Construct a time line of historical, economic, and political events that took place between 1900–1950. View your time line and write an analysis paper of how one key event of your choice affected the time period. Place your time line and analysis paper in your portfolio.

POINTS TO PONDER

What items would you include in a daily reading portfolio? In a formal reading portfolio? Discuss your choices with other teachers. Did you agree? Explain any differences.

Read "A Literacy Poem Phonics Lesson." How does this poem reinforce the need for the use of portfolio assessments? Using specific examples, justify your answer.

A Literacy Poem Phonics Lesson

Lisa Lenz

When I entered first grade, I wanted to read
And assumed that it all might be fun.
I like hearing stories (Knew some by heart!)
My mom thought the battle half won.

But that was before Ms. Jackson appeared
With her phonics, her rules and her charts.
Worksheets came prior to books in her room—
By November I began to lose heart.

In September we'd practice our three letter words
Like **CAT, BIT, TOM, CUT, BUT,** and **RED.**
We thought that **"short vowels"** referred to word length
And not to their sound, as she'd said.

But by late November, we learned **"silent e"**
Could change anything **"short"** to a **"long"**

She asked for a reader one day; I stood up,
Thinking I couldn't go wrong.

She gave me these cards and I started out well
With word family: **HOME, ROME** and **DOME.**
Then I boldly flipped back that first card to **c**
And announced to the class it was **CŌME.**

"No dear!" sighed Ms. J. "That word isn't **COMB** . . .
COMB ends with a **b** you can't hear."
So I flipped the **e** over and put in the **b.**
My grasp of this getting less clear.

For if **COMB** has a **"long o"** and no **"silent e"**
And the **"short u"** sound is in **COME.**
The **DOME** should be spelled **D-O-M-B**
And **D-O-M-B** pronounced **DUMB.**

Ms. Jackson protested my little ad lib
And restored **"silent e"** to its place.
I never spoke up in her classroom again,
I'd been hushed by the look on her face!

My remedial teacher now drills me
On things I'm not able to do.
We spend endless hours practicing vowel sounds
A, E, I, O, and **U.**

I may not be able to make sense of those rules;
At school, the die has been cast . . .
But at home I devour books—just love to read!
(At school they don't know; no one's asked!)

Lisa Lenz, "A Literacy Poem Phonetics Lesson" *The Reading Teacher*, vol. 44, no. 8 (April 1991), p. 622. Copyright 1991. International Reading Association. By permission.

EVALUATING YOURSELF: A CLIMATE AUDIT

Parents will tell you that if their child has a teacher who is sensitive and caring, and can motivate their child, it is a wonderful year. The child looks forward to school, completes homework, and does extra assignments. Learning takes place and the child feels good about the year. School is grand!

The dream of every creative teacher is to have every child love school. After the students leave the room at 3:05 and you have time to reflect on the day, you know the students who got 100 percent on the spelling test, wrote the extra reports, and participated in class discussion, but you really do not know how your students feel about school, your class, your assignments, and you. You will never know unless you ask.

You can develop a survey that asks questions about the attitudes students have about the school, your classroom, your assignments, and you. It is up to you to find out what they like best, what they like least, and why.

Teachers complete student report cards at regular intervals during the school year. This is a perfect time to have your students evaluate you. Even upper elementary students can be helpful in designing a teacher's report card. You can use the same form each grading period or create new ones that reflect new projects and activities. If the students feel you want the information to improve the class, they will be very serious about the evaluation. If you have lower elementary students, you can read the questions to the students and have them mark a face that corresponds with their feelings. You can also meet with the students in small groups or individually to access their ideas. By getting feedback on a regular basis, you can adjust your approach, types of projects, length of homework assignments, and teaching style to meet the needs of your students.

It takes an interested and concerned teacher with a strong self-concept to pursue teacher evaluation. You will receive some glowing remarks and some cutting comments. Be prepared. It takes a thick skin and a willing heart, but creative teachers realize that there is always a different way to do something—and it may be better.

If you decide to give teacher evaluations only twice during the year, consider the first and middle grading periods. An early evaluation will give you the information you need from the students to make necessary changes. You certainly would not want to go through an entire school year, only to find out that a student was unhappy most of the year with a procedure or a concept that could have been changed or altered. If you wait until the end of school, it is too late. Your class will move to the next grade level. Start your evaluations early so you can be the best teacher ever.

Sending evaluation surveys to parents is extremely beneficial. You will want to know if they have concerns about your educational program, teaching style, and rapport. It is also helpful to know what was most helpful for their child, what activities were motivating, how long their child spent doing homework, and the attitude of their child about school and the classroom. This information is valuable to creative teachers who care about the intellectual and psychological needs of students. Parent surveys also open the door for communication between the teacher and parents. They send a clear message to parents that says, "I care and I am interested in your feedback."

Creative teachers take time to evaluate themselves. They do an individual climate audit at the end of each day to determine if they are meeting the needs of their students. Questions and statements that you may want to include on your list are:

Did I greet each student as he/she entered the class?

Did I make each student feel welcome?

Did I respond positively to questions?

Did I ask thought-provoking questions that made students think, analyze, compare, and evaluate?

Did I allow an appropriate waiting time for questions?

Did I meet the intellectual needs of each child in my class today?

Did I make each student feel important?

Did I allow my students to teach each other today?

Did I move about the classroom to assist students?

Did I read to the students?

Did any students confide in me today?

Did the students have an opportunity to speak in front of the class?

Did I get angry? Why? How could I avoid this feeling?

Were any of my students angry? Why? How could I help to resolve the conflict?

Did I urge students to help others?

Did I laugh with the students?

Did I send positive messages to students during the day?

Did I do at least one activity that was new or different?

Was I a positive role model for my students today?

The reactions to these questions and statements are used as aids by creative teachers in preparing for the next day. Creative teachers encourage evaluation and feedback from their peers, parents, administrators, and students.

FRAMES OF REFERENCE FOR INDIVIDUAL PROGRESS: EVALUATING AND GRADING STUDENT PERFORMANCE

Stories abound about students and teachers and the act of evaluating academic progress—and the assignment to grade, to communicate, and to record such progress. Students have been heard to mutter, "I worked very hard. I learned a great deal. And I only received a grade of C." Or, "I did not learn a thing in that class, but I made an A." Evaluation and the assignment of grades are not easy. Teachers are often heard to say, "I love teaching, but I hate to assign grades." All year long teachers work hard encouraging chidren. They compliment children for their persevering effort. They smile at their idiosyncrasies. They touch hands with affection to instill trust. And, when the occasion is right, they have even been known to hug children. Then the agony arrives. Grades are due. The honeymoon is over. The moment of truth is here. Grades are assigned. Some children are elated, some pleased, and some are terribly disappointed. Some children do not understand. You have been nice all along, and now the BOMB. How could this have happened? The student often thinks, "I thought she liked me. If so, how come I received these grades?"

Evaluation and the associated grading are difficult because emotions often enter into the process. Teachers enjoy their students. They become attached to them. For a year (and occasionally, for one or two students, two years) they see more of the children than the parents do. It is difficult to dispense love and academic justice from the same pulpit. Teachers resolve this dilemma in several ways. Some teachers do a careful job of telling children that "grades are what you earn," and affection, attention, encouragement, and other kudos are "what is given." The two are not necessarily connected. They further state that the notion of grades is not something the teacher gives to you, but something you earn by and for yourself. In essence, you give yourself the grades; the teacher merely records them. This approach gains in validity when the teacher makes available, at any time, a child's (not the class's) current grade status. This behooves the teacher to keep accurate, current records, and to provide sufficient scores so that a final grade allows children to determine where they are in light of the ongoing grading process. When children are apprised of their current status, final grades do not come as a surprise. They will know in which direction they are moving. If extra efforts need to be made, they can make them. They can correct mistakes or complete additional work. They will know what must be done. And, if they choose to do nothing, they are usually aware of the consequence. Using this approach, there are few surprises. Creative teachers trust children enough to allow them to compute their individual scores, which leads children to be more responsible for their own actions. And teachers become more cognizant of individual progress, attitudes, and concerns. Guessing is removed from grading. The accumulating evidence is visible for each child to review and to use for planning future progress. The onus is off the teacher and, where it belongs, on the children.

Schools evaluate many things. Children are weighed and their height recorded early, and again late, in the school year. The difference in these measures is the growth (or the lack of growth) of each child. The same concept holds true for academic evaluations. In order to evaluate, one must have an initial frame of reference. Various test scores should be obtained early in the school year and compared to similar scores at the end of the academic year. Without an initial frame of reference, gains cannot be accurately measured. To simply test only reveals where they are. Gains cannot be established unless one knows where the students were at some prior point. Thus the need for pretests.

Some textbook series have commercially designed pretests and posttests, but if they are not available it is easy to write your own. You can determine the key skills or concepts that need to be mastered by looking through the table of contents. Once you have determined the 10 to 30 types of problems, parts of speech, science process skills, or periods of history that you deem important, you can devise a pretest by selecting a representative question from each area.

The pretest can be given to find out what the students know and what they "forgot to remember." You will find a range of students in your class. Some will have already mastered a majority of skills, while others will know only a few skills. The pretest will help you to determine what needs to be taught and to whom.

After you have determined where each student should start, it is important to monitor progress. You can do this by constructing survey sheets that include one question related to each skill (Figure 5.8). These questions can be easily found at the end of the chapter or book. (Students feel more comfortable about taking a survey than a test because the goal is to improve their score, not to get a perfect paper.)

Surveys can be given at regular intervals to check progress: once a week, every two weeks, or twice during a grading period. Each time a survey is taken, the teacher and student can see if progress has been made. A goal for the next survey can also be set.

It helps to construct a Progress Chart. (Figure 5.9) Down the side of the chart, list the skills that need to be mastered during the grading period, semester, or year. Across the top, mark the date each survey is given.

The progress chart says it all. When parents come for conferences, you can show the progress each child has made in a specific area and what each child still needs to accomplish. Parents will view you as a very organized teacher who knows the strengths and weaknesses of their child. Your students will also see what they have to accomplish. The goal for each student is to learn at least one new skill on each survey. Little by little, week by week, each skill is mastered. The students feel wonderful because they can see and chart their own progress.

If you plan to give weekly or biweekly surveys, it is helpful to make several surveys at one time. You can use the questions at the back of the book or at the end of the chapters. Use the same format for each survey. Copy and place each survey in a labeled and numbered folder. Once organized, this system can be used from year to year.

The weekly or biweekly review sharpens and reinforces skills, challenges students, and provides the teacher with a record of progress. This method of charting progress can be used at any grade level or in any subject. Bonus: Because of the constant review, your students will perform remarkably well on standardized tests.

POINTS TO PONDER

During a grading period, student A mastered four beginning-level math skills. Student B mastered four higher-level math skills. Both students reached their individual goals. Have both students earned an A? Why or why not? How would you defend the grades to the parents, the principal, or the child?

PARENT CONFERENCES

You have feverishly graded stacks of papers, tabulated all of the grades, and completed the report cards. You have had the students wash the tops of the desks,

Figure 5.8

MATHEMATICS SURVEY SHEET

Name _____

1. $\begin{array}{r} 423651 \\ + 217688 \\ \hline \end{array}$

2. $\begin{array}{r} 4836 \\ - 2867 \\ \hline \end{array}$

3. $\begin{array}{r} 572 \\ \times \;\; 86 \\ \hline \end{array}$

4. $\begin{array}{r} 839 \\ \times 550 \\ \hline \end{array}$

5. $5\overline{)326}$

6. $70\overline{)6508}$

7. $853\overline{)73824}$

8. $\begin{array}{r} \frac{3}{8} \\ + \frac{3}{4} \\ \hline \end{array}$

9. $\begin{array}{r} \frac{4}{5} \\ - \frac{3}{10} \\ \hline \end{array}$

10. $\frac{5}{2} \times \frac{3}{10} =$

11. $\frac{5}{9} \div \frac{2}{3} =$

12. $\begin{array}{r} 8\frac{2}{3} \\ + 6\frac{2}{5} \\ \hline \end{array}$

13. $\begin{array}{r} 9 \\ - 6\frac{5}{6} \\ \hline \end{array}$

14. $2\frac{1}{2} \times 3\frac{1}{2} =$

15. $5\frac{1}{2} \div 2\frac{1}{2} =$

16. $\begin{array}{r} 4.636 \\ + 3.294 \\ \hline \end{array}$

17. $\begin{array}{r} 8 \\ - 3.94 \\ \hline \end{array}$

18. $\begin{array}{r} 9.31 \\ \times \;\; 60 \\ \hline \end{array}$

19. $3\overline{)6.24}$

20. Average
    126
    124
    132
    428
    130
    ‾‾‾

21. Perimeter
22. Area
23. Volume

    L = 2 cm.
    W = 5 cm.
    H = 10 cm.

24. 10% of 80 =

25. $\begin{array}{l} \text{3 ft. 4 in.} \\ + \text{2 ft. 11 in.} \\ \hline \end{array}$

1. _____
2. _____
3. _____
4. _____
5. _____
6. _____
7. _____
8. _____
9. _____
10. _____
11. _____
12. _____
13. _____
14. _____
15. _____
16. _____
17. _____
18. _____
19. _____
20. _____
21. _____
22. _____
23. _____
24. _____
25. _____

Figure 5.9

PROGRESS CHART

Student _____

+ mastered skill.
− skill not mastered.
The goal for the end of the sixth grade is mastery in all 25 areas.

Math Skills	*Dates of Surveys*									
Addition										
Subtraction										
Multiplication by tens										
Multiplication by hundreds										
Division by ones										
Division by tens										
Division by hundreds										
Addition of fractions										
Subtraction of fractions										
Multiplication of fractions										
Division of fractions										
Addition of mixed fractions										
Subtraction of mixed fractions										
Multiplication of mixed fractions										
Division of mixed fractions										
Addition of decimals										
Subtraction of decimals										
Multiplication of decimals										
Division of decimals										

Averages									
Perimeter									
Area									
Volume									
Percent									
Measurement									

erase the chalkboard, and clean out the guinea pig cage. It is time for parent conferences.

The halls are lined with chairs, the classrooms are empty, the parents sit nervously, time lingers, the classroom door opens and closes, and the heart of every parent is at your mercy. The parents have waited a full six to nine weeks for the teacher to give the verdict. "Is my child above or below average?" "Does my child have friends?" "Will my child succeed?" Parents inherently know the answers, but they want a second opinion: yours. They want to hear it from a professional.

Be prepared, be polite, and, first and foremost, be positive. Start by walking to the door to greet the parents; introduce yourself, and, if appropriate, shake their hands. Be friendly and cordial. Most of the time the parents are more nervous than you are. Make them feel comfortable and at ease. Set your materials on a table instead of your desk, and have adult-sized chairs arranged so you can have good eye contact.

Start your conference with several positive comments about the child, and let the parents know you enjoy working with their child. Next ask the parents if they have questions or concerns. Some parents will come with organized lists while others will just want to listen to what you have to say. Some parents will be interested in the social aspects of their child, others will focus on the academic. If a parent asks a question and you do not know the answer or if it will take you some time to find the answer, write the question on a piece of paper and tell the parent you will call him or her later with the information. Once the parent concerns are answered, the parents will be more interested in listening to your comments.

Have everything well organized. Compile a folder of materials for each child and arrange these in order of your conferences. You may even want to put the time of the conference on each folder to keep you on schedule. In the folder, place progress charts and examples of the child's work so you can show the parents which skills their child has mastered and what he/she still needs to accomplish.

Creative teachers keep the conversation positive. If the child has deficiencies, be specific and give examples. Tell the parents that you are concerned and explain how you are trying to encourage and assist their child. Remember that it is your responsibility and not the parents'. If the parents say they would like to help, record on your pad of paper what you plan to do to get information or materials to them. If the parents begin to blame all of the past teachers, refocus them on the present situation and assure them that you plan to work with their child. For every problem there is at least one solution. Concentrate on solutions.

Be cognizant of the time. You will have other parents waiting. Politely look at your watch and mention that you appreciate their taking time to come to the conference and if they need to talk with you about other concerns, you will be glad to schedule another conference. Slowly rise, hand them their child's report card, a packet of selected papers, and walk the parents to the door.

Keep an open mind during conferences. Parents may tell you things about your teaching that you do not want to hear. Listen patiently and try not to be defensive. If a parent says you give too much homework, or hurt their child's feelings, or graded a paper incorrectly, jot the information on your notepad. If a parent brings up a concern, it is important. After parent conferences are over, review your notepad. If a comment has been mentioned by several parents, see how you can improve the situation. If it was only mentioned by one set of parents, be sensitive to their child's needs. It may be helpful to talk with the class about concerns. As a group you can discuss problems and brainstorm solutions.

Creative teachers make parent conferences as positive as possible. It is your opportunity to communicate with the parents. Put some students' poems, a student newsletter, or positive articles about parents and education in the hallway. This simple form of communication gets a conference off to a good start and gives parents something to read while they are waiting. For yourself, order a small bouquet of flowers and place them on the conference table. It will brighten your day. Dress neatly and professionally. That will bolster your self-confidence. Have a supply of candy bars in your desk for a quick energy break, and plan to go out for dinner. You will be too exhausted to cook.

ON BECOMING A CREATIVE TEACHER

Previous sections of this book dealt with the changing curriculum, changing schools, changing students, and changing teachers. Change is universal, constant, and continuous. Things must change so they can remain the same. Otherwise our lives and the world as we know it would not be the same. We adjust to change, and the key to surviving these adjustments is flexibility. Creative teachers are flexible. They bend, they rebound, but they don't break. They accept change in stride.

Creative teachers produce new, original, unique learning situations wherein students can create new, original, unique solutions to problems and discover new patterns, ideas, or products. Creativity flourishes in a classroom atmosphere where thinking processes are automatic, swift, and spontaneous when not disturbed by other influences. Schools as they are currently organized interfere with the natural flow of creativity. Teachers perceive "good teaching" as interactive relationships. The teacher fields a question, and responses from children are forthcoming. Or conversely, the child poses a question and the teacher responds. The teacher is the gateway through which all things must pass. The action is one-on-one, the teacher always being one of the two individuals involved. Emphasis is not on the correctness of the response to the stimulus, but on the thinking process. Creative teachers supplant stimulus-response situations with broad-based, cooperative interaction guided by the teacher, but not necessarily involving the teacher as a final authority in a decision-making situation.

Creativity is recognized as a highly desirable component of learning—a hallmark of all that is good and vital to the learning process. Creativity is drawing on all past experiences and selecting from them components that yield a construct of new patterns, ideas, products, or solutions. Creativity is a thinking process. It is something everyone possesses in varying degrees. Everyone is born with some creative potential. Creativity can be developed, and its development depends upon the environment into which it is introduced and circumstances that condition it. It cannot be learned like geography or demonstrated like shooting a basketball through a hoop. It can only be developed and nurtured. Creativity is what creative people do, and create we must. Creativity can and should permeate all of learning.

Characteristic Traits of Creative Teachers

How do you know a creative teacher when you see one? Invariably they are distinguished by their actions. Creative teachers are generators. They produce a product, an idea, a unique learning climate, or resolve a thirst for an accepted challenge. As a group, they exhibit some common traits. These are not necessarily developed traits, and many of these traits are not necessarily deemed desirable. Nonetheless, they exist.

Creative persons usually:

have strong egos. They appear satisfied with their uniqueness.

enjoy the knowledge that they are identified as being creative. They may even relish it.

search for challenges. They enjoy thinking, wrestling with ideas, and resolving dilemmas, problems, or situations.

revel in manipulating ideas and objects to see what is revealed when the manipulation is completed.

have the ability to endure. They are often single-minded in their pursuit of solutions to problems. They hang tough.

have abundant energy. They pursue tasks in a disciplined manner, mindful of energy expenditures.

have a healthy appetite for work. They enjoy shuffling, rearranging, gyrating, and expanding ideas.

exhibit an impatience to get on with the task at hand, yet are not anxious to conclude tasks prematurely. They prefer to investigate various irregularities of a problem on the chance that some small influences might need to be considered before closure can be effected.

are not overly concerned about inconsistencies. They search them out on the chance that an explanation of these inconsistencies might prove interesting.

resist an overabundance of supervision. They feel confident enough to operate independently.

challenge existing solutions to problems. They prefer to offer their own.

can simultaneously handle diverse variables or considerations in the flow of ideas directed toward the solution of problems.

are easily irritated and resist change that alters what they consider is right.

are satisfied with their identity. They wonder about the way of the world.

are risk takers and accept the responsibilities that are engendered by extending their thinking beyond conventional boundaries.

Reviewing these traits and noting other interesting descriptive traits of highly creative people, such as discontented, introversive, avoids conventions of courtesy, different, one might question how desirable a creative teacher really is. This question might be partially answered by how creative teachers might react to educational statements such as:

It will never work!

It has been tried before.

Whose idea was this?

The kids and the parents, let alone the administration will never go for it.

Its time has not come. Let's sit on it.

Put it on the back burner. We are not ready for this.

We tried this before, and it did not work.

If it ain't broke, don't fix it.

We could never swing it. We don't have the time, the money, or the energy. Bring it up next year.

POINTS TO PONDER

How desirable is a creative teacher? What do you think?

Improving Your Creativity

Creative people are problem seekers and problem solvers. As teachers we must acquire, then promote creative talents in ourselves and in our students. Creativity comes naturally to some people; for most individuals, however, creativity is a do-it-yourself achievement. It is personal. It appears most readily available when one is oneself. So relax. Be yourself. Discover yourself. Many people have never taken time to become acquainted with themselves. People who have discovered and accepted the parameters of their personalities appear more free to concentrate on developing their creativities. Here are suggestions for involving yourself in your creativity:

Ask yourself questions. Don't always accept what you see or hear as final. Delve into each situation. Challenge yourself to come up with several searching questions about any situation. Think of extending the scope of the problem or situation by asking provocative questions of yourself, of others about the situation. This should encompass a thorough understanding of the problem, a plan for actively embracing the problem, and a verification of results.

Vary your perspective. When viewing a problem, look for ways of modifying it, substituting variables, rearranging components of the problem to arrive at new relationships, or occasionally reversing processes. Remember that a cow doesn't look the same viewed from opposite ends. Try magnifying components of the problem; minimizing components. What does this do for trying out recombinations or new relationships?

Get involved. Creative spontaneity springs from fresh insights that mingle with old ideas and exit from the mind as new expressions. Keep fresh discoveries coming by getting involved in something—preferably something new. Become an expert in some area, but keep reaching out for new experiences. Quiz people. Wonder about everything. Observe. Associate with people who exhibit the creative spark. Creativity rubs off. It is infectious.

Live happily. Happiness with a pinch of frustration, stirred well with a germ of an idea, drenched in perseverance, is highly conducive to creative production.

Take a chance. Become a calculated risk taker. Creativity demands daring personalities. Engineer dreams down to reality. Don't be bashful. Kick at stars. Run with the wind. Try something. Remember: If you think you are, you are. And, after all, you really are.

Immerse yourself. Work! Persevere! Think! Reflect! Create something! Reach up. Reach out. Alter your perspective. Challenge yourself to grow. Remember that you are someone's creation.

Barriers to Creative Teaching

To initiate a creative teaching and learning environment, several constraints must be considered and subsequently removed. Prime among these constraints are:

> a lack of strong desire of all concerned for creative change

> a lack of information on how to initiate and sustain creative instruction and learning

> a grave concern for releasing oneself from the traditional approach to a more cavalier, creative teaching style

a fear of failure

predetermined methods of teaching and teaching plans, replacing them with a creative style

staid lesson plans (the same plan for all children)

the overuse of low-level questions, supplanting them with a broad mix of the full range of established taxonomical categories

the overuse of textbooks as a teaching device with the same assignments for everyone

efficiency in education, substituting quality in education, and instituting an evaluation system commensurate with creative teaching.

Creative teaching sometimes conflicts with many well-established school rules. By nature the school setting, with finite hours, days, and weeks of attendance in the school year, is uncreative. The automatic mass progression of children from one grade level to the next, use of the same books for the entire grade, uniform assignments, and common lessons are all uncreative. Schools are replete with uncreative acts. Teachers have adjusted their teaching to the so-called normal student; by contrast, the creative individual is usually dubbed the deviate who taxes our energy and tries our patience. Teachers have not always favored, and some may have even disfavored, the more creative student. We operate with contradictions. We want children to be free to express themselves, but not too free. We invite children to talk, but not too much and only at the right time. We appreciate student independence, but not too much. We wish students to conform, but not too much. And we want them to be creative, but not too creative. Dilemmas do exist. Schools by nature are restrictive. With concerns for children's safety, their physical and social involvements, and extracurricular concerns, schools must operate within a prescribed network of rules and regulations. Creative teachers recognize the problems, observe the rules, and devise methods and techniques for operating within these parameters.

Providing a Creative Classroom Setting

As the creative teacher, you must work at being creative; you serve as the creative model in action. If creativity is to be a joy to children, this joy must be reflected in your behavior and actions. Some actions that you might take are:

1. Be constantly aware of the existence of individual differences, and accommodate them by appropriate praise, attention, and assignments.
2. Convince the class that creative action is welcomed, recognized, and rewarded.
3. Recognize creative contributions and communicate your acceptance and approval.
4. Be receptive to all creative contributions; be tolerant of every contribution, no matter how insignificant it may appear to be.
5. Eliminate evaluation or judgment; occasionally engage the entire class in off-the-wall brainstorming.

6. Reduce reliance on authority; promote individual investigations, experimentations, and inventions.
7. Assist highly creative individuals to relax their fears and anxieties, integrating them into more group activities.
8. Downplay perfection at early levels of thinking.
9. Help individuals to express themselves more freely and to worry less about making mistakes.

Children are more creative when they operate in a relaxed, democratic environment where individual contributions are accepted and respected. They perform most creatively when ideas are allowed to flow in a natural manner, devoid of criticism, and their efforts are rewarded and encouraged.

As you begin involving children in creative experiences, as you disenfranchise yourself from the traditional approach to teaching in favor of a more creative approach, you will have more time to observe children in action. Here are some salient questions to consider in evaluating how successful your creative teaching/creative learning is:

Are the students operating more on their own?

Are leadership roles evolving from the class?

Are children looking to other children for assistance and are they getting it?

Does more talking exist, child-to-child, about the task at hand?

Do children want to carry on or extend the lesson despite the time period ending?

Are the children interacting more, listening more, planning more on their own and with each other?

Do you as a teacher feel less needed?

Has your role changed from teacher to facilitator?

Are the children finding out that independent activities are more difficult, involve more personal responsibility, but are more enjoyable than the traditional approach? Has this resulted in a greater tolerance for each other's contributions?

Are you becoming a director more than a corrector?

Do the children only call on you for help as a last resort?

When the children do not know something and want to know something, do they formulate a plan of action and carry it forward on their own?

Do the children exhibit novel, unique, creative solutions to resolve problems being studied?

Look for signs to guide you as to when, how much, and for how long you need to intervene to bring things back on track and focused in a positive direction.

RESEARCH SAYS . . .

In an article entitled, "You can't have authentic assessment without authentic content" (Peters 1991), it is pointed out that "when the appropriateness of content is not attended to, comprehension is impeded, strategies cannot be used effectively, learning is fragmented, and transfer of content knowledge to new learning situations is impaired. Therefore, it is not enough to use trade books, textbooks, and children's magazines. Authentic content must be reflective of subjects that make up the elementary curriculum material that goes to the heart of a discipline and material that allows for personal application of ideas that go beyond school-related activities." (p. 590)

The author provides five guidelines to assist teachers in the selection of material that will contain important content, the heart of authentic assessment. They are:

1. Material should reflect important themes and ideas.
2. Materials should be consistent with the goals of the subject area curriculum in your district.
3. Material should be rooted in real-world experiences and have application to the world both inside and outside of school.
4. Materials should be sensitive to the developmental progression of students.
5. Materials should allow students to engage in higher order thinking. (pp. 590–591)

The article concludes, "Through careful content selection, we communicate our definitions and goals of reading and learning and ensure that assessment is authentic and meaningful." (p. 590)

POINTS TO PONDER

Select a theme or idea.

Develop a teaching strategy, activities, and an assessment that utilizes this theme. Check the five guidelines for authentic assessment and discuss with a colleague whether or not each of these guidelines has been satisfied.

PAUSE FOR A SUMMARY

If we expect to teach the whole child, then we should expect to teach and evaluate in all three learning domains—cognitive (content), affective (attitude), and psychomotor (physical motion).

Cognitive learning is accumulating content knowledge and may be classified into six levels.

The most important of the three domains of learning is the affective domain.

The psychomotor domain is concerned with the development of muscular skill and coordination.

Creative teachers preassess children according to a set of performance objectives (criterion-referenced tests). They also provide each child with a profile of their skills so that everyone can be informed of the child's progress.

Creative teachers utilize portfolios as one method of assessment.

Creative teachers first evaluate themselves and their instruction to determine if they are meeting the needs of their students.

Creative teachers encourage evaluation of themselves and their classrooms by their peers, by the administration, by parents, and by their students.

Creative teachers develop authentic assessments for their students.

Epilogue

An older gentleman sitting on the bench noticed a young man hurling what looked like stones into the water.

He would bend down, pick one up and fling it as far as he could into the sea. Finally, the older man asked what he was doing.

"Well, you see," smiled the young man, "the tide is now out. There are so many of these poor starfish who are washed up on the beach"—he had one in his hand—"and they will die unless they are put back into the water.

"So, I wanted to save them, and that is why I am putting them back into the sea."

"But that's crazy," the older man exclaimed. "There are thousands more starfish on the beach, maybe millions. There is no way you can make a difference."

The young man gazed at the starfish in his hand.

"I can make a difference to this one," he said, and he hurled the starfish back into the sea.

Source: Editorial page, "The Future Is Students," *Indianapolis News,* May 10, 1991. Lisa Coffey, Writer. ©1991 The Indianapolis News. By permission.

REFERENCES

Bloom, B. S., ed. (1956). *Taxonomy of Educational Objectives: Handbook I: Cognitive Domain.* New York: McKay.

Cangelosi, J. S. (1990). *Designing Tests for Evaluating Student Achievement.* White Plains: Longman.

Cangelosi, J. S. (1988). *Classroom Management Strategies: Gaining and Maintaining Students' Cooperation.* White Plains: Longman.

Kubiszyn, T., and Bosich, G. (1987). *Educational Testing and Measurement: Classroom Application and Practice.* Glenview: Scott, Foresman.

Science Curriculum Improvement Study. (1973). *Energy sources evaluation supplement.* Regents of the University of California.

Appendix
I
Education-Related Journals and Organizations

Action in Teacher Education   Available only to members. $40. q (ISSN 0162-6620) Association of Teacher Educators, Office of Publication, Suite ATE, 1900 Association Dr., Reston, VA 22091

Administrator's Notebook $17. 9 times a yr (ISSN 0001-8430) University of Chicago, Midwest Administration Center, 5835 S. Kimbark Ave., Chicago, IL 60637

Adolescence $64. q (ISSN 0001-8449) Libra Publishers, Inc., 3089C Clairemont Dr., Suite 383, San Diego, CA 92117

American Annals of the Deaf $40. 5 times a yr (ISSN 0002-726X) American Annals of the Deaf, ADARA, Box 55369, Little Rock, AK 72225-0369

The American Biology Teacher $48. 8 times a yr (ISSN 0002-7685) National Association of Biology Teachers, 11250 Roger Bacon Dr., No. 19, Reston, VA 22090

American Educational Research Journal $35. q (ISSN 0002-8312) American Educational Research Association, 1230 17th St., N.W., Washington, DC 20036-3078

American Journal of Education $38. q (ISSN 0195-6744) University of Chicago Press, Journals Division, P.O. Box 37005, Chicago, IL 60637

---

q	= quarterly publication	w	= weekly publication
m	= monthly publication	a	= annual publication
yr	= yearly publication	irr	= irregular publication
bi-m	= bimonthly publication		

American Libraries   Free to members; $40 to libraries. m (bi-m Jl/Ag) (ISSN 0002-9769) American Library Association, 50 E. Huron St., Chicago, IL 60611

The American Music Teacher $16. 6 times a yr (ISSN 0003-0112) Music Teachers National Association, Inc., 617 Vine St., Suite 1432, Cincinnati, OH 45202-2434

The American School Board Journal $38. m (ISSN 0003-0953) National School Board Association, 1680 Duke St., Alexandria, VA 22314

American Teacher $7. m (bi-m D/Ja, My/Je) (ISSN 0003-1380) American Federation of Teachers, 555 New Jersey Ave., N.W., Washington, DC 20001

Arithmetic Teacher   Available only to members. $40. m (S-My) (ISSN 0004-136X) National Council of Teachers of Mathematics, 1906 Association Dr., Reston, VA 22091

Art Education $50. bi-m (ISSN 0004-3125) National Art Education Association, 1916 Association Dr., Reston, VA 22091

Arts & Activities $20. m (S-Je) (ISSN 0004-3931) Arts & Activities, Subscriptions Manager, 591 Camino de la Reina, Suite 200, San Diego, CA 92108

Bilingual Review $26. 3 times a yr (ISSN 0094-5366) The Bilingual Review/La Revista Bilingue, Hispanic Research Center, Arizona State University, Tempe, AZ 85287

British Journal of Educational Studies $142.50. 4 times a yr (ISSN 0007-1005) Basil Blackwell, Publishers, Ltd., 108 Cowley Rd., Oxford OX4 1JF, England

British Journal of Educational Technology $62. 3 times a yr (ISSN 0007-1013) National Council for Educational Technology, 3 Devonshire St., London W1N 2BA, England

Bulletin of the Council for Research in Music Education $22.50. q (ISSN 0010-9894) Council for Research in Music Education, School of Music, University of Illinois, 1205 W. California, Urbana, IL 61801

Business Education Forum   Available only to members. $38. m (O-My) (ISSN 0007-6678) National Business Education Association, 1906 Association Dr., Reston, VA 22091

Canadian Journal of Education $60. q (ISSN 0380-2361) CSSE/SCEE, 14 Henderson Ave., Ottawa, Ontario K1N 7P1, Canada

Child & Youth Care Forum $130. bi-m (ISSN 1053-1890) Human Sciences Press, 233 Spring St., New York, NY 10013-1578

Childhood Education   Available only to members. $65. 5 times a yr (ISSN 0009-4056) Association for Childhood Education International, 11141 Georgia Ave., Suite 200, Wheaton, MD 20902

Children Today $12.50. bi-m (ISSN 0361-4336) Superintendent of Documents, U.S. Government Printing Office, Washington, DC 20402

Children's Literature in Education $42. q (ISSN 0045-6713) Human Sciences Press, Inc., 233 Spring St., New York, NY 10013-1578

Chinese Education $187. q (ISSN 0009-4560) M.E. Sharpe, Inc., 80 Business Park Dr., Armonk, NY 10504

The Chronicle of Higher Education $62.50. w (except last 2 wks in Ag and last 2 wks in D) (ISSN 0009-5982) Chronicle of Higher Education, Inc., P.O. Box 1955, Marion, OH 43302

Classroom Computer Learning $24. 8 times a yr (ISSN 0746-4223) Classroom Computer Learning, 19 Davis Dr., Belmont, CA 94002

Communication Education $90. q (ISSN 0363-4523) Speech Communication Association, 5105 Backlick Rd., Suite E, Annandale, VA 22003

Counselor Education and Supervision $12. q (ISSN 0011-0035) American Association for Counseling Development, 5999 Stevenson Ave., Alexandria, VA 22304

Day Care and Early Education $65. q (ISSN 0092-4199) Human Sciences Press, 233 Spring St., New York, NY 10013-1578

Early Child Development and Care $250. q (ISSN 0300-4430) Gordon and Breach Science Publishers, Inc., 270 8th Ave., New York, NY 10011-1613

Early Childhood Education $8.95. a (ISSN 0272-4456) Dushkin Publishing Group, Sluice Dock, Guilford, CT 06437

Education and Training in Mental Retardation $28. a (ISSN 0013-1237) Council for Exceptional Children, Division on Mental Retardation, 1920 Association Dr., Reston, VA 22091

Education and Treatment of Children $62. q (ISSN 0748-8491) Clinical Psychology Publishing Co., Inc., 4 Conant Sq., Brandon, VT 05733

Education and Urban Society $100. q (ISSN 0013-1245) Sage Publications, Inc., 2111 W. Hillcrest, Newbury Park, CA 91320

Education (Chula Vista, Calif.) $21. q (ISSN 0013–1172) Education, 1362 Santa Cruz Ct., Chula Vista, CA 92010

Education Canada $20. q (ISSN 0013–1253) Canadian Education Association, Suite 8-200, 252 Bloor St., W., Toronto, Ontario M5S 1V5, Canada

The Education Digest $27. m (S-My) (ISSN 0013-127X) Prakken Publications, Inc., 416 Longshore Dr., P.O. Box 8623, Ann Arbor, MI 48107

Education Week $49.94. w (for 40 weeks) (ISSN 0277-4232) Editorial Projects in Education Inc., 4301 Connecticut Ave., N.W., Suite 250, Washington, DC 20008

Educational Administration Quarterly $36. q (ISSN 0013-161X) Sage Publications, Inc., 211 West Hillcrest Dr., Newbury Park, CA 91320

Educational Evaluation & Policy Analysis $23. 4 times a yr (ISSN 0162-3737) American Educational Research Association, 1230 17th St., N.W., Washington, DC 20036-3078

The Educational Forum $12. q (ISSN 0013-1725) Kappa Delta Pi, 1601 W. State St., P.O. Box A, West Lafayette, IN 47906

Educational Horizons $18. q (ISSN 0013-175X) Pi Lambda Theta, P.O. Box 6626, Bloomington, IN 47407-6626

Educational Leadership $32. 8 times a yr (ISSN 0013-1784) Association for Supervision and Curriculum Development, 225 N. Washington St., Alexandria, VA 22314-1403

Educational Media International $50. q (ISSN 0004-7597) Kogan Page Ltd., 120 Pentonville Rd., London N1 9JN, England

Educational Record $25. q (ISSN 0013-1873) American Council on Education, Publication Sales Dept., One Dupont Circle, Washington, DC 20036

Educational Research $90. 3 times a yr (ISSN 0013-1881) Carfax Publishing Co., 85 Ash St., Hopkinton, MA 01748

Educational Research Quarterly $23. q (ISSN 0196-5042) Educational Research Quarterly, University of Southern California, School of Education, Phillips Hall, University Park, Los Angeles, CA 90089-0031

Educational Researcher $35. m (bi-m Ja/F, Je/Jl–Ag/S) (ISSN 0013-189X) American Educational Research Association, Subscription Dept., 1230 17th St., N.W., Washington, DC 20036-3078

Educational Review (Abingdon, England) $210. 3 times a yr (ISSN 0013-1911) Carfax Publishing Co., 85 Ash St., Hopkinton, MA 01748

Educational Studies (Abingdon, England) $232. 3 times a yr (ISSN 0305-5698) Carfax Publishing Co., 85 Ash St., Hopkinton, MA 01748

Educational Studies (American Educational Studies Association) $15. q (ISSN 0013-1946) c/o R. Sherman, College of Education, University of Florida, Gainesville, FL 32311

Educational Studies in Mathematics $219.50. q (ISSN 0013-1954) Kluwer Academic Publishers Group, P.O. Box 17, Dordrecht 3300 AA, Netherlands

Educational Technology $119. m (ISSN 0013-1962) Educational Technology Publications, Inc., 720 Palisade Ave., Englewood Cliffs, NJ 07632

Educational Technology Research and Development $45. q (ISSN 1042-1629) Association for Educational Communications and Technology, Inc., 1126 16th St., N.W., Washington, DC 20036
Merger of *Educational Communication and Technology Journal* and *Journal of Instructional Development*, with vol. 37, 1989

Educational Theory $20. q (ISSN 0013-2004) Educational Theory, Education Bldg., University of Illinois, 1310 S. Sixth St., Champaign, IL 61820

Electronic Education $36. 7 times a yr (ISSN 0278-5293) Electronic Communications, Inc., 1311 Executive Center Dr., Suite 220, Tallahassee, FL 32301

Electronic Learning $23.95. 8 times a yr (ISSN 0278-3258) Electronic Learning, Scholastic Inc., 730 Broadway, New York, NY 10003

Elementary School and Guidance & Counseling $30. 4 times a yr (ISSN 0013-5976) American Association for Counseling and Development, 5999 Stevenson Ave., Alexandria, VA 22304

The Elementary School Journal $43. bi-m (ISSN 0013-5984) University of Chicago Press, Journals Division, P.O. Box 37005, Chicago, IL 60637

English Education $18. 4 times a yr (ISSN 0007-8204) National Council of Teachers of English, 1111 Kenyon Rd., Urbana, IL 61801

Equity & Excellence $30. q (ISSN 0894-0681) The School of Education, 109 Montague House, University of Massachusetts, Amherst, MA 01003

Exceptional Children $40. 6 times a yr (ISSN 0014-4029) Council for Exceptional Children, 1920 Association Dr., Reston, VA 22091-1589

The Exceptional Parent $24. 8 times a yr (ISSN 0046-9157) The Exceptional Parent, P.O. Box 657, Kenmore Station, Boston, MA 02215
   Includes Sections: *Family Support Bulletin* and *Networking*, beginning with Ja/F 1991

Focus on Exceptional Children $36. m (S-My) (ISSN 0015-511X) Love Publishing Co., 1777 S. Bellaire St., Denver, CO 80222

The French Review $27. 6 times a yr (ISSN 0016-111X) American Association of Teachers of French, 57 E. Armory Ave., Champaign, IL 61820

The German Quarterly $35. q (ISSN 0016-8831) American Association of Teachers of German, 112 Haddontowne Court, No. 104, Cherry Hill, NJ 08034

Gifted Child Quarterly   Available only to members. $45. q (ISSN 0016-9862) National Association for Gifted Children, 1155 15th St., N.W., Suite 1002, Washington, DC 20005

The Gifted Child Today $30. 6 times a yr (ISSN 0892-9580) GCT Inc., P.O. Box 6448, Mobile, AL 36660-0448

Guidance and Counselling $30. 6 times a yr (ISSN 0831-5493) Guidance Centre, University of Toronto, 10 Acorn Ave., Toronto, Ontario M4V 228, Canada

Harvard Educational Review $60. q (ISSN 0017-8055) Harvard Educational Review, Subscriber Service Dept., Gutman Library, Suite 349, 6 Appian Way, Cambridge, MA 02138-3752

Health Education $50. 6 times a yr (ISSN 0097-0050) American Alliance for Health, Physical Education, Recreation, and Dance, 1900 Association Dr., Reston, VA 22091

Hispania (American Association of Teachers of Spanish and Portuguese) $30. 4 times a yr (ISSN 0018-2133) American Association of Teachers of Spanish and Portuguese, Inc., c/o James R. Chatham, Mississippi State University, Lee Hall, P.O. Box 6349, Mississippi State, MS 39762-6349

History of Education Quarterly $47. q (ISSN 0018-2680) History of Education Quarterly, School of Education, Indiana University, Bloomington, IN 47405

The History Teacher (Long Beach, Calif.) $28. q (ISSN 0018-2745) Society for History Education, Inc., Department of History, California State University, Long Beach, 1250 Bellflower Blvd., Long Beach, CA 90840

Human Development $212. 6 times a yr (ISSN 0018-716X) S. Karger Publishers, Inc., 26 W. Avon Rd., P.O. Box 529, Farmington, CT 06085

Human Development $8.95. a (ISSN 0278-4661) Dushkin Publishing Group, Guilford, CT 06437

Industrial Education $20. m (S-My) (ISSN 0091-8601) Industrial Education, 26011 Evergreen Rd., Suite 204, Southfield, MI 48076-9862

Instructor $16. 9 times a yr (ISSN 0892-9122) Instructor, 545 Fifth Ave., New York, NY 10017

International Journal of Early Childhood $10. 2 times a yr (ISSN 0020-7187) Ontario Institute for Studies in Education, Dept. of Applied Psychology, 252 Bloor St., W., Toronto, Ontario M5S 1V5, Canada

International Journal of Instructional Media $25. q (ISSN 0092-1815) Westwood Press, Inc., 251 Park Ave. South, New York, NY 10010

International Journal of Mathematical Education in Science and Technology $280. bi-m (ISSN 0020-739X) Taylor & Francis Inc., 1900 Forest Rd., Suite 101, Bristol, PA 19007

International Journal of Mathematics and Mathematical Sciences $80. q (ISSN 0161-1712) University of Central Florida, Department of Mathematics, Orlando, FL 32816-6990

International Journal of Physical Education $16; air mail, $20. q (ISSN 0341-8685) Velag Karl Hofmann, D-7060 Schorndorf, Postfach 1360, Germany

International Review of Education $106. 4 times a yr (ISSN 0020-8566) Kluwer Academic Publishers Group, Distribution Center, P.O. Box 17, 3300 AA Dordrecht, Netherlands
    Text and title in English, French, and German

Interracial Books for Children Bulletin $18. 8 times a yr (ISSN 0146-5562) Council on Interracial Books for Children, Inc., 1841 Broadway, New York, NY 10023

Jewish Education $15. q (ISSN 0021-6429) Council for Jewish Education, c/o Board of Jewish Education, Inc., 426 W. 58th St., New York, NY 10019

Journal for Research in Mathematics Education $30. 4 times a yr (ISSN 0021-8251) National Council of Teachers of Mathematics, 1906 Association Dr., Reston, VA 22091

The Journal of Aesthetic Education $25. q (ISSN 0021-8510) University of Illinois Press, Subscription Dept., 54 E. Gregory Dr., P.O. Box 5081, Champaign, IL 61820

Journal of Alcohol and Drug Education $35. 3 times a yr (ISSN 0090-1482) Journal of Alcohol and Drug Education, 1120 East Oakland, P.O. Box 10212, Lansing, MI 48901

Journal of American College Health $52. bi-m (ISSN 0744-8481) Heldref Publications, 4000 Albemarle St., N.W., Washington, DC 20016

Journal of American Indian Education $14. 3 times a yr (ISSN 0021-8731) Center for Indian Education, College of Education, Arizona State University, Tempe, AZ 85281-1311

Journal of Autism and Developmental Disorders $195. q (ISSN 0162-3257) Plenum Press Corp., 233 Spring St., New York, NY 10013-1578

Journal of Biological Education $75. q (ISSN 0021-9266) Journal of Biological Education, Institute of Biology, 20 Queensberry Pl., London SW7 2DZ, England

Journal of Chemical Education $28. m (ISSN 0021-9584) Journal of Chemical Education, Subscription and Book Order Dept., 20th & Northampton Sts., Easton, PA 18042

Journal of Child Language $49. 3 times a yr (ISSN 0305-0009) Cambridge University Press, 110 Midland Ave., Port Chester, NY 10573

The Journal of Computers in Mathematics and Science Teaching Available only to members. $36. q (ISSN 0731-9258) Association of Computers in Mathematics and Science Technology, JCNST, P.O. Box 2966, Charlottesville, VA 22902-2966

Journal of Counseling and Development $65. bi-m (ISSN 0748-9633) American Association for Counseling and Development, 5999 Stevenson Ave., Alexandria, VA 22304

The Journal of Creative Behavior $25. q (ISSN 0022-0175) Managing Editor, Journal of Creative Behavior, Creative Education Foundation, 1050 Union Rd., Buffalo, NY 14224

Journal of Developmental Education $24. 3 times a yr (ISSN 0894-3907) National Center for Developmental Education, Appalachian State University, Reich College of Education, Boone, NC 28608

Journal of Drug Education $96. q (ISSN 0047-2379) Baywood Publishing Co., Inc., 26 Austin Ave., P.O. Box 337, Amityville, NY 11701

The Journal of Economic Education $48. q (ISSN 0022-0485) Heldref Publications, 4000 Albemarle St., N.W., Washington, DC 22016

Journal of Education for Library and Information Science $50. 5 times a yr (Summer, Fall, Winter, directory issue, Spring) (ISSN 0748-5786) Journal of Education for Library and Information Science, Publications Office, 5623 Palm Aire Dr., Sarasota, FL 34243-3702
   Formerly *Journal of Education for Librarianship;* name changed with Summer 1984

Journal of Educational Measurement $50. q (ISSN 0022-0655) National Council on Measurement in Education, 1230 17th St., N.W., Washington, DC 20036-0663

Journal of Educational Psychology $120. bi-m (ISSN 0022-0663) Subscription Section, American Psychological Association, 1400 N. Uhle St., Arlington, VA 22201

The Journal of Educational Research (Washington, DC) $55. bi-m (S-J1) (ISSN 0022-0671) Heldref Publications, Suite 504, 4000 Albemarle St., N.W., Washington, DC 20016

Journal of Educational Technology Systems $96. 4 times a yr (ISSN 0047-2395) Baywood Publishing Co., Inc., 26 Austin Ave., P.O. Box 337, Amityville, NY 11701

Journal of Educational Thought $27. 3 times a yr (ISSN 0022-0701) University of Calgary, Faculty of Education, 2500 University Dr., N.W., Calgary, Alberta T2N 1N4, Canada

The Journal of Environmental Education $47. q (ISSN 0095-8964) Heldref Publications, Suite 500, 4000 Albemarle St., N.W., Washington, DC 20016

The Journal of Experimental Education $52. q (ISSN 0022-0973) Heldref Publications, Suite 500, 4000 Albemarle St., N.W., Washington, DC 20016

The Journal of General Education $9. q (ISSN 0021-3667) Pennsylvania State University Press, 215 Wagner Bldg., University Park, PA 16802

Journal of Geography   Available only to members. $55. bi-m (ISSN 0022-1341) National Council for Geography Education, Indiana University of Pennsylvania, Indiana, PA 15705

Journal of Geological Education $33. 4 times a yr (ISSN 0022-1368) National Association of Geology Teachers, 1041 New Hampshire St., P.O. Box 368, Lawrence, KS 66044

Journal of Health Education $60. 6 times a yr (ISSN 0097-0050) American Alliance for Health, Physical Education, Recreation, and Dance, 1900 Association Dr., Reston, VA 22091
    Formerly *Health Education;* name changed with Ja/F 1991

Journal of Industrial Teacher Education   Available only to members. $15. q (ISSN 0022-1864) National Association of Industrial and Technical Teachers Education, Center for Vocational and Adult Education, Auburn University, Auburn, AL 36849

Journal of Learning Disabilities $45. m (bi-m Je/Jl, Ag/S) (ISSN 0022-2194) PRO-ED Journals, 8700 Shoal Creek Blvd., Austin, TX 78758-6897

Journal of Moral Education $85. 3 times a yr (ISSN 0305-7240) Carfax Publishing Co., 85 Ash St., Hopkinton, MA 01748

Journal of Multicultural Counseling and Development $10. 4 times a yr (ISSN 0883-8534) American Association for Counseling and Development, 5999 Stevenson Ave., Alexandria, VA 22304

The Journal of Negro Education $20. q (ISSN 0022-2984) The Journal of Negro Education, Circulation Dept., P.O. Box 311, Howard University, Washington, DC 20059

Journal of Nutrition Education $85. bi-m (ISSN 0022-3182) Society for Nutrition Education, P.O. Box 64380, Baltimore, MD 21264-4380

Journal of Outdoor Education   Free. a (ISSN 0022-3336) Northern Illinois University, Dept. of Outdoor Teacher Education, Taft Field Campus, P.O. Box 299, Oregon, IL 61061

Journal of Physical Education, Recreation, and Dance $65. m (Ja-My/Je, Ag-N/D) (ISSN 0730-3084) American Alliance for Health, Physical Education, Recreation, and Dance, 1900 Association Dr., Reston, VA 22091

Journal of Reading   Available only to members. $33. 8 times a yr (ISSN 0022-4103) International Reading Association, Inc., 800 Barksdale Rd., P.O.Box 8139, Newark, DE 19714-8139

Journal of Reading Behavior $50. q (ISSN 0022-4111) National Reading Conference, Inc., 11 E. Hubbard St., Suite 200, Chicago, IL 60611

Journal of Research and Development in Education $15. q (ISSN 0022-426X) Journal of Research and Development in Education, 823 Aderhold Bldg., University of Georgia, Athens, GA 30602-6780

Journal of Research in Music Education $21. q (ISSN 0022-4294) Music Educators National Conference, 1902 Association Dr., Reston, VA 22091-1597

Journal of Research in Science Teaching $175. m (S-My) (ISSN 0022-4308) John Wiley & Sons, Inc., Subscription Dept., 605 Third Ave., New York, NY 10158-0012

Journal of Research on Computing in Education $38. q (ISSN 0888-6504) International Society for Technology in Education, University of Oregon, 1787 Agate St., Eugene, OR 97403-1923

The Journal of Special Education $35. q (ISSN 0022-4669) PRO-ED Journals, 8700 Shoal Creek Blvd., Austin, TX 78758-6897

The Journal of Special Education Technology $7. q (ISSN 0162-6434) Journal of Special Education Technology, Peabody College of Vanderbilt University, P.O. Box 328, Nashville, TN 37203

Journal of Teacher Education $35. 5 times a yr (ISSN 0022-4871) Publications Department, Journal of Teacher Education, AACTE, 1 Dupont Circle, Suite 610, Washington, DC 20036-2142

Journal of Teaching in Physical Education $28. q (ISSN 0273-5024) Human Kinetics Publishers Inc., P.O. Box 5076, Champaign, IL 61825-5076

Language Arts   Available only to members. $43. m (S-Ap) (ISSN 0360-9170) National Council of Teachers of English, 1111 Kenyon Rd., Urbana, IL 61801

Language Learning $36. q (ISSN 0023-8333) Language Learning, c/o Irene Zadonsky, Business Manager, 178 Henry S. Frieze Bldg., 105 S. State St., Ann Arbor, MI 48109-1285

Language, Speech, and Hearing Services in Schools $33. q (ISSN 0161-1461) Journal Subscriptions Office, American Speech-Language-Hearing Association, 10801 Rockville Pike, Rockville, MD 20852

Learning $18. 9 times a yr (ISSN 0090-3167) Education Today, P.O. Box 2606, Boulder, CO 80322

Learning Disability Quarterly $40. q (ISSN 0731-9487) Council for Learning Disabilities, P.O. Box 40303, Overland Park, KS 66204

The Mailbox $20. 6 times a yr (ISSN 0199-6045) The Education Center, Inc., 1607 Battleground Ave., P.O. Box 9753, Greensboro, NC 27429

Mathematics Teacher   Available only to members. $40. m (S-My) (ISSN 0025-5769) National Council of Teachers of Mathematics, 1906 Association Dr., Reston, VA 22091

Mathematics Teaching   Available only to members. $75. q (ISSN 0025-5785) Association of Teachers of Mathematics, 7 Shaftesbury St., Derby DE3 8YB, England

Middle School Journal $20. 5 times a year (ISSN 0094-0771) National Middle School Association, c/o Dennis D. Smith, Executive Director, 4807 Evanswood Dr., Columbus, OH 43229-6292

Music Educators Journal $41. m (S-My) (ISSN 0027-4321) Music Educators National Conference, Center for Educational Associations, 1902 Association Dr., Reston, VA 22091

NASSP Bulletin $65. m (S-My) (ISSN 0192-6365) National Association of Secondary School Principals, 1904 Association Dr., Reston, VA 22091

The Negro Educational Review $15. q (ISSN 0548-1457) Negro Educational Review, Inc., P.O. Box 2895, General Mail Center, Jacksonville, FL 32203

New Directions for Teaching and Learning $36. q (ISSN 0271-0633) Jossey-Bass, Inc., Publishers, 350 Sansome St., San Francisco, CA 94104

The New England Reading Association Journal $5. 3 times a yr (ISSN 0028-4882) New England Reading Association, Business Manager, University of Rhode Island, Kingston, RI 02881

Oxford Review of Education $130. 3 times a yr (ISSN 0305-4985) Carfax Publishing Co., 85 Ash St., Hopkinton, MA 01748

Peabody Journal of Education $60. q (ISSN 0161-956X) Peabody Journal of Education, Editorial Assistant, Peabody College of Vanderbilt University, 113 Payne Hall, P.O. Box 41, Nashville, TN 37203

Phi Delta Kappa Fastbacks $.90 each. irr (ISSN 8756-6494) Phi Delta Kappa, Inc., 8th & Union, P.O. Box 789, Bloomington, IN 47402-0789

Phi Delta Kappan $30. m (S-Je) (ISSN 0031-7217) Phi Delta Kappa, Inc., 8th & Union, P.O. Box 789, Bloomington, IN 47402-0789

The Physical Educator $22.50. 4 times a yr (ISSN 0031-8981) Subscription Office, The Physical Educator, 901 W. New York St., Indianapolis, IN 46202

The Physics Teacher (Stony Brook, N.Y.) $112. m (S-My) (ISSN 0031-921X) American Association of Physics Teachers, Subscription Fulfillment Dept., 5112 Berwyn Rd., College Park, MD 20770

Preventing School Failure $52. q (ISSN 1045-988X) Heldref Publications, 4000 Albemarle St., N.W., Washington, DC 20016
    Formerly *The Pointer;* name changed with Fall 1989

Principal (Reston, VA)   Available only to members. $55. 5 times a yr (ISSN 0271-6062) National Association of Elementary School Principals, 1615 Duke St., Alexandria, VA 22314

The Psychology of Learning and Motivation $65. a (ISSN 0079-7421) Academic Press, P.O. Box 6208, Duluth, MN 55806-0208

Reading Improvement $17. q (ISSN 0034-0510) Project Innovation of Mobile, P.O. Box 8508, Spring Hill Station, Mobile, AL 36608

Reading Research and Instruction $30. q (ISSN 0886-0246) College Reading Association, c/o Robert B. Cooter, Jr., 576 Education Bldg., Bowling Green State University, Bowling Green, OH 43403

Reading Research Quarterly   Available only to members. $38. 4 times a yr (ISSN 0034-0553) International Reading Association, 800 Barksdale Rd., P.O. Box 8139, Newark, DE 19714

The Reading Teacher Available only to members. $30. m (O-My; with Winter supp) (ISSN 0034-0561) International Reading Association, Inc., 800 Barksdale Rd., P.O. Box 8139, Newark, DE 19711-8139

Remedial and Special Education $35. 6 times a yr (ISSN 0741-9325) PRO-ED Journals, 8700 Shoal Creek Blvd., Austin, TX 78758-6897
　　Merger of *Exceptional Education Quarterly; The Journal of Special Educators;* and *Topics in Learning and Learning Disabilities*

Research in Education $83. 2 times a yr (ISSN 0034-5237) Manchester University Press, Oxford Rd., Manchester M13 9PL, England

Research in the Teaching of English $20. 4 times a yr (ISSN 0034-527X) National Council of Teachers of English, 1111 Kenyon Rd., Urbana, IL 61801

Research Quarterly for Exercise & Sport $55. q (ISSN 0270-1367) American Alliance of Health, Physical Education, Recreation, and Dance, 1900 Association Dr., Reston, VA 22091

Review of Educational Research $35. q (ISSN 0034-6543) American Educational Research Association, Subscriptions, 1230 17th St., N.W., Washington, DC 20036-3078

Roeper Review $40. q (ISSN 0278-3193) Roeper City and Country School, P.O. Box 329, Bloomfield Hills, MI 48304

Scholastic Coach $23.95. m (bi-m My/Je) (ISSN 0036-6382) Scholastic Magazines, P.O. Box 2042, Mahopac, NY 10541

School Arts $21. m (S-My) (ISSN 0036-6463) School Arts, 50 Portland St., Worcester, MA 01608

The School Counselor $37.50. 5 times a yr (ISSN 0036-6536) American Association for Counseling and Development, 5999 Stevenson Ave., Alexandria, VA 22304

School Library Journal $63. m (ISSN 0362-8930) School Library Journal, P.O. Box 1978, Marion, OH 43302-1978

School Library Media Quarterly Free to members; nonmembers $35. q (ISSN 0278-4823) American Library Association, 50 E. Huron St., Chicago, IL 60611

School Science and Mathematics $32. m (O-My) (ISSN 0036-6803) c/o Darrel W. Fyffe, Executive Secretary, School Science and Mathematics, Bowling Green State University, 126 Life Science Bldg., Bowling Green, OH 43403-0256

Science Activities $38. q (ISSN 0036-8121) Heldref Publications, 4000 Albemarle St., N.W., Washington, DC 20016

Science and Children Available only to members. $45. 8 times a yr (ISSN 0036-8148) National Science Teachers Association, 1742 Connecticut Ave., N.W., Washington, DC 20009

Science Education $135. 6 times a yr (ISSN 0036-8326) John Wiley & Sons, Inc., 605 Third Ave., New York, NY 10158

The Science Teacher Available only to members. $42. m (S-My) (ISSN 0036-8555) National Teachers Association, 1742 Connecticut Ave., N.W., Washington, DC 20009

SIECUS Report $70. bi-m (ISSN 0091-3995) Sex Information and Education Council of the U.S., Inc., 32 Washington Pl., New York, NY 10003-6638

Social Education $50. 7 times a yr (ISSN 0037-7724) National Council for the Social Studies, 3501 Newark St., N.W., Washington, DC 20016-3167

The Social Studies (Washington, DC) $39. bi-m (ISSN 0037-7996) Heldref Publications, 4000 Albemarle St., N.W., Washington, DC 20016

Sociology of Education $60. q (ISSN 0038-0407) American Sociological Association, 1722 N St., N.W., Washington, DC 20036

Studies in Art Education   Available only to members. $25. 4 times a yr (ISSN 0039-3541) National Art Education Association, 1916 Association Dr., Reston, VA 22091-1590

T.H.E. Journal   Free on limited basis. 11 times a yr (ISSN 0192-592X) Information Synergy, Inc., 150 El Camino Real, Tustin, CA 92680

Teacher Education and Special Education $22. q (ISSN 0888-4064) Special Press, Suite 3205, 11230 West Ave., San Antonio, TX 78213

The Teacher Educator   Free. q (ISSN 0887-8730) The Teacher Educator, TC 810, Ball State University, Muncie, IN 47306

Teaching Exceptional Children $25. q (ISSN 0040-0599) Council for Exceptional Children, 1920 Association Dr., Reston, VA 22091-1589

Teaching PreK–8 $19.77. 8 times a yr (ISSN 0891-4508) Teaching PreK–8, Box 912, Farmingdale, NY 11737-9612

Technology & Learning $24. 8 times a yr (ISSN 0890-7889) Lawrence Albaum Associates, 365 Broadway, Hillsdale, NJ 07642
   Formerly *Classroom Computer Learning;* name changed with S 1990

The Technology Teacher $55. 8 times a yr (ISSN 0746-3537) International Technology Education Association, 1914 Association Dr., Reston, VA 22091-1502

Unterrichtspraxis $20. semi-a (ISSN 0042-062X) American Association of Teachers of German, 112 Haddontowne Court, No. 104, Cherry Hill, NJ 08034

Urban Education $110. q (ISSN 0042-0859) SAGE Publications, Inc., 2111 W. Hillcrest, Newbury Park, CA 91320

The Urban Review $50. q (ISSN 0042-0972) Human Sciences Press, Inc., P.O. Box 2580, New York, NY 10013-1578

Vocational Education Journal $24. 8 times a yr (ISSN 0884-8009) American Vocational Association, Inc., 1410 King St., Alexandria, VA 22314-2715

The Volta Review $42. 7 times a yr (ISSN 0042-8639) Alexander Graham Bell Association for the Deaf, Inc., Subscription Dept., 3417 Volta Pl., N.W., Washington, DC 20007-2778

Western European Education $235. q (ISSN 0043-3675) M. E. Sharpe, Inc., 80 Business Park Dr., Armonk, NY 10504

Women's Studies Quarterly $14. q (ISSN 0732-1562) Feminist Press, City University of New York, 311 E. 94th St., New York, NY 10128

Yearbook (Association for Supervision and Curriculum Development) a (ISSN 0066-9199) Association for Supervision and Curriculum Development, 225 N. Washington St., Alexandria, VA 22314

Yearbook (Claremont Reading Conference) $20. a (ISSN 0886-6880) Center for Developmental Studies, Claremont Graduate School, Harper 200, 150 E. 10th St., Claremont, CA 91711-6160

Yearbook (Council on Technology Teacher Education) a (ISSN 1048-4779) Glencoe Publishing Co., 15319 Chatsworth St., Mission Hills, CA 91345

Yearbook (National Council of Teachers of Mathematics) $18. a (ISSN 0077-4103) National Council of Teachers of Mathematics, 1906 Association Dr., Reston, VA 22091

Yearbook (National Society for the Study of Education) a (2 parts) (ISSN 0077-5762) National Society for the Study of Education, Kenneth J. Rehage, Secretary-Treasurer, 5835 Kimbark Ave., Chicago, IL 60637

The Yearbook of Education Law $34. a (ISSN 1049-0264) National Organization on Legal Problems of Education, 3601 Southwest 29th St., Suite 223, Topeka, KS 66614

   Formerly *The Yearbook of School Law;* name changed with 1988

Young Children $20. bi-m (ISSN 0044-0728) National Association for the Education of Young Children, 1834 Connecticut Ave., N.W., Washington, DC 20009-5786

Appendix
II

Museum Resources

The addresses of the following types of museums can be accessed from:

The Official Museum Directory
The American Association of Museums
MacMillan Directory Division
National Register Publishing Co.
  3004 Glenview Rd.
  Wilmette, IL 60091
  Telephone: 708-441-2210 or 1-800-323-6772

This directory is updated yearly, and may be found in local public libraries.

Institutions may be accessed by category

List of Categories

Art
Art Associations, Councils and Commissions, Foundations, and Industries
Art Museums and Galleries
Arts and Crafts Museums
China, Glass, and Silver Museums
Civic Art and Cultural Centers
Decorative Arts Museums
Folk Art Museums
Textile Museums

Children's and Junior Museums

College and University Museums

Company Museums

Exhibit Areas

General Museums

History
Historic Agencies, Councils, Commissions, Foundations, and Research Institutes
Historic Houses and Historic Buildings
Historic Sites
Historical and Preservation Societies
Historical Society Museums
History Museums
Maritime and Naval Museums and Historic Ships
Military Museums
Preservation Projects

Libraries Having Collections of Books

Libraries Having Collections Other Than Books

National and State Agencies, Councils, and Commissions

Nature Centers

Park Museums and Visitor Centers

Science
Academies, Associations, Institutes, and Foundations
Aeronautics and Space Museums
Anthropology, Ethnology, and Indian Museums
Aquariums, Marine Museums, and Oceanariums
Arboretums
Archaeology Museums and Archaeological Sites
Aviaries and Ornithology Museums
Botanical and Aquatic Gardens, Conservatories, and Horticultural Societies
Entomology Museums and Insect Collections
Geology, Mineralogy, and Paleontology Museums
Herbariums
Herpetology Museums
Medical, Dental, Health, Pharmacology, Apothecary, and Psychiatry Museums
Natural History and Natural Science Museums
Planetariums, Observatories, and Astronomy Museums
Science Museums (General Science, Physical Science)
Wildlife Refuges and Bird Sanctuaries
Zoos, Children's Zoos

Specialized Museums

Agricultural

Antiques

Architecture

Audiovisual and Film

Circus

Comedy

Communications

Costume

Crime

Electricity

Fire-Fighting

Forestry

Furniture

Gun

Hobby

Horological

Industrial

Lapidary Arts

Logging and Lumber

Mappariums

Mining

Money and Numismatics

Musical Instruments

Philatelic

Photography

Religious

Scouting

Sports

Technology

Theater

Toy and Doll

Transportation

Typography

Village

Wax

Whaling

Woodcarving

III

Directory of State Teacher-Certification Offices in the United States

A certificate is valid only in the state for which it is issued. Therefore, applicants who wish to move to another state are advised to contact the certification office listed below for additional information, application procedures, and forms.

Alabama

Division of Professional Services
Department of Education
404 State Office Building
Montgomery 36130-3901, 205-261-5290

Alaska

Department of Education
Teacher Education and Certification
P.O. Box F
Goldbelt Building
Juneau 99811-0500, 907-465-2810

Arizona

Teacher Certification Unit
Department of Education
1535 W. Jefferson
P.O. Box 85002
Phoenix 85007, 602-542-4368

Arkansas

Department of Education
Teacher Certification & Education
#4 Capitol Mall, Rooms 106B/107B
Little Rock 72201, 501-682-4368

California

Commission on Teacher Credentialing
1812 9th St.
Sacramento 94244-2700, 916-445-7254

Colorado

Teacher Certification
Colorado Department of Education
201 E. Colfax Ave.
Denver 80203, 303-866-6628

Connecticut

State Department of Education
Division of Curriculum and Professional
Development
P.O. Box 2219
Hartford 06115, 203-556-4561

Delaware

Department of Public Instruction
Supervisor of Certification and Personnel
Townsend Building
P.O. Box 1402
Dover 19903, 302-726-4688

District of Columbia

Division of Teacher Services
District of Columbia Public Schools
415 12th St., N.W.
Room 1013
Washington 20004-1994, 202-724-4250

Florida

Department of Education
Division of Human Resource Development
Teacher Certification Offices
325 W. Gaines St.
Tallahassee, 32399-0400, 904-488-5724

Georgia

Georgia Department of Education
Division of Teachers Certification
1452 Twin Towers East
Atlanta 30334, 404-656-2604

Hawaii

State Department of Education
Office of Personnel Services
P.O. Box 2360
Honolulu, 96804, 808-548-5802

Idaho

State Department of Education
Teacher Education and Certification
Len B. Jordan Office Building
Boise 82720, 208-334-3475

Illinois

Illinois State Board of Education
100 N. First St.
Springfield 62777, 217-782-2805

Indiana

Department of Education
Center for Professional Development
Room 229, State House
Indianapolis 46204, 317-232-9010

Iowa

Board of Education Examiners
State of Iowa
Grimes State Office Building
Des Moines 50319-0146, 515-281-3245

Kansas

State Department of Education
Certification, Teacher Education, &
Accreditation
120 E. 10th St.
Topeka 66612, 913-296-2288

Kentucky

State Department of Education
Teacher Education and Certification
18th Floor, Capital Plaza Tower
Frankfort 40601, 502-564-4606

Louisiana

State Department of Education
Bureau of Higher Education and Teacher
Certification
P.O. Box 94064
Baton Rouge 70804-9064, 504-342-3490

Maine

Department of Education and Cultural Services
Teacher Education and Higher Education
State House Station 23
Augusta 04333, 207-289-5992

Maryland

State Department of Education
Division of Certification and Accreditation
200 W. Baltimore St.
Baltimore 21201-2595, 301-333-2142

Massachusetts

Division of Educational Personnel
Department of Education
Quincy Center Plaza
1385 Hancock St.
Quincy 02169, 617-770-7517

Michigan

Department of Education
Teachers/Preparation and Certification Services
P.O. Box 30008
Lansing 48909, 517-373-3310

Minnesota

State Department of Education
Capitol Square Building
550 Cedar St.
St. Paul 55101, 612-296-2046

Missouri

Teacher Education
Missouri Teacher Certification Office
Department of Elementary & Secondary
Education
P.O. Box 480
Jefferson City 65102, 314-751-3486

Montana

Certification Services
Office of Public Instruction
State Capitol
Helena 59620, 406-444-3150

Nebraska

Department of Education
Teacher Certification/Education
310 Centennial Mall South
Box 94987
Lincoln 68509, 402-471-2496

Nevada

State Department of Education
1850 Sahara, Suite 200
State Mail Room
Las Vegas 89158, 702-486-6457

New Hampshire

Bureau of Teacher Education and Professional
Standards
State Office Park South
101 Pleasant St.
Concord 03301-3860, 603-271-2407

New Jersey

State Department of Education
Teacher Certification and Academic Credentials
3535 Quakerbridge Road, CN 503
Trenton 08625-0503, 609-588-3100

New Mexico

New Mexico State Department of Education
Educator Preparation & Licensure
Education Building
Santa Fe 87503, 505-827-6587

New York

Office of Teachers Certification
Cultural Education Center Room 5A 11
Nelson A. Rockefeller Empire State Plaza
Albany 12230, 518-474-3901

North Carolina

State Department of Public Instruction
Division of Certification
114 W. Edenton St.
Raleigh 27603-1712, 919-733-4125

North Dakota

State Department of Public Instruction
Teacher Certification
State Capitol, 9th Floor
Bismarck 58505, 701-224-2264

Ohio

Department of Education
Teacher Certification
64 S. Front St., Room 1012
Columbus 43266-0308, 614-466-3593

Oklahoma

Department of Education
Hodge Education Building
2500 N. Lincoln Blvd., Room 211
Oklahoma City 73105-4599, 405-521-3337

Oregon

Teacher Standards and Practices Commission
630 Center St. N.E., Suite 200
Salem 97310, 503-378-3586

Pennsylvania

Department of Education
Bureau of Teacher Preparation and Certification
333 Market St., 3rd Floor
Harrisburg 17126-0333, 717-787-2967

Rhode Island

Department of Education
School and Teacher Accreditation, Certification,
and Placement
Roger Williams Building
22 Hayes St.
Providence 02908, 401-277-2675

South Carolina

State Department of Education
Teacher Education and Certification
1015 Rutledge
1429 Senate St.
Columbia 29201, 803-734-8466

South Dakota

Division of Education & Cultural Affairs
Office of Certification
Kneip Office Building
700 Governor's Dr.
Pierre 57501, 605-773-3553

Tennessee

Department of Education
Office of Teacher Licensing
6th Floor, North Wing
Cordell Hull Building
Nashville 37243-0377, 615-741-1644

Texas

Division of Teacher Certification
William B. Travis State Office Building
1701 N. Congress Ave.
Austin 78701, 512-463-8976

Utah

State Office of Education
Certification and Personnel Development
250 East 500 South
Salt Lake City 84111, 801-533-5965

Vermont

State Department of Education
Certification Division
Montpelier 05602, 802-828-3124

Virginia

Department of Education
Division of Teacher Education and Certification
Box 60, James Monroe Building
Richmond 23216, 804-225-2094

Washington

Office of the Superintendent of Public
Instruction
Director of Professional Certification
Old Capitol Building, Mail Stop FG-11
Olympia 98504-3211, 206-753-6775

West Virginia

Department of Education
Office of Professional Education
Capitol Complex, Room B-337, Bldg. 6
Charleston 25305, 304-348-2703

Wisconsin

Bureau of Teacher Education, Licensing, and
Placement
Teacher Certification
State Department of Public Instruction
125 S. Webster St., P.O. Box 7841
Madison 53707-7841, 608-266-1027

Wyoming

State Department of Education
Certification and Licensing Unit
Hathaway Building
Cheyenne 82002-0050, 307-777-6261

Puerto Rico

Teacher Certification Division
Department of Education
Box 759
Hato Rey 00919, 809-758-4949

St. Croix District

Department of Education
Educational Personnel Services
No. 21, 22, & 23 Hospital St.
St. Croix, Virgin Islands 00802, 809-773-1095

St. Thomas/St. John District

Department of Education
Educational Personnel Services
44-46 Kongens Gad
St. Thomas, Virgin Islands 00802, 809-774-0100

United States Department of Defense Overseas Dependent Section

Recruitment and Assignment Section
2461 Eisenhower Ave.
Alexandria, VA 22331-1100, 202-325-0885

Appendix
IV

Personal Computer Communication Resources

CompuServe
CompuServe Information Service, Inc.
5000 Arlington Centre Blvd.
Columbus, OH 43220
617-457-8600
Customer Service 1-800-848-8990

Delphi
General Videotex Corporation
3 Blackstone St.
Cambridge, MA 02139
617-491-3393
Customer Service 1-800-544-4005

DIALOG
DIALOG and the Knowledge Index
Information Services, Inc.
3460 Hillview Ave.
Palo Alto, CA 94304
415-858-3792
Customer Service 1-800-334-2564

EdLINC
P.O. Box 14325
Columbus, OH 43214
Customer Service 614-793-0698

GEnie
GE Information Services, Dept. 02B
401 N. Washington St.
Rockville, MD 20850
301-340-4000
Customer Service 1-800-544-4005

NASA Spacelink
NASA Educational Affairs Division
Public Services and Education Branch
Marshall Center Public Affairs Office
Huntsville, AL 35801
Computer Access Number 205-895-0028

NewsNet
NewsNet, Inc.
945 Haverford Rd.
Bryn Mawr, PA 19010
215-527-8030
Customer Service 1-800-345-1301

Prodigy
Prodigy Services Company
445 Hamilton Ave.
White Plains, NY 10601
914-993-8848
Customer Service 1-800-776-3552

Additional information about these services and others may be found in:

The Complete Handbook of Personal Computer Communications
by Alfred Glossbrenner,
St. Martin's Press, 175 Fifth Ave.
New York, NY 10010
ISBN 0-312-03312-5

This handbook is updated on a regular basis. The third edition was published in 1990.

A sourcebook for communication resource funding opportunities is:

United States Distance Learning Association (USDLA) Funding Sourcebook
New Orbit Communications
39 Plaza Street
Brooklyn, NY 11217
(718) 857-3713
$42.75

Appendix
V

Sources for Ordering Creative Teaching Materials

Baker and Taylor Books, 652 E. Main St., P.O. Box 6920, Bridgewater, NJ 08807-0920, 1-800-435-5111 or 1-800-892-1892 (in IL)—Recommended books for school libraries in all subject areas, K–12.

Carolina Biological Supply, 2700 York Rd., Burlington, NC 27215, 1-800-334-5551—Living plants, animals, microorganisms, and viral cultures plus slides, filmstrips, videos, books, dissecting tools, models, glassware, posters, microscopes, and computer software related to biological sciences, K–12.

Co-op Artist's Materials, P.O. Box 53097, Atlanta, GA, 30340, 1-800-877-3242—Art materials for classroom use.

Creative Publications, 5040 W. 111th St., Oak Lawn, IL 60453, 1-800-624-0822—Manipulatives and books for mathematics, language arts, and science.

Creative Ventures, Inc., P.O. Box 2286, West Lafayette, IN 47906, 317-743-3564—Innovative books for teachers on how to teach science; loaded with useful, thought-provoking activities.

Cuisenaire Co. of America, Inc., 12 Church St., Box D, New Rochelle, NY 10802, 1-800-237-3142—Manipulatives, games, and books for mathematics and science.

Dale Seymour Publications, P.O. Box 10888, Palo Alto, CA 94303, 1-800-872-1100—Features math manipulatives, problem-solving kits, posters, enrichment books, and calculators. Also has materials for science, language arts, art, and graphics, K–12.

Dandy Lion Publications, 3563 - L Sueldo, San Luis Obispo, CA 93401, 1-805-543-3332—Enrichment books for creative and critical thinking, K–12.

Davis Publications, Inc., 50 Portland St., Worcester, MA 01608, 1-800-533-2847—Art books and textbooks for elementary and secondary teachers.

Dick Blick, P.O. Box 1267, Galesburg, IL 61401, 309-343-6181 or 1-800-373-7575—All types of art supplies.

D.O.K. Publishers, P.O. Box 605, East Aurora, NY 14052, 1-800-458-7900—Books to enhance thinking skills and creative problem solving in math, science, social studies, and language arts, K–12.

Edmund Scientific, 101 E. Gloucester Pike, Barrington, NJ 08007, 609-547-3488—Tools and equipment to stimulate thinking.

The Education Center, Inc., 16078 Battleground Ave., P.O. Box 9753, Greensboro, NC 27429, 1-800-334-0298—Publish *The Mailbox* ($19.95 per year) and *Worksheet Magazine* ($13.95 per year), which are activity-based magazines with many ready-to-use, creative, and practical ideas for preschool/K, primary, and intermediate levels. They also sell bulletin-board supplies, stickers, stamp pads, and game pieces.

Fisher Scientific Company, Educational Materials Division, 4901 W. LeMoyne St., Chicago, IL 60651, 1-800-621-4769—Equipment and supplies for biology, chemistry, and physics, including microscopes, slides, models, chemicals, balances, glassware, and instructional kits, K–12.

Free Spirit Publishing, Inc., 123 N. Third St., Suite 716, Minneapolis, MN 55401, 1-800-735-7323—Books on self-esteem, stress management, perfectionism, and other affective issues, K–12.

Fresno Pacific Bookshop, AIMS Education Foundation, 1717 S. Chestnut, Fresno, CA 93702—Integrated math and science activities and posters. Some selections in Spanish, K–9.

Good Apple, 1204 Buchanan St., P.O. Box 299, Carthage, IL 62321-0299, 1-800-435-7234—Bulletin-board books and activity books for all areas of the curriculum, K–8.

Greenhaven Press, Inc., P.O. Box 289009, San Diego, CA 92128-9009, 1-800-231-5163—Presents books of opposing viewpoints on social, science, and health-related topics. Excellent for controversial issues at the middle-school level, 5–12.

Interact, P.O. Box 997-Y90, Lakeside, CA 92040, 1-800-359-0961—Simulation games in language arts, science, social studies, counseling, mathematics, and health, K–12.

J. Weston Walch, Publisher, P.O. Box 658, Portland, ME 04104-0658, 1-800-341-6094—Activity books and multimedia materials in all subject areas, K–12.

J. S. Latta Company, 2218 Main St., Box 128, Cedar Falls, IA 50613, 1-800-553-1761—Art and craft materials, K–12.

Jamestown Publishers, P.O. Box 9168, Providence, RI 02940, 1-800-872-7323—Books and tapes to improve reading and spelling skills. They have high-interest, low-vocabulary materials as well as advanced-level poem and short-story series, K–12.

Joint Council on Economic Education, 2 Park Ave., New York, NY 10016, 1-212-685-5499—Materials to teach economic education, K–12.

Let's Get Growing, General Feed and Seed Company, 1900-B Commercial Way, Santa Cruz, CA 95065—Tools, seeds, supplies, and books for classroom gardening.

MECC Distribution Center (Minnesota Educational Computing Consortium), 2520 Broadway Dr., St. Paul, MN 55113-5199, 1-612-638-0600—Catalog of available Apple and IBM software in all subject areas.

Midwest Publications, P.O. Box 448, Dept. 17, Pacific Grove, CA 93950, 1-800-458-4849—Critical-thinking activities in mathematics, reading, writing, and social studies, K–12.

National Clearing House for Alcohol and Drug Information, P.O. Box 2345, Rockville, MD 20850, 1-800-729-6686—Videos, books, and filmstrips on alcohol and drug prevention, K–12.

National Geographic Society, Educational Services, P.O. Box 2895, Washington, DC 20036, 1-800-368-2728—Filmstrips, learning kits, videos, films, books, maps, globes, and atlases for science and geography.

Office for Substance Abuse Prevention, 5600 Fishers La., Rockville, MD 20857, 301-443-0365—Books, tapes, and posters for substance-abuse prevention, K–12.

Opportunities for Learning, Inc., 20417 Nordoff St., Dept. GF7, Chatsworth, CA 91311, 1-818-341-2535—Multimedia materials for gifted, K–12.

Sax Arts and Crafts, 2405 Calhoun Rd., P.O. Box 51710, New Berlin, WI 53151, 414-784-6880 or 1-800-558-6696, open 24 hours a day and 7 days a week—Full line of art supplies and teacher idea books.

Sunburst Communication, 39 Washington Ave., Pleasantville, NY 10570-2898, 1-800-628-8897—Computer coursewear for all subject areas, K–12.

Tom Snyder Production, 90 Sherman St., Cambridge, MA 02140, 1-800-342-0236—Computer simulations and learning games for social studies, math, and science, K–12.

Warner Books, Educational Department, 666 Fifth Ave., New York, NY 10103, 212-484-2900—Literature books for classroom use and books for parents and teachers, K–12.

Zephyr Press, 3316 N. Chapel Ave., P.O. Box 13448-C, Tucson, AZ 85732-3448, 1-602-322-5090—Innovative books on global awareness, whole language, thinking skills, arts and humanities, and whole-brain learning, K–12.

Credits

p. 16   Yager, R. E. (1990). "Instructional Outcomes Change with STS," *Iowa Science Teachers Journal*, Spring, pp. 20–23. By permission.

p. 41   McTighe, Jay, and Frank T. Lyman, Jr. (1988). Figure 3, Cueing Bookmark, from "Cueing Thinking in the Classroom: The Promise of Theory-embedded Tools," *Educational Leadership* 45, 7. Language and Learning Improvement Branch, Division of Instruction, Maryland State Department of Education. Reprinted with permission of the Association for Supervision and Curriculum Development. Copyright 1988 by ASCD. All rights reserved.

pp. 44–45   Patricia R. Burgette, "Listen to the Sounds a Child Makes." By permission.

pp. 87–88   T. Scruggs and M. Mastropieri (in press). "Effective Mainstreaming Strategies for Mildly Handicapped Students." *Elementary School Journal.* The University of Chicago Press.

pp. 90–91   Fig. 3.2, "A Poet Inside," by Nelson Price, *The Indianapolis News*, Feb. 12, 1991, pp. C1–C6. By permission.

p. 92   Poems by Ian Hudson. By permission.

p. 93   Pang, Valerie Ouka, "Ethnic Prejudice: Still Alive and Hurtful," *Harvard Educational Review*, 58:3, pp. 375–379. Copyright © 1988 by President and Fellows of Harvard College. All rights reserved.

p. 132   *Science Activities*, vol. 10, no. 3, pp. 38–39, November 1973. Reprinted with permission of the Helen Dwight Reid Educational Foundation. Published by Heldref Publications, 4000 Albermarle St., N.W., Washington, D.C. 20016. Copyright © 1973.

pp. 240–241   Lisa Lenz, "A Literary Poem Phonetics Lesson." *The Reading Teacher*, vol. 44, no. 8 (April 1991), p. 622. Copyright © 1991. Reprinted with permission of the International Reading Association.

p. 254   Peters, Charles W. (1991). "You can't have authentic assessment without authentic content." *The Reading Teacher*, vol. 44, no. 8 (April 1991), pp. 590–591. Copyright © 1991. Reprinted with permission of Charles W. Peters and the International Reading Association.

Index